FORENSIC APPLICATIONS of the MMPI-2-RF
A Casebook

FORENSIC APPLICATIONS of the MMPI-2-RF

A Casebook

Martin Sellbom, PhD

Dustin B. Wygant, PhD

Foreword by Yossef S. Ben-Porath, PhD

UNIVERSITY OF MINNESOTA PRESS

Minneapolis | London

Published by the University of Minnesota Press
111 Third Avenue South, Suite 290
Minneapolis, MN 55401-2520
http://www.upress.umn.edu

ISBN 978-1-5179-0352-7
A Cataloging-in-Publication record for this book is available from the Library of Congress.

Printed in the United States of America on acid-free paper

The University of Minnesota is an equal-opportunity educator and employer.

24 23 22 21 20 19 18   10 9 8 7 6 5 4 3 2 1

FROM DR. SELLBOM

To Yossi Ben-Porath, Jack Graham, Mike Bagby, Kathy Stafford, and Gary Meunier—mentors without whom writing this book would never have been possible.

FROM DR. WYGANT

To Jenny, Elise, and Lauren—you motivate me to do my best every day. Thank you for your unending support and love.

CONTENTS

PART III
Civil Forensic Applications of the MMPI-2-RF

PART IV
Conclusions about the Forensic Use of the MMPI-2-RF

LIST OF TABLES

LIST OF FIGURES

FOREWORD

Yossef S. Ben-Porath

It is with a combined sense of pride and joy that I write this foreword to a volume of forensic *Minnesota Multiphasic Personality Inventory-2-Restructured Form* (MMPI-2-RF) case studies by Martin Sellbom and Dustin B. Wygant, two individuals uniquely qualified to author this book. Sellbom and Wygant epitomize the forensic clinical scientist. They have contributed substantially to the empirical and conceptual forensic psychology literature, and they are leading MMPI-2-RF researchers. Both were graduate students at Kent State at the time the instrument was developed, and they have made multiple impactful contributions to the literature on general clinical applications as well as specific forensic uses of the inventory. Perhaps what is most important, these authors are active, practicing psychologists, able to draw on their wealth of forensic assessment experience using the MMPI-2-RF.

The book is divided into four parts. In the first, Sellbom and Wygant provide a general introduction to the MMPI-2-RF, including a description of the test scales and material available to support its use. This is followed by a detailed discussion of how the MMPI-2-RF is used in forensic evaluations. The authors' analysis of the legal and empirical foundations for relying on this instrument in forensic assessments includes a thoughtful debunking of unsubstantiated critiques of forensic uses of the MMPI-2-RF. This will be of particular value to forensic psychologists who may be confronted with this material in trial testimony or deposition. A final chapter in Part I provides a comprehensive treatment of the topic of validity scales and their role in forensic psychological evaluations. This includes a forensically focused discussion of the conceptual model underlying the MMPI-2-RF Validity Scales and an up-to-date review of the literature guiding and supporting their use. A sophisticated discussion of the topic of malingering will be of particular value to the reader.

Parts II and III of this volume focus respectively on use of the MMPI-2-RF in criminal and civil forensic evaluations. The standard structure of these chapters includes a discussion of psycho-legal matters related to the specific forensic topic covered (e.g., assessments of criminal responsibility), followed by analysis of general assessment-related considerations, then MMPI-2-RF-specific material (including a review of the relevant empirical literature), culminating in a detailed case study. The authors' extensive forensic assessment experience shines through in these case studies. The richness of their description of the background and psychological history of the subject of each evaluation, and their sophisticated analyses of the forensic referral issues in general and how MMPI-2-RF findings may (or, in some instances, may not) be integrated in the evaluating expert's opinion provide instructive models for empirically grounded forensic practice.

An appealing feature of the case studies is their breadth and diversity. The cases include individuals evaluated in the United States, Australia, and New Zealand, with legal analyses focused on both U.S. statutory and case law as well as elements of English common law, making the volume applicable throughout the English-speaking world. The examples include members of ethnic minority and marginalized groups and a discussion of the special considerations when using the MMPI-2-RF with these populations. All are instructive, but among the most compelling are the two competency-to-stand-trial assessments of the same individual separated in time by several years, which nicely illustrate the ability of MMPI-2-RF scale scores to reflect both stable features of chronic psychological disorders and more transient findings related to symptom severity. Another important feature of the case studies is the authors' illustration of using standard MMPI-2-RF comparison groups that are available for several of the forensic evaluations illustrated in this book.

The criminal forensic evaluations covered include assessments of competence to stand trial, criminal responsibility, violence risk, sex-offending risk, and mitigating factors in sentencing. The two risk assessment chapters provide good illustrations of how MMPI-2-RF findings may be integrated with those of forensically focused measures often used in these assessments, such as the Structured Professional Judgment model embodied in the Historical, Clinical, Risk Management-20 (Douglas, Hart, Webster, & Belfrage, 2013) and the Risk for Sexual Violence Protocol (Hart et al., 2003). Civil forensic assessments covered include child custody, parental fitness, personal injury, and disability evaluations. The child custody chapter presents a detailed analysis of MMPI-2-RF protocols of a divorcing couple. The test data illustrate effectively how differences in psychological functioning can be reflected in test scores as well as in the daily lives of the individuals assessed. The chapter on personal injury and disability evaluations provides a comprehensive review of a substantial body of MMPI-2-RF research available to guide and support these evaluations. The case described represents a good example of how MMPI-2-RF findings can document credible sequela of psychological injury, leading to settlement of litigation.

In chapter 12, Sellbom and Wygant offer concluding remarks highlighted by identification of future directions for forensically focused MMPI-2-RF research. Among the interesting topics discussed in this chapter is the need for systematic research on how evaluators might most effectively and validly integrate MMPI-2-RF findings when formulating and communicating their opinions, how MMPI-2-RF findings may best be used in the context of retrospectively and future-oriented forensic evaluations, and specifically how test findings can inform the practice of structured professional judgment in forensic assessments.

It is fitting that Sellbom and Wygant conclude with identification of future research efforts, which they are among those most likely to lead, along with their students, my "grandstudents," and the other many dedicated scholars who make up the next generation of MMPI researchers and practitioners. I'll conclude this foreword where I began, by conveying a sense of pride and joy related to seeing my former students produce a scholarly work that will undoubtedly shape future research and practice of forensic assessments with the MMPI-2-RF and, more broadly, the field of forensic psychology.

PREFACE

The *Minnesota Multiphasic Personality Inventory-2-Restructured Form* (MMPI-2-RF; Ben-Porath & Tellegen, 2008/2011; Tellegen & Ben-Porath, 2008/2011) was developed to capture the essential clinical substance of the MMPI-2 in a more concise and psychometrically sound manner. Since its release in 2008, the MMPI-2-RF has garnered an impressive amount of attention in the research literature and is used frequently in clinical and forensic assessments. Both of us were graduate students at Kent State University under the mentorship of Yossef Ben-Porath when the MMPI-2-RF was in the process of being developed, and we were both heavily involved from the beginning in contributing to its extensive research literature. Moreover, we have both continued to engage in clinical practice in parallel with our academic positions, with our respective practices focusing largely on forensic psychological assessment. We were therefore excited about writing a timely applied MMPI-2-RF interpretive text to guide forensic clinicians in using the instrument to address various psycho-legal questions.

Our goal is that this book serve as an illustrative guide to using the MMPI-2-RF in a variety of forensic assessment contexts. Our primary aim is to educate the reader on the most common forensic applications of the instrument and, in doing so, provide a brief overview of the various psycho-legal issues being addressed. The book is organized into two main substantive sections. The first provides an introduction to the MMPI-2-RF and discusses broader considerations for using the test in forensic psychological evaluations. The introduction, chapter 1, describes the MMPI-2-RF scales and provides guidelines for administration, scoring, and interpretation. Chapter 2 discusses general considerations for using the MMPI-2-RF in forensic psychological evaluations. Each type of forensic psychological evaluation comes with challenges, both general (e.g., the potential for response bias) and unique (e.g., retrospective assessment in criminal responsibility evaluations). We consider the impact such challenges have on the use of the MMPI-2-RF in such contexts, address how to deal with challenges to the admissibility of MMPI-2-RF information in court, and respond to recent critiques of using the instrument in forensic practice.

The second section, chapters 4 to 11, focuses on MMPI-2-RF interpretation through specific case analyses. Eight common psycho-legal questions are discussed in each chapter. These are divided into criminal court evaluations (e.g., competency to stand trial, criminal responsibility, violence risk) in Part II and civil litigation (child custody, parental fitness, personal injury, and disability) in Part III. The chapters begin with an introduction and overview of each psycho-legal issue and conclude with a case study that includes full MMPI-2-RF profiles to illustrate interpretation and integration of test data into clinical and diagnostic impressions and generating forensic opinions.

The book concludes with a brief summary and discussion of using the MMPI-2-RF in forensic evaluations. We discuss future directions for research on the MMPI-2-RF in these contexts.

We believe this book will appeal to three main audiences. The first and primary audience is professional psychologists (and related mental health professionals) who use the MMPI-2-RF clinically, in particular in forensic contexts. The second audience is graduate students who are completing advanced training in psychological assessment, with a focus on forensic settings. The book may also provide an introduction to forensic psychological evaluations for practitioners/students with little expertise in conducting such evaluations. Finally, a third audience may be lawyers who want to gain a better appreciation for how personality testing (especially the MMPI-2-RF) should be appropriately used in forensic mental health evaluations.

We hope readers will enjoy this book and find it a valuable learning tool for using the MMPI-2-RF in forensic psychological practice.

ACKNOWLEDGMENTS

We would like to acknowledge the contributions of those who assisted us in making this book possible. From the University of Minnesota Press, we appreciate the guidance of Beverly Kaemmer, who was influential in bringing this project to fruition and providing excellent feedback and editing on the manuscript, and Tami Brown, for her assistance throughout the project. We appreciate Yossef Ben-Porath, Robert Archer, Scott Bresler, Roger Gervais, and Patricia Zapf for taking the time to give us feedback on several of our chapters. We thank Tayla Lee for assistance with our personal injury case example. Finally, we appreciate the work of Imogen Kaack and Sydney Abell in proofreading the book.

We extend our sincere gratitude to our mentors in this area, Yossi Ben-Porath, Scott Bresler, Jack Graham, and Kathy Stafford, who helped us develop the skills and knowledge to write this book as well as guide our work in forensic clinical psychology more broadly.

PART I

Introduction and Broader
Considerations for Use of the
MMPI-2-RF in Forensic Contexts

Chapter 1

Introduction to the MMPI-2-RF

The *Minnesota Multiphasic Personality Inventory-2-Restructured Form* (MMPI-2-RF; Ben-Porath & Tellegen, 2008/2011; Tellegen & Ben-Porath, 2008/2011) is an updated 338-item version of the MMPI-2 (Butcher et al., 2001), the most recent of the MMPI family of instruments for adults that began with the original MMPI, developed in the 1930s and published in 1943 (Hathaway & McKinley, 1943). The MMPI-2-RF items aggregate into 9 Validity Scales and 42 scales that measure substantive clinical content. The MMPI-2-RF normative sample consists of 1,138 men and 1,138 women, combined to represent a nongendered reference group.

The MMPI has a long history of being used in forensic psychological evaluations. Indeed, early use of the MMPI focused primarily on the characterization and explanation of criminal behavior (see Dahlstrom, Welsh, & Dahlstrom, 1975, for a review). Studies by Capwell (1945a, 1945b) and Hathaway and Monachesi (1953, 1957) examined personality patterns of juvenile delinquents. A number of early researchers also focused on the etiology of criminal behavior, using the MMPI as a proxy for underlying personological explanations for various crimes, including heroin dependency (Sutker & Allain, 1973) and aggression (e.g., Megargee & Mendelsohn, 1962). This pattern continued with the MMPI-2 (see Sellbom & Anderson, 2013, for a review). The focus of the current text is to articulate the evidence-base and, more substantially, the applied use of the MMPI-2-RF in these contexts.

DEVELOPMENT OF THE MMPI-2-RF

The first step in the development of the MMPI-2-RF was the restructuring of the eight original MMPI Clinical Scales (Tellegen et al., 2003), which were constructed in the 1930s using an empirical keying method. This method involved selecting items that differentiated diagnostic groups from a healthy comparison group to derive scales measuring eight target disorders. Even with the substantial strengths of the Clinical Scales, which include extensive empirical validation and decades of clinical experience by practitioners, it has been widely known for a long time that the scales were not psychometrically optimal as measures of diagnostic constructs (e.g., Loevinger, 1972; Norman, 1972; see Tellegen & Ben-Porath, 2008/2011; Tellegen et al., 2003). The primary step in developing these scales was to identify and isolate a shared general distress dimension (labeled demoralization) that saturates the Clinical Scales and then to identify distinct target constructs from each scale, thereby improving their convergent and especially discriminant validity. This process ultimately resulted in nine Restructured Clinical Scales (RC Scales; Tellegen et al., 2003): a measure of demoralization and eight scales assessing key components of the Clinical Scales (except for Scale 5 [Masculinity/Femininity] and Scale 0 [Social Introversion], which do not measure psychopathology constructs). The RC Scales are scored on both the MMPI-2 and the MMPI-2-RF.

Subsequent to the RC Scale development and introduction in the MMPI-2, Ben-Porath and Tellegen continued their work on additional scales for the new version of the MMPI, the MMPI-2-RF. This version was designed to capture the clinical substantive content in the MMPI-2 item pool using as efficient and psychometrically up-to-date measures as possible. They also sought to enhance the overall construct validity by linking the scales to contemporary models of psychopathology and personality (Tellegen & Ben-Porath, 2008/2011). Additional MMPI-2-RF scales were intended to assess: (a) distinctive core components from the original Clinical Scales not covered by the RC Scales; (b) facets of the broader RC Scales; (c) clinically significant attributes not directly covered or assessed by the Clinical or RC Scales (e.g., suicidal ideation). A set of Higher-Order (H-O) Scales was also developed to provide a hierarchical interpretive framework for the test (Ben-Porath, 2012b; Tellegen & Ben-Porath, 2008/2011).

MMPI-2-RF SCALES

Table 1-1 includes a list of the 51 MMPI-2-RF scales, abbreviated scale names, number of items, and a brief description of the content of the scales.

TABLE 1-1
MMPI-2-RF Scale Labels, Abbreviations, Number of Items, and Brief Description

Scale	Abbreviation	Items	Description
Validity Scales			
Variable Response Inconsistency	VRIN-r	53 pairs	Random responding
True Response Inconsistency	TRIN-r	26 pairs	Fixed responding
Infrequent Responses	F-r	32	Responses infrequent in the general population
Infrequent Psychopathology Responses	Fp-r	21	Responses infrequent in general and psychiatric populations
Infrequent Somatic Responses	Fs	16	Somatic complaints infrequent in medical patient populations
Symptom Validity	FBS-r	30	Noncredible somatic and cognitive complaints
Response Bias Scale	RBS	28	Self-reported symptoms associated with failure on performance validity tests
Unlikely Virtues	L-r	14	Rarely claimed moral attributes or activities
Adjustment Validity	K-r	14	Avowals of good psychological adjustment
Higher-Order (H-O) Scales			
Emotional/Internalizing Dysfunction	EID	41	Pervasive problems associated with mood and affect
Thought Dysfunction	THD	26	Pervasive problems associated with disordered thinking
Behavioral/Externalizing Dysfunction	BXD	23	Pervasive problems associated with under-controlled behavior
Restructured Clinical (RC) Scales			
Demoralization	RCd	24	Nonspecific emotional distress; general unhappiness and dissatisfaction
Somatic Complaints	RC1	27	Preoccupation with a diverse set of health complaints
Low Positive Emotions	RC2	17	Lack of positive emotional experiences; anhedonia
Cynicism	RC3	15	Non-self-referential beliefs expressing distrust and a generally low opinion of others
Antisocial Behavior	RC4	22	Social deviance, rule breaking, impulsivity, and irresponsible behavior
Ideas of Persecution	RC6	17	Self-referential beliefs that others pose a threat; paranoid delusions
Dysfunctional Negative Emotions	RC7	24	Maladaptive anxiety, anger, irritability
Aberrant Experiences	RC8	18	Unusual perceptions or thoughts
Hypomanic Activation	RC9	28	Hyperactivation, aggression, impulsivity, and grandiosity
Specific Problem (SP) Scales			
Somatic/Cognitive Scales			
Malaise	MLS	8	Overall sense of physical debilitation, poor health
Gastrointestinal Complaints	GIC	5	Complaints about nausea, recurring upset stomach, and poor appetite
Head Pain Complaints	HPC	6	Complaints about head and neck pains

(continued on next page)

Scale	Abbreviation	Items	Description
Neurological Complaints	NUC	10	Complaints about dizziness, weakness, paralysis, loss of balance, etc.
Cognitive Complaints	COG	10	Memory problems, difficulties concentrating
Internalizing Scales			
Suicidal/Death Ideation	SUI	5	Direct reports of suicidal ideation and suicide attempts
Helplessness/Hopelessness	HLP	5	Belief that goals cannot be reached or problems solved
Self-Doubt	SFD	4	Lack of confidence, feelings of uselessness
Inefficacy	NFC	9	Belief that one is inefficacious; indecisiveness
Stress/Worry	STW	7	Stress reactivity; preoccupation with disappointments; difficulty with time pressure
Anxiety	AXY	5	Pervasive anxiety; frights; frequent nightmares
Anger Proneness	ANP	7	Becoming easily angered; impatient with others
Behavior-Restricting Fears	BRF	9	Fears that significantly inhibit normal activities
Multiple Specific Fears	MSF	9	Fears of a diverse set of stimuli, such as blood, fire, thunder, etc.
Externalizing Scales			
Juvenile Conduct Problems	JCP	6	Difficulties at school and at home; stealing as a youngster
Substance Abuse	SUB	7	Current and past misuse of alcohol and drugs
Aggression	AGG	9	Verbally and physically aggressive; violent behavior
Activation	ACT	8	Heightened excitation and energy level; euphoria; racing thoughts
Interpersonal Scales			
Family Problems	FML	10	Conflictual family relationships
Interpersonal Passivity	IPP	10	Being unassertive and submissive with others
Social Avoidance	SAV	10	Avoiding or not enjoying social events
Shyness	SHY	7	Bashful; prone to feel inhibited and anxious around others
Disaffiliativeness	DSF	6	Disliking people and being around them
Interest Scales			
Aesthetic-Literary Interests	AES	7	Interests in literature, music, the theater
Mechanical-Physical Interests	MEC	9	Interested in fixing and building things, the outdoors, sports
Personality Psychopathology Five (PSY-5) Scales			
Aggressiveness-revised	AGGR-r	18	Instrumental, goal-directed aggression; dominance and assertiveness; grandiosity
Psychoticism-revised	PSYC-r	26	Disconnection from reality
Disconstraint-revised	DISC-r	20	Undercontrolled behavior; impulsivity; sensation-seeking
Negative Emotionality/ Neuroticism–revised	NEGE-r	20	Dispositional proclivity to experience anxiety, insecurity, worry, anger, and fear
Introversion/Low Positive Emotionality–revised	INTR-r	20	Dispositional proclivity for social disengagement and anhedonia

Note. MMPI-2-RF = *Minnesota Multiphasic Personality Inventory-2-Restructured Form.*

The set of 9 Validity Scales assess various forms of response bias, whereas the 42 substantive scales assess clinical and personality content. Most of the substantive scales are organized in a hierarchy that reflects both content breadth and interpretive organization. More specifically, this hierarchy of scales includes the 3 H-O Scales on the first tier, the 9 RC Scales at the mid-tier level, and the 23 Specific Problems (SP) Scales at the bottom. Parallel to this hierarchy are the Personality Psychopathology Five (PSY-5) Scales, which are dimensional measures of personality pathology, and the two Interest Scales. We will discuss the scales in the following, but for much more detail on the scales and their underlying constructs we refer readers to Ben-Porath (2012b).

Validity Scales

The description, interpretation, and application of the Validity Scales will be discussed in detail in chapter 3. In brief, the nine Validity Scales assess various forms of response bias that can broadly be divided into three domains: non-content-based responding, overreporting, and underreporting (see e.g., Ben-Porath, 2013c, for a thorough description of these concepts). The non-content-based response bias refers to unintentional or intentional responding that manifests as an unscorable random/inconsistent/careless response or an indiscriminant fixed (acquiescent or counteracquiescent) response.

The MMPI-2-RF Score Report provides the number of unscorable responses as well as the percentage of such responses for each MMPI-2-RF scale. The Variable Response Inconsistency (VRIN-r) and True Response Inconsistency (TRIN-r) scales are designed to measure inconsistent and fixed indiscriminant responding, respectively. Five scales assess overreporting: Infrequent Responses (F-r) and Infrequent Psychopathology Responses (Fp-r), revised versions of their MMPI-2 counterparts, assess overreporting of psychopathology, the latter focused specifically on severe psychopathology; Infrequent Somatic Responses (Fs), Symptom Validity (FBS-r), and Response Bias Scale (RBS) assess various forms of noncredible somatic and cognitive responding, Fs and RBS being new scales in the MMPI-2-RF.

H-O Scales

The three H-O Scales, Emotional/Internalizing Dysfunction (EID), Thought Dysfunction (THD), and Behavioral/Externalizing Dysfunction (BXD) index broadband psychopathology constructs of internalizing, externalizing, and thought disorder, respectively. They map onto broader level dimensions that have been identified in a wide range of psychopathology research (see, e.g., Kotov et al., 2017, for a review). At the top of the MMPI-2-RF interpretive hierarchy, they reflect general and pervasive dysfunction in their respective areas. The narrowband levels of the interpretive hierarchy warrant consultation for a more fine-tuned interpretation of a test-taker's symptoms and traits.

RC Scales

The nine RC Scales are identical to their MMPI-2 counterparts. Unlike the original Clinical Scales, the RC Scales reflect underlying transdiagnostic and dimensional psychological constructs rather than psychiatric syndromes. Demoralization (RCd) is a measure of nonspecific emotional distress that is relevant to a range of internalizing psychopathology, including depression and anxiety, but it is also reflective of the distress that frequently accompanies other forms of psychopathology. Somatic Complaints (RC1) reflects a broad-based index of somatization, including preoccupation with somatic functioning and anxiety about health. Low Positive Emotions (RC2) measures low positive emotionality/anhedonia, a transdiagnostic construct related to deficiency in reward processing and interpersonal sensitivity and disengagement. This construct has been linked to depression, schizophrenia, social anxiety disorder, and avoidant personality disorder. Cynicism (RC3) reflects a worldview that other people are motivated by their selfish needs and cannot be trusted. It is important to distinguish RC3 from Ideas of Persecution (RC6). Unlike RC6, this construct is non-self-referential. High-scorers do not necessarily believe that they themselves are targets of maleficence. Antisocial Behavior (RC4) measures an antisocial personality lifestyle, including a deviation from social norms and standards, impulsivity, irresponsibility, substance abuse, and familial discord. Unlike RC3, as noted, the underlying construct for RC6 is a self-referential belief that one is being targeted and victimized by others (i.e., persecutory and interpersonal suspiciousness) and, at extreme levels, indicates paranoid delusions. Dysfunctional Negative Emotions (RC7) measures negative emotionality, including the maladaptive experience of anxiety, worry, sadness, guilt, and anger, as well as a hypersensitivity to criticism and rumination. The underlying construct for Aberrant Experiences (RC8) is a proclivity toward aberrant experiences, including nonpersecutory psychotic symptoms and dissociative experiences. Finally, Hypomanic Activation (RC9) is a measure of interpersonal antagonism, aggression, grandiosity, and excessive energy at lower levels of the clinical range and may be indicative of mania symptoms (e.g., racing thoughts, excessive euphoria) in the higher range of scores.

SP Scales

The 23 SP Scales are the most narrowband symptom and trait measures on the instrument. The scale labels are self-explanatory and reflect the underlying item content of the scales. Table 1-1 provides descriptions of the scales and we will not go into details here. Rather, we will discuss the organization of these scales and make specific points about scales that are particularly relevant in forensic settings. The SP Scales are organized into the four thematic domains of somatic/cognitive, internalizing, externalizing, and interpersonal, which also reflect the general interpretive organization of the instrument.

The Somatic/Cognitive SP Scales reflect specific manifestations of somatization, with the exception of Malaise (MLS), which assesses a nonspecific preoccupation with physical debilitation and poor health. These scales can be important in personal injury and disability evaluations, but it is critical to rule out noncredible somatic and cognitive responding before interpreting them.

The Internalizing SP Scales consist of various measures of emotional problems and proclivities. These scales can be further divided into facets of demoralization and negative emotionality. It is important to note that "facets" are not subscales, but, rather, these narrowband constructs indicate specific manifestations of a higher-order construct.[1] Suicidal/Death Ideation (SUI), Helplessness/Hopelessness (HLP), Self-Doubt (SFD), and Inefficacy (NFC) are all facets of demoralization, whereas Stress/Worry (STW), Anxiety (AXY), Anger Proneness (ANP), Behavior-Restricting Fears (BRF), and Multiple Specific Fears (MSF) are manifestations of negative affect, that is, RC7 facets. It is important to consider that hopelessness is a good predictor of suicide attempt (e.g., Kovacs & Garrison, 1985); as such, clinicians should be concerned about an elevated HLP scale score even if SUI items are not explicitly endorsed. STW and AXY can be differentiated in that the former is a more generalized measure of anxious apprehensiveness and stress reactivity, including rumination and obsessiveness, whereas AXY refers to intense fright and trauma symptoms (Ben-Porath, 2012b). Indeed, the latter scale is the best MMPI-2-RF predictor of posttraumatic stress disorder (PTSD) symptoms (Sellbom, Lee, Ben-Porath, Arbisi, & Gervais, 2012). Finally, BRF assesses fearfulness that inhibits normal activity, whereas MSF is a more generalized tendency toward fearfulness.

The four externalizing SP Scales (JCP, SUB, AGG, and ACT) can be divided into RC4 and RC9 facets. JCP items are all worded in the past tense and reflect conduct problems as a child; this scale is the best marker of general externalizing (Sellbom, 2016a). The SUB items are all face valid; therefore, it is important to consider the potential denial of such symptoms in settings in which individuals may have an incentive to deny alcohol and drug problems or in treatment settings in which these individuals may be in denial. The AGG and ACT items can both be reflective of severe manic symptoms at very high scores, but structurally the AGG items are better indicators of general externalizing, whereas ACT items are more specific to manic symptoms (Sellbom, 2016a; Sellbom, Bagby, Kushner, Quilty, & Ayearst, 2012). Indeed, empirical research has demonstrated that ACT is the best individual MMPI-2-RF scale at differentiating bipolar disorder from unipolar depression and schizophrenia (Sellbom, Bagby, et al., 2012; Watson, Quilty, & Bagby, 2011).

The five interpersonal SP Scales (FML, IPP, SAV, SHY, and DSF) reflect individual differences and dysfunction in several related but distinct domains. FML is nonspecific and considers familial discord and alienation, as the name implies. The remaining four are different manifestations of interpersonal detachment. SAV and DSF both indicate avoidance of others; however, the former scale measures pure introversion and lack of desire to socialize, whereas the latter reflects a disdain for bonding and closely affiliating with others. Neither measure social anxiety per se, which is the target construct of SHY. Individuals with psychopathic personality traits tend to score low on IPP, SAV, and SHY, but high on DSF (Sellbom et al., 2012), which is consistent with a superficial domineering, gregarious, and socially nonanxious presentation in light of limited capacity and desire for developing close emotional bonds with others.

Interest Scales

The two Interest Scales (Aesthetic-Literary Interests [AES] and Mechanical-Physical Interests [MEC]) primarily measure personality and attitudinal constructs rather than clinical symptoms. Early research has indicated that AES is moderately associated with empathy, whereas high scores on MEC are associated with sensation-seeking and thrill-seeking (Tellegen & Ben-Porath, 2008/2011).

PSY-5 Scales

The five PSY-5 Scales are revised versions of their MMPI-2 counterparts. They are measures of the PSY-5 constructs originally articulated by Harkness and McNulty (1994). They represent dimensional personality traits with an abnormal range and were presented as a dimensional alternative to the categorical personality disorder system, which has dominated the *Diagnostic and Statistical Manual of Mental Disorders* (DSM). Currently, these constructs and associated MMPI-2-RF scales align well with the trait domains included in the Alternative Model for Personality Disorders (AMPD; American Psychiatric Association, 2013) in Section III of the DSM-5 (Anderson et al., 2013; Anderson, Sellbom, Ayearst, et al., 2015). More specifically, Aggressiveness-revised (AGGR-r) (which measures instrumental aggression, grandiosity, dominance, and to a lesser degree callousness) parallels the antagonism domain in the DSM-5-AMPD. Psychoticism-revised (PSYC-r) indexes a broad proneness to disconnect from reality, similar to its DSM-5-AMPD counterpart of the same name. Disconstraint-revised (DISC-r) measures a somewhat broader dimension than the disinhibition domain within the DSM-5-AMPD and, in particular, reflects impulsivity, sensation-seeking, thrill-seeking, deceitfulness, and manipulativeness. NEGE-r is closely aligned with negative emotionality, and, unlike RC7, it is conceived as a personality proclivity to negative emotionality (Ben-Porath, 2012b). Finally, Introversion/Low Positive Emotionality–revised (INTR-r) reflects two related subconstructs of social disengagement and anhedonia and maps onto the DSM-5-AMPD domain.

MMPI-2-RF DOCUMENTATION

Three manuals guide the use and understanding of the MMPI-2-RF: *Manual for Administration, Scoring, and Interpretation; Technical Manual;* and *User's Guide for Reports.* It is recommended that readers who use the MMPI-2-RF clinically read these manuals carefully before administering the MMPI-2-RF. In this section, we provide some highlights of important information contained in each manual.

The *Manual for Administration, Scoring, and Interpretation* covers what the title implies. In addition, it provides an introduction to the instrument, contains an important chapter on intended uses, user qualifications, and test security, as well as a description of the normative reference group and a calculation of standardized scores. In terms of administration, the manual informs the reader that it is important, first and foremost, to assess the test-ability of the test-taker; this might include a formal reading assessment. The MMPI-2-RF has a reading level of grades 4.5 to 6, depending on the methodology used (Ben-Porath, 2012b). If this level is not met, or the examiner has other concerns about reading proficiency, an audio-recorded CD version of the test is available. The administration modalities available for the MMPI-2-RF are a standard paper booklet with an answer sheet (with audio CD, when needed, as previously mentioned) and a computer via web interface (Pearson Q-global) or software (Pearson Q Local). It is optimal to administer the test in a quiet and private setting under supervision. Supervision is particularly important in forensic evaluations. One issue that can sometimes arise in a forensic evaluation is less than optimal motivation on the part of the examinee to complete the test. Occasionally, examinees might be resistant to completing the MMPI-2-RF, particularly if they are compelled to complete the evaluation by the court. It is important for the examiner to explain the purpose of the testing (as part of the overall evaluation). If the examinee exhibits significant resistance to completing the MMPI-2-RF, testing should be discontinued, which would be noted in the report or testimony to the court.

The *Manual for Administration, Scoring, and Interpretation* also includes a good summary section on protection of test materials, which is quite relevant to forensic settings, where attorneys make frequent requests for test results (including raw data and test items) as part of the discovery process. The manual notes that it is contingent on psychologists to maintain test integrity and security by not releasing copy-protected materials. The manual also provides a sample letter to aid in litigation-related demands for MMPI-2-RF materials. When responding to a request for records, it is important for the examiner to ensure that the materials are only released to another qualified individual who can score and interpret them. Jurisdictions vary with how strict these rules are followed. Some courts will compel a psychologist to release test records even if another psychologist is not involved in the case. In those cases, the psychologist should take efforts to ensure that test materials are protected (e.g., placed under seal in the court file).

Several scoring procedures are available for the MMPI-2-RF. Two computerized reports (Score Report and Interpretive Report), to be described later, can be generated via Q-global, Q Local, or by mailing the score sheets to Pearson Assessments. The MMPI-2-RF can also be scored by converting an MMPI-2 to an MMPI-2-RF protocol with the same report options. Finally, hand-scoring materials are available, including paper profile sheets, for those who find the cost of computerized scoring prohibitive or who simply wish to do their own scoring. Forensic examiners should be aware that hand-scoring is more prone to errors and, thus, to erroneous scale scores.

The *MMPI-2-RF Technical Manual* includes information about the rationale for developing the test, scale development, and a plethora of psychometric and validity data. More specifically, it provides 136 tables of external correlates that are derived from a range of settings, including mental health (both inpatient and outpatient), medical, substance abuse treatment, civil and criminal forensic, and nonclinical. Overall, 605 independent external criteria are included, derived from several different criterion modalities (e.g., clinician-ratings, self-report questionnaires, history data), which translate into almost 54,000 correlations. The *Technical Manual* also includes descriptive data from a wide range of settings that serve as the basis for comparison groups, which are continuously updated in Pearson Assessments' scoring software. They include, but are not limited to, psychiatric inpatients; outpatient mental health; various presurgery and personnel screening; and, most important to the current context, forensic pretrial, forensic neuropsychology, forensic disability claimant, forensic child custody, and forensic parental fitness. These comparison groups supplement the normative reference group by allowing the clinician to determine the degree to which an evaluee's responses are typical or atypical for a particular context. The *Technical Manual* also includes the important information that the MMPI-2-RF normative sample, which was collected in the 1980s, is still representative of the current population.

The *MMPI-2-RF User's Guide for Reports* provides information about how to use the Score and Interpretive Reports.[2] The Score Report contains the score profiles for all MMPI-2-RF scales. Information on the profile includes raw scores, standardized *T* scores (uniform *T* scores for 40 of the 42 Substantive Scale scores, linear *T* scores are provided for the two Interest Scales), and percentage of scorable responses. The Score Report also includes a page that organizes all MMPI-2-RF scale scores by interpretive domain as recommended by the test authors (see e.g., Ben-Porath, 2012b, chapter 8). Item-level information is also provided, which includes a list of all items to which the test-taker produced an unscorable response, as well as a list of "critical responses." The latter are organized by the seven default scales, which are listed when a scale is clinically elevated. The software allows the report user to add scales—the default scale items are always reported—if deemed important for a particular setting or evaluee. Finally, the inclusion of a comparison group provides the average *T* score for each MMPI-2-RF scale (plotted in the profile and presented numerically) as well as the *T*-score values that fall ± 1 standard deviation from the comparison group mean. Also provided is the percentage of comparison group members who score at or below the test-taker, values that are analogous to percentiles.

The MMPI-2-RF Interpretive Report includes all the features of the Score Report as well as an interpretive narrative that is organized according to the authors' recommended strategy. Diagnostic considerations as well as potential targets for treatment are presented on the basis of MMPI-2-RF scale scores. The narrative interpretation is transparent: superscripts (with corresponding endnotes) document which MMPI-2-RF scale(s) resulted in a particular statement being made and whether the statement is based on an empirical correlate associated with the scale in question or on author inference. References supporting the correlates are provided.

MMPI-2-RF INTERPRETIVE STRATEGY

Two sources document the MMPI-2-RF interpretive strategy recommended by the test authors: the *MMPI-2-RF Manual for Administration, Scoring, and Interpretation* (Ben-Porath & Tellegen, 2008/2011) and Ben-Porath's (2012b) *Interpreting the MMPI-2-RF* book. The latter is highly recommended to the reader, since Ben-Porath (2012b) was able to incorporate research not yet available when the test manual was originally published. We assume that the reader has at least the manual available to obtain the formal interpretive strategy. However, in the following, we provide a succinct summary of the interpretive framework and organization.

The first step in any interpretation is determining protocol validity. The Validity Scales and their interpretation, of particular importance in forensic contexts, will be discussed in detail in chapter 3. If a protocol is deemed valid for clinical interpretation, the Substantive Scales can be examined.

Five broad domains provide a framework for the interpretation: emotional dysfunction, thought dysfunction, behavioral dysfunction, somatic/cognitive dysfunction, and interpersonal functioning. The H-O Scales, representing the first three domains, is the first scale set to be consulted. The most elevated H-O Scale determines which domain is interpreted first; for instance, if THD is the most (or only) elevated H-O Scale, then this scale and all scales contained within the domain (i.e., RC6, RC8, and PSYC-r) are interpreted first. The second-most elevated H-O Scale dictates the next domain to be interpreted, and so forth. If no more H-O Scales are elevated (or if none of the H-O Scales are elevated in the profile), the RC Scales are consulted. The most elevated RC Scale determines the next domain of interpretation. For instance, if RC4 is elevated, then the behavioral dysfunction domain and all of its affiliated SP Scales (i.e., JCP, SUB, AGG, ACT) and the PSY-5 Scales (i.e., AGGR-r, DISC-r) are interpreted before moving onto the next domain. If no more RC Scales are elevated, then all elevated SP Scales that have not already been covered are interpreted, with information from additional elevated PSY-5 Scales where applicable, in their respective remaining domains.

A few additional comments are in order. There are no H-O Scales for the somatic/cognitive and interpersonal domains. RC1 and RC3, respectively, serve as the anchor scales for these domains. Ben-Porath (2012b) recommended that the somatic/cognitive domain be interpreted immediately after the emotional dysfunction domain. It is also recommended that the interpersonal domain be interpreted last, regardless of RC Scale elevation order. Furthermore, most of the RC Scales are associated with diagnostic and treatment-related considerations, which should be consulted, though integrated with other extratest information. We strongly recommend that no diagnosis ever be generated on the basis of self-report questionnaire information alone.

Chapter 2

General Considerations for Using the MMPI-2-RF in Forensic Evaluations

FORENSIC APPLICATIONS IN BRIEF

There are numerous contexts in forensic psychological assessment in which MMPI-2-RF information can be useful. In criminal court, psychologists are often called upon to address questions related to competency to stand trial (and, less frequently, other competencies such as understanding Miranda rights, sentencing to be executed, etc.), criminal responsibility, risk assessment (for sentencing as well as custodial release), sexual offender assessment, and mitigation of sentencing. Furthermore, the MMPI-2-RF is frequently used in civil litigation when individuals claim psychological or neurocognitive injury. Similarly, individuals who file for disability status (to receive a benefit) can be evaluated psychologically using the MMPI-2-RF. In family court, the instrument can be used by psychologists to examine parents' mental health status or maladaptive personality traits, which can be important factors for consideration by judges in ruling on custody arrangements that are in the best interests of the child. Finally, the MMPI-2-RF can be used by psychologists working in correctional settings, in which they are often called upon to conduct mental health evaluations to identify targets for invention or other forms of management and to evaluate risk status for security classification.

As a broadband measure of psychological functioning, the MMPI-2-RF can augment a forensic evaluation in a number of ways. If the circumstances and logistics of the evaluation allow the MMPI-2-RF to be administered prior to the clinical interview, the clinician will gain an indication of the individual's psychological functioning in a variety of relevant areas. Moreover, the clinician can utilize the test results to formulate clinical hypotheses about diagnostic issues as well as forensic matters (e.g., evidence of delusions and competency to stand trial). The test results can also yield important inquiries for the clinician to utilize in clinical and collateral interviews. Avoiding confirmatory bias is an important issue in forensic assessment, as well as in clinical assessment generally (Borum, Otto, & Golding, 1993). By covering a wide range of psychological constructs, the MMPI-2-RF enhances the clinician's ability to consider various hypotheses about the evaluee's functioning.

When using the MMPI-2-RF in a forensic psychological evaluation, it is very important for psychologists to consider that this instrument (and its predecessors) was not designed to address psycho-legal questions and it cannot specifically address them. Nonetheless, the MMPI-2-RF can be very useful in forensic evaluations because it can yield important information about a person that is highly relevant to the question at hand, such as self-presentation, symptoms of psychopathology, personality traits, and specific behavioral styles. Of course, the degree to which MMPI-2-RF information is relied upon varies—as does its use. For instance, competency evaluations focus on current capacity and functioning, whereas a criminal responsibility evaluation examines mental state at the time of the offense. A risk assessment evaluation is focused on the prediction of future behavior. In personal injury (and, to some degree, disability) evaluations, the focus is often on change in psychological status in light of a precipitating event (e.g., a car accident or accident at work).

Most forensic evaluations come with an external incentive to misrepresent oneself psychologically. The MMPI-2-RF Validity Scales can be quite useful in detecting whether a person is responding to the test in an inconsistent, exaggerated, or defensive manner (e.g., Handel, Ben-Porath, Tellegen, & Archer, 2010; Sellbom & Bagby, 2008; Sellbom, Toomey, Wygant, Kucharski, & Duncan, 2010; see Wygant, Walls, Brothers, & Berry, 2018, for a review). In addition, corroborating information can assist with a judgment about whether the person is cooperating with the evaluation, possibly malingering, or being intentionally defensive. The evaluation of response bias will be covered in greater detail in Chapter 3.

The MMPI-2-RF scales that measure substantive clinical content can aid in characterizing the level of psychopathology and/or personality functioning of the test-taker. For instance, in evaluations of competency to stand trial or criminal responsibility, a significant issue is frequently the mental state of the defendant and, in particular, whether the individual is suffering from disordered thinking. Several MMPI-2-RF scales are useful in identifying thought disturbance, and the test can differentiate paranoid from non-paranoid psychosis (e.g., RC6 and RC8; see Arbisi, Sellbom, & Ben-Porath, 2008; Handel & Archer, 2008; Romero, Toorabally, Burchett, Tarescavage, & Glassmire, 2017; Tellegen et al., 2003). For risk assessment evaluations, several MMPI-2-RF scales measure externalizing proclivities, including RC4 and RC9, which have been associated with psychopathy (e.g., Haneveld, Kamphuis, Smid, & Forbey, 2017; Phillips, Sellbom, Ben-Porath, & Patrick, 2014; Sellbom et al., 2012), increased risk for violent reoffending (e.g., Sellbom, Ben-Porath, Baum, Erez, & Gregory, 2008; Tarescavage, Cappo, & Ben-Porath, 2016; Tarescavage, Glassmire, & Burchett, 2016), and substance abuse (e.g., Arbisi et al., 2008; Forbey & Ben-Porath, 2007; Sellbom, Ben-Porath, & Stafford, 2007; Sellbom, Ben-Porath, Baum, et al., 2008).

In sum, the MMPI-2-RF has gained widespread use in forensic settings (e.g., Neal & Grisso, 2014) owing to its utility in assisting clinicians in forensic psychological evaluations. However, a significant issue arises when MMPI-2-RF information is used as evidence to inform a psycho-legal opinion to be offered in court testimony and whether this evidence is admissible in court.

GENERAL ADMISSIBILITY ISSUES IN COURT

When an expert relies on the MMPI-2-RF to form an opinion to be offered in testimony, the basis for this opinion may be scrutinized and admissibility denied if it fails to meet certain standards. In U.S. federal court cases and in many U.S. state courts, these standards for admissibility are outlined in the U.S. Supreme Court decision in *Daubert v. Merrell Dow Pharmaceuticals, Inc.* (1993). The court unanimously ruled that the preceding *Frye v. U.S.* (1923) requirement that expert evidence should be admissible in court only if it was generally accepted by its scientific community was too stringent when applied to newly tested and validated techniques. Therefore, the court highlighted the *Federal Rules of Evidence Rule 702* to guide a more flexible determination of admissibility that included an emphasis on the scientific reliability and validity of the technique in question, rather than on general acceptance. It is also important to note that considering the *Daubert* factors may have implications for the international reader as well. U.S. Supreme Court cases have significant influence in commonwealth countries (see, e.g.,

Makita v. Sprowles, 2001, New South Wales Court of Appeal, Australia), and many jurisdictions consider highly similar factors. Such consideration is often applied in states that continue to rely predominately on the *Frye v. U.S.* (1923) test of general acceptance, in that case law often dictates trial judges to consider *Daubert*-like criteria (see Ben-Porath, 2012a). We therefore center our discussion of defending MMPI-2-RF–based opinions in court on the *Daubert* criteria.

In its ruling on *Daubert,* the Supreme Court established that trial judges must determine the validity of inferences based on scientific techniques by considering whether: (a) the technique can be and has been tested empirically, (b) the technique has been subjected to peer review, (c) the error rates of the technique are known, (d) there are standards for applying the technique, and (e) the technique is generally accepted in its scientific discipline. The last criterion refers back to the *Frye v. U.S.* (1923) ruling regarding expert testimony, which still applies in several states.

The MMPI-2-RF is next considered in regard to each of these *Daubert* criteria (see Ben-Porath, 2012a, and Sellbom, 2012, who have offered similar and more detailed discussions in this regard; see also Ben-Porath, 2013a). It is important to keep in mind that we are referring to general use of the MMPI-2-RF in a forensic psychological evaluation. In any given case, the question is whether a specific MMPI-2-RF–based conclusion reached by an expert can meet the standards for admissibility. The reader should bear in mind that because any MMPI-2-RF interpretive statement can be scrutinized and challenged, the forensic examiner should be ready to defend such statements in court. Interpretations that are not consistent with the empirical literature on the MMPI-2-RF should always be avoided (e.g., using MMPI-2-RF information to draw conclusions about deviant sexual preferences).

HAS THE MMPI-2-RF BEEN TESTED?

The MMPI-2-RF had very likely undergone more extensive testing to determine its psychometric properties at the time of its release than has any other psychological test instrument. In addition to information about the MMPI-2-RF normative sample (the MMPI-2 nongendered normative sample; Ben-Porath & Forbey, 2003), the *MMPI-2-RF Technical Manual* (Tellegen & Ben-Porath, 2008/2011) presents a substantial amount of information about internal consistency and test–retest reliability estimates in several normative and clinical samples. Moreover, the *Technical Manual* includes validity data from a range of settings, such as criminal defendants and forensic disability claimants, community mental health center clients, psychiatric inpatients, substance abuse patients, medical outpatients, and university students. External criterion measurement modalities include therapist ratings, intake information, record review data, and other self-report instruments. These validity data made it possible for the test authors to elaborate on individual scale interpretations.

In addition to inferential statistics, the *MMPI-2-RF Technical Manual* (Tellegen & Ben-Porath, 2008/2011) provides descriptive group data for numerous settings, including (but not limited to) pretrial criminal, civil forensic disability, correctional, outpatient mental health, inpatient mental health, outpatient medical, substance abuse treatment, personnel selection, and nonclinical settings. This list of settings is continuously evolving and being incorporated into the Pearson Assessments' scoring software. Overall, these samples include well over 60,000 men and women. These group means and standard deviations can be highly informative to clinicians who wish to compare a test-taker's scores with those from a particular setting. In terms of forensic psychological evaluations, the large pretrial, civil disability, and correctional samples are particularly applicable. As such, the forensic examiner can determine whether MMPI-2-RF scale scores, in addition to being consistent with or deviant from normative data, are typical or atypical of a particular setting in which he or she practices.

HAS THE MMPI-2-RF BEEN SUBJECTED TO PEER REVIEW?

Subsequent to the release of the *Technical Manual,* over 300 peer-reviewed publications have appeared on the MMPI-2-RF, including a large number that contain empirical data on MMPI-2-RF scale scores across a wide range of settings.[1] We recommend that readers consult the continuously updated reference list hosted by the test publisher, the University of Minnesota Press (see https://www.upress.umn.edu/test-division/MMPI-2-RF/mmpi-2-rf-references).

A large proportion of the MMPI-2-RF publications have focused on the RC Scales. Overall, this research indicates that the RC Scales capture the core components of the original MMPI and MMPI-2 Clinical Scales with little or no loss of convergent information, but with a substantial gain in discriminant validity (e.g., Forbey & Ben-Porath, 2007; Handel & Archer, 2008; Sellbom & Ben-Porath, 2005; Sellbom, Ben-Porath, & Graham, 2006; Sellbom, Ben-Porath, McNulty, Arbisi, & Graham, 2006; Sellbom, Graham, & Schenk, 2006; Simms, Casillas, Clark, Watson, & Doebbeling, 2005; Wygant et al., 2007; see also Tellegen, Ben-Porath, & Sellbom, 2009, for a review of this literature).

In terms of peer-reviewed research directly relevant to forensic psychological evaluations, Ben-Porath (2012a) estimated that 25 percent of MMPI-2-RF studies have focused on the Validity Scales. Indeed, a large body of research has examined the detection of various forms of overreporting (e.g., see Hoelzle, Nelson, & Arbisi, 2012; Sleep, Petty, & Wygant, 2015; Wygant et al., 2018, for reviews), whereas far fewer have examined the detection of underreporting (e.g., Crighton, Marek, Dragon, & Ben-Porath, 2015; Marion et al., 2013; Sellbom & Bagby, 2008).

With regard to specific forensic issues beyond the detection of overreporting (and by extension, malingering), the area of risk assessment and forensic treatment outcomes has garnered the most attention. Several studies have begun to document both concurrent associations between MMPI-2-RF scale scores and risk assessment instruments (e.g., Tarescavage, Cappo, et al., 2016), and in the prediction of violent reoffending (e.g., Rock, Sellbom, Ben-Porath, & Salekin, 2013; Sellbom et al., 2008; Tarescavage, Glassmire, et al., 2016; Tarescavage, Luna-Jones, & Ben-Porath, 2014). Other studies have indicated that MMPI-2-RF scale scores can be useful in predicting negative outcomes in various court-mandated treatment programs (Mattson, Powers, Halfaker, Akenson, & Ben-Porath, 2012; Sellbom et al., 2008).

Psychopathy is often considered an important clinical construct in forensic settings (e.g., Hare, 2016). Over the past decade, a plethora of studies have shown that psychopathic personality traits can be assessed by MMPI-2-RF scales (Haneveld et al., 2017; Phillips et al., 2014; Sellbom, Ben-Porath, Lilienfeld, Patrick, & Graham, 2005; Sellbom, Ben-Porath, et al., 2007; Sellbom et al., 2012; Wygant & Sellbom, 2012). Specific psychopathy scales for the MMPI-2-RF have also been developed (Sellbom et al., 2012; Sellbom et al., 2016). Furthermore, Rock et al. (2013) showed that psychopathy indices that reflect psychopathic personality traits were predictive of poor treatment outcomes as well as future reoffending in a male domestic violence offender sample.

The MMPI-2-RF has also been validated in several studies using prison inmates. More specifically, empirical data from these settings show evidence of good convergent and discriminant validity (e.g., Forbey, Ben-Porath, & Gartland, 2009; Gottfried, Anestis, Dillon, & Carbonell, 2016). Other studies report evidence for prediction of treatment compliance and outcomes (e.g., Clegg, Fremouw, Horacek, Cole, & Schwartz, 2010; McAnulty, McAnulty, Sipp, Demakis, & Heggestad, 2014). A recent study demonstrated that MMPI-2-RF scale scores can be used to identify subgroups of offenders (Sellbom, 2014).

A final salient area of forensic-relevant peer-reviewed research comes from studies using the MMPI-2-RF for family court evaluations. A number of studies have been published that illustrate MMPI-2-RF scale scores in child custody and parental fitness evaluations (e.g., Archer, Hagan, Mason, Handel, & Archer, 2012; Kauffman, Stolberg, & Madero, 2015; Pinsoneault & Ezzo, 2012; Resendes & Lecci, 2012; Stredny, Archer, & Mason, 2006). These studies allow forensic examiners to distinguish typical from atypical scores in these settings, which is important in light of the inherent levels of underreporting present in such evaluations.

In sum, there is extensive peer-reviewed literature on the MMPI-2-RF to guide its clinical and forensic use.

ARE THE ERROR RATES OF THE MMPI-2-RF KNOWN?

This question can be directly answered with reliability data and, in particular for individuals' scores, standard error of measurement (SEM) data (Ben-Porath, 2012a; Sellbom, 2012). The *MMPI-2-RF Technical Manual* (Tellegen & Ben-Porath, 2008/2011) presents reliability and SEM data for the normative sample, as well as for several clinical samples. It is noted in the manual that internal consistencies and test–retest reliability estimates for almost all MMPI-2-RF scales are well within acceptable standards and are comparable or better relative to similar self-report inventories.

The most important statistic for an individual's score on an MMPI-2-RF scale is SEM. According to the *MMPI-2-RF Technical Manual,* these values (in *T*-score units) range from 4 to 9 (normative sample) and 6 to 12 (clinical samples) for the Validity Scales;[2] from 3 to 5 (normative sample) and 4 to 6 (clinical samples) for the H-O Scales; from 3 to 6 (normative sample) and 3 to 7 (clinical samples) for the RC Scales; from 4 to 8 (normative sample) and 5 to 11 (clinical samples) for the SP and Interest Scales; and from 3 to 6 (normative sample) and 5 to 6 (clinical samples) for the PSY-5 Scales. These values are acceptable to excellent by psychometric standards and at least comparable to those of other self-report inventories of personality and psychopathology. The somewhat lower reliabilities of the SP Scales suggest that clinicians should look for more extreme scores to have sufficient confidence in inferences based on these scales relative to those based on the H-O, RC, and PSY-5 Scales—at least when interpreted in isolation. Tellegen and Ben-Porath (2008/2011) recognized this issue and stated:

> SEMs are predominantly eight T-score points or lower, and a majority are six points or lower. Exceptions are SEMs of shorter and/or highly truncated measures like Suicidal/Death Ideation (SUI), Helplessness/Hopelessness (HLP), Anxiety (AXY), Behavior Restricting Fears (BRF), and Disaffiliativeness (DSF), which in the clinical samples range from 9 to 11 points. Larger SEM values imply that more extreme T scores are needed to justify clinically significant inferences. (p. 26)

Furthermore, error rates can also be determined for scales used directly for categorical decision making. Such error rates are particularly applicable to the MMPI-2-RF Validity Scales, which are used to make decisions about a test-taker's approach to the test and/or evaluation. A large number of studies reported on the MMPI-2-RF Validity Scales indicate that they are associated with very good overall classification accuracy (see, e.g., Wygant et al., 2018).

ARE THERE STANDARDS FOR APPLYING THE MMPI-2-RF?

The *MMPI-2-RF Manual for Administration, Scoring, and Interpretation* (Ben-Porath & Tellegen, 2008/2011) described these standards. As Ben-Porath (2012a) noted, the manual provides detailed instructions for the administration, scoring, and interpretation of the test. These were covered in detail in Chapter 1 and will therefore not be repeated here. It is safe to assume that, if the procedures outlined in this manual were followed, it is unlikely that the forensic examiner would be successfully challenged on these grounds.

IS THE MMPI-2-RF GENERALLY ACCEPTED?

Ben-Porath (2012a) provided an impressive array of evidence to support general acceptance of the MMPI-2-RF, which has continued to evolve. Indeed, we think we are now at a point, almost 10 years since the instrument was published, where we can state with a great deal of confidence that the MMPI-2-RF is generally accepted in the scientific and professional community. Nevertheless, because forensic examiners could still be challenged on this basis, particularly in jurisdictions that emphasize this criterion (i.e., "*Frye*" states), we will review some indicators of general acceptance.

In a recent article of evidenced-based assessment in forensic psychology, Archer, Wheeler, and Vauter (2016) highlighted five criteria that they believed should be met for a clinical assessment instrument to be considered evidence-based (e.g., adequate standardization, acceptable reliability/validity when used in forensic settings). The MMPI-2-RF was a frequently noted example by Archer, Wheeler, et al. and possibly one of the few instruments currently available to psychologists that could meet all five (as noted by Sellbom & Hopwood, 2016).

As Ben-Porath (2012a) pointed out, substantial space is devoted to the MMPI-2-RF in major interpretive texts, most notably the leading ones by Greene (2011) and Graham (2012). The instrument is also covered in several chapters in edited books (e.g., Ben-Porath, 2013a, 2013b; Ben-Porath & Archer, 2014; Ben-Porath, Corey, & Tarescavage, 2017; Sellbom & Lee, 2013; Wygant, Applegate, & Wall, 2015; Wygant et al., 2018).

The MMPI-2-RF has also been recommended for use by several government and professional organizations (Ben-Porath, 2012a). For instance, it is listed among measures in proposed practice guidelines for assessments of child sexual abusers (Chu & Ogloff, 2012). The MMPI-2-RF is also a recommended measure in a guide to establishing a practice on police preemployment psychological evaluations (Gallo & Haglin, 2011). Moreover, the test was the only personality inventory included among measures for assessing mental health as part of the National Football League settlement with retired players (see, e.g., Conidi, 2015). And the MMPI-2-RF was highlighted in the Institute of Medicine report to U.S. Congress: *Psychological Testing in the Service of Disability Determination* (Committee on Psychological Testing, 2015) in which the Validity Scales were featured.

Ben-Porath (2012a) also indicated that the MMPI-2-RF is being increasingly used internationally. The American English version is available and being used in Australia, New Zealand, Canada, South Africa, and the United Kingdom. Translations into Spanish, Korean, French, and Dutch, among other languages, have also been completed.

Finally, the MMPI-2-RF has been continuously cited in a growing number of U.S. federal and state appellate court cases. To our knowledge, none of these cases have specifically rejected the reliance on this instrument for supporting opinions about psycho-legal questions (see, e.g., *Adams v. Astrue*, 2012; *Michigan v. Espinoza*, 2011; *Wood v. Haler*, 2011).

A RECENT CRITIQUE OF USING THE MMPI-2-RF IN FORENSIC SETTINGS

Several critiques of the MMPI-2-RF have been published, almost exclusively by the same core group of people. Reviews of these critiques and how they have been clearly and impressively rebutted are available elsewhere (e.g., Ben-Porath, 2012a, 2012b, 2013a; Ben-Porath & Flens, 2012). Most recently, however, Butcher, Hass, Greene, and Nelson (2015) authored a book on using the MMPI-2 in forensic evaluations and devoted a chapter to critiquing the MMPI-2-RF. Unfortunately, we find the criticisms to be unfounded and, in many cases, very misleading. It is nevertheless important that forensic examiners be aware of them, as they might be challenged on or confronted with this material during testimony. We will review some key criticisms the authors made, but note that all of them have been repeatedly published (and rebutted) elsewhere.

Butcher et al. (2015) complained that the MMPI-2-RF uses only 60 percent of the 567 MMPI-2 items, and, as a result, forensic examiners using the MMPI-2-RF would not have information about important mental health problems and personality traits relevant to forensic assessments. The authors appear to have ignored the fact that the main goal of the MMPI-2-RF was to capture the important clinical substance in the MMPI-2-RF item pool using a more efficient set of scales that are psychometrically up-to-date (Tellegen & Ben-Porath, 2008/2011). Butcher et al. also did not mention that the *MMPI-2-RF Technical Manual* shows correlations between all MMPI-2 and MMPI-2-RF scale scores across several normative and mental health samples (Tellegen & Ben-Porath, 2008/2011), which allows the forensic examiner to demonstrate that the clinical substance of each MMPI-2 scale is indeed likely to be covered by the more efficient measure.

Next, Butcher et al. (2015) claimed that the MMPI-2-RF could not be considered a version of the MMPI-2 because the scales are different and the Clinical Scales are not included. This argument has been rebutted extensively elsewhere (e.g., Ben-Porath, 2012a, 2013a; Ben-Porath & Flens, 2012). Briefly, MMPI-2 items (the majority from the original MMPI) are exclusively used as is the MMPI-2 normative sample. Given this, calling it "anything but a restructured version of the MMPI-2 would, in fact, be misleading" (Ben-Porath, 2013a, p. 475).

Butcher et al. (2015) questioned whether the MMPI-2-RF is generally accepted, particularly when compared with the MMPI-2. There are a number of problems with their misleading arguments. First, general acceptance, especially from the perspective of *Frye v. U.S.,* is an absolute consideration, not a relative one. Second, the authors argued that the lack of surveys on the use of the MMPI-2-RF versus the MMPI-2 brings into question the relative acceptance of these instruments. The authors neglected to mention the recent surveys in forensic neuropsychology practice that show that the MMPI-2-RF is preferred over the MMPI-2 for symptom validity testing in such evaluations (Martin, Schroeder, & Odland, 2015; Schroeder, Martin, & Odland, 2016). Third, Butcher et al. also cited misleading data about the sales of MMPI-2 versus MMPI-2-RF materials, suggesting that sales of the former outweigh the latter 3:1. However, recently published fully updated sales data show that sales of the instruments are roughly equal (Ben-Porath, 2016).

Butcher et al. (2015) argued that there is limited evidence available on the MMPI-2-RF Validity Scales: "Rogers and Granacher (2011) concluded that 'with minimal data on their effectiveness for assessing feigned mental disorders, it is likely to be years before the body of research justifies their use with suspected malingering in forensic cases'" (p. 667). Unfortunately, they neglected to note that the very next sentence in Rogers and Granacher (2011) is: "Initial forensic studies (Sellbom et al., 2010; Rogers et al., 2010) produced promising yet disparate results," as well as more recent literature by both Rogers and Granacher that has been more supportive (Rogers, Gillard, Berry, & Granacher, 2011; Wygant et al., 2011). More broadly, Butcher et al. (2015) neglected to take into account the existing empirical literature on the MMPI-2-RF Validity Scales, including their use in forensic settings. Indeed, at the time of this writing, there are 67 published studies that have included the MMPI-2-RF Validity Scales, not 15 as cited by the authors when they published their chapter in 2015. Also, Butcher et al. did not mention that an overview of the MMPI-2-RF research literature would clearly indicate that the MMPI-2-RF versions of the Validity Scales perform comparably to their MMPI-2 counterparts in the assessment of overreported psychopathology. Moreover, the MMPI-2-RF would be preferred for the assessment of response bias in forensic neuropsychology settings owing to two new scales indexing response styles directly relevant to such settings (Martin et al., 2015; Schroeder et al., 2016).

Butcher et al. (2015) recommended against use of the SP Scales in forensic settings owing to the lack of information about their development, low reliability, and limited research base. They failed to mention that similar (albeit invalid) arguments could be made about many MMPI-2 scales as well, but these were not held to the same standard. Once again, the authors did not mention the substantial research base of the MMPI-2-RF. The *Technical Manual* presents 605 correlations for each SP Scale from a range of settings using diverse criterion modalities, which includes a large number of correlates from a forensic setting using a database that has met the threshold for publication in top-tier assessment and psychopathology journals (e.g., Sellbom, 2016a; Sellbom, Ben-Porath, and Stafford, 2007). In addition, a plethora of studies in forensic and correctional psychology settings have now included the SP Scales (e.g., Anderson, Sellbom, Pymont, et al., 2015; Glassmire, Jhawar, Burchett, & Tarescavage, 2016; Mattson et al., 2012; Sellbom, 2011, 2014; Sellbom, Lee, et al., 2012; Tarescavage et al., 2014; Tarescavage, Glassmire, et al., 2016). Moreover, low reliability (which is a result of shorter scales) does indeed lead to greater SEM values, but Butcher et al. ignored the fact that reliability is much greater in clinical settings (in which there is greater variability in scores) than in the normative sample and that the SEM falls in the acceptable range for the majority of scales.

A final point made by Butcher et al. (2015) is that the MMPI-2-RF RC Scales exhibit a low sensitivity to psychopathology relative to the MMPI-2 Clinical Scales. They supported this contention by citing a plethora of unpublished materials, as well as the case of Ted Kaczynski, known as "the Unibomber." They also erroneously interpreted findings from family court settings. To use a single case as evidence to make a scientific point is quite unhelpful, and regardless of whether the case is consistent with their arguments or not (one cannot actually determine that from the information presented), there are always exceptions to scientific group data. Butcher et al. ignored the only systematic study that directly addresses the issue of discrepancies in Clinical and RC Scale elevations. Sellbom, Ben-Porath, McNulty, et al. (2006) showed in two large inpatient and outpatient samples that discrepancies in Clinical and corresponding RC Scale elevations were actually quite rare. When such discrepancies did occur, the external validity criteria favored the RC Scale scores over the Clinical Scale scores. For instance, psychiatric inpatients who had an RC6 elevation in the absence of a Clinical Scale 6 elevation were far more likely to be independently rated as delusional than were inpatients exhibiting the opposite pattern. Furthermore, Butcher et al. (2015) cited higher rates of elevations on Clinical Scale scores than on RC Scale scores in family court settings (e.g., Archer et al., 2012; Stredny et al., 2006) as evidence for sensitivity to psychopathology of the Clinical Scales, while not taking into account the fact that the RC Scales are much more consistent with the average level of underreporting exhibited in these settings (Ben-Porath & Flens, 2012). Indeed, it is likely (at least in part) that the higher elevations on the Clinical Scales are the result of the arbitrary influence of the *K* correction.

In sum, the preponderance of information presented in the Butcher et al. chapter in support of their recommendation that the MMPI-2-RF not be used in forensic settings is both inaccurate and misleading. We recommend that readers of this book consult the empirical literature on the MMPI-2-RF before making decisions on whether to use the test in forensic settings. We believe, as illustrated in our discussion of *Daubert* criteria, that the test would easily be upheld when faced with an admissibility challenge in court, at least for general purposes of use (e.g., assessment of response bias and psychopathology). Moreover, if the use of the MMPI-2-RF is challenged in court on the grounds of these criticisms, we hope that readers now also have some general guidelines for how to respond to such challenges.

Chapter 3

Assessment of Malingering and Defensiveness with the MMPI-2-RF

One way in which forensic psychological assessment differs from traditional clinical assessments (conducted primarily for treatment planning) is that evaluees typically have a greater incentive to misrepresent themselves with respect to psychological functioning (Wygant & Granacher, 2015). Given the role that self-report plays in clinical assessment, whether through clinical interview or objective personality testing, it is important to assess the validity of symptoms reported during the evaluation. Moreover, the principles of forensic mental health assessment (e.g., Heilbrun, Grisso, & Goldstein, 2008) note the importance of utilizing psychological testing to assess response style in forensic evaluations. Following in the tradition started with the original MMPI (Hathaway & McKinley, 1943), the MMPI-2-RF effectively captures various threats to protocol validity, which is important for forensic psychologists, who must defend their interpretations in court. The assessment of response bias is important not only in support of formulating opinions about the presence of malingering or defensiveness, but also from a psychometric perspective in that the presence of overreporting and underreporting attenuates the correlations between the clinically substantive scales of the MMPI-2-RF and clinically relevant criteria (Burchett & Ben-Porath, 2010; Wiggins, Wygant, Hoelzle, & Gervais, 2012).

ASSESSMENT OF RESPONSE BIAS

Self-report inventories of personality and psychopathology are based on the notion that individuals are sufficiently introspective about their psychological functioning to respond to items characterizing various traits and symptoms. Such introspection requires that individuals can adequately read and understand the item, reflect with sufficient insight on whether it characterizes their functioning, and respond in a genuine, unbiased manner.

Ben-Porath (2013c) characterized invalid responding on self-report inventories such as the MMPI-2-RF as falling into two broad categories: non-content-based and content-based. Non-content-based invalid responding occurs when the evaluee does not attend to the content of the items in a meaningful way (e.g., random or fixed responding). Content-based invalid responding occurs when the evaluee responds to the content of the items in a way that distorts his or her actual level of psychological functioning or impairment (e.g., overreporting/faking bad, underreporting/defensive responding). The MMPI-2-RF includes Validity Scales that assess both of these forms of invalid responding. Burchett and Bagby (2014) noted further that within each of these categories of invalid responding, the evaluee may act in an intentional or unintentional manner. For example, intentional overreporting is characterized as feigning (Rogers, 2018; Rogers & Bender, 2013). The term malingering goes one step further than feigning (which does not make any assumptions about the motivation for overreporting), by denoting intentional overreporting that is motivated by external circumstances, such as involvement in a forensic case (American Psychiatric Association, 2013). Burchett and Bagby (2014) noted that individuals may unintentionally overreport symptoms owing to poor insight or negative emotionality. It is important to note that although the MMPI-2-RF Validity Scales can be used to detect overreporting and underreporting, they must not be used as a sole indicator of malingering, which is much broader in its scope and requires careful consideration of additional factors, such as evaluation context and secondary gain. Scores on the MMPI-2-RF Validity Scales should always be examined in light of clinical observations, scores on other response bias measures, and clinical factors, such as current and historical psychopathology.

Richard Rogers and others (e.g., Rogers, 2018; Rogers & Bender, 2013) have advanced our understanding of response bias and malingering by identifying strategies for assessing the ways in which individuals misrepresent their presentation during a clinical or forensic evaluation. Three specific strategies of particular relevance to MMPI-2-RF Validity Scales include quasi-rare symptoms, rare symptoms, and erroneous stereotypes. Essentially, the quasi-rare symptoms approach identifies items that are rarely endorsed in a particular keyed direction by nonclinical samples. This strategy is analogous to the development of the original Infrequency (F) scale on the MMPI.

The rare symptoms strategy is similar, but utilizes a clinical comparison group to identify infrequently endorsed items. This comparison group is important because items deemed "rare" among nonclinical evaluees may be less uncommon in clinical settings, a point noted by Arbisi and Ben-Porath (1995) in the development of the MMPI-2 Infrequency Psychopathology (Fp) scale. These two approaches work as response-bias detection strategies because individuals overreporting symptoms on the test might not recognize that they are rare among patients with genuine mental illness. The erroneous stereotypes detection strategy assumes that individuals feigning on the test will not be able to discriminate between erroneous stereotypes and genuine symptoms of psychopathology. Gough's (1954) Dissimulation scale was one of the original scales to utilize this approach. The Fake Bad Scale (FBS; Lees-Haley, English, & Glenn, 1991), later renamed the Symptom Validity scale, also employs this approach. Conceptually, FBS (FBS-r on the MMPI-2-RF) detects erroneous stereotypes of postinjury distress in a personal injury setting while also minimizing preinjury pathology. Understanding the conceptual basis underlying each of the MMPI-2-RF Validity Scales is important for the forensic clinician to effectively explain the nature of an evaluee's response bias when it occurs on the test. Assessing underreporting and guarded responding is more challenging than identifying overreporting. Two particular detection strategies for assessing underreporting are defensiveness (denial of psychopathology) and social desirability (Rogers, 2018).

MMPI-2-RF VALIDITY SCALES

Non-Content-Based Invalid Responding

The idea of tabulating unscorable responses (either left blank or responded to both true and false) goes back to the original MMPI, when evaluees were asked to respond true, false, or cannot say to each of the test items. The MMPI-2-RF Score Report includes a list of every item either unanswered or double-marked so that the clinician can discern whether there is any pattern to these responses. Occasionally, defendants in criminal forensic evaluations will intentionally leave an item unanswered because they believe it will incriminate them in some way. For instance, during a sexual offender risk assessment, an evaluee may refuse to respond to any item on the test pertaining to sexual behavior. As stated in the *Manual for Administration, Scoring, and Interpretation,* scales for which at least 90 percent of the items had scorable responses can be interpreted without any problem. When more than 10 percent of the items on a scale are unscorable, one might mistakenly assume that a nonelevation indicates the absence of psychopathology, whereas it might be the result of items being left unanswered.

The VRIN-r and TRIN-r scales are similar to the MMPI-2 VRIN and TRIN scales in assessing random and fixed (acquiescent or nonacquiescent) responding. VRIN-r includes 53 item pairs with similar content to measure consistent responding. Evaluees obtain a raw-score point on VRIN-r when they endorse the paired items in a conceptually and statistically inconsistent manner. TRIN-r is composed of 23 pairs of items that have opposite content. A raw-score point on TRIN-r occurs when the evaluee responds to each item in the pair in the same direction (true or false). Thus, endorsement of both items in the same direction suggests a fixed response pattern that is inconsistent with the logic of the item pairs.

Handel et al. (2010) examined VRIN-r and TRIN-r by inserting various degrees of inconsistent responding and found that a cut score of 80T on either scale invalidates the remainder of the protocol, which is consistent with the *Manual for Administration, Scoring, and Interpretation* (Ben-Porath & Tellegen, 2008/2011).

Content-Based Invalid Responding: Overreporting

The MMPI-2-RF includes five overreporting indicators that employ several strategies to detect response bias. The first of these scales is F-r, which is composed of 32 items rarely endorsed in the keyed direction in the MMPI-2-RF normative sample. Similar to its MMPI-2 counterpart (Infrequency), elevated scores on F-r can result from overreporting, inconsistent responding, or significant psychopathology. Any elevation on this scale would therefore need to be examined in light of scores on VRIN-r/TRIN-r, the Fp-r scale, and the individual's history of mental illness.

The Fp-r scale is similar in design to the MMPI-2 Fp scale. It is composed of items that are infrequently (i.e., rarely) endorsed in a clinical psychiatric sample, thus mitigating one of the confounds of elevations on F-r. Fourteen of the 21 Fp-r items come from the MMPI-2 version of the scale. Several items were removed from Fp, including four that were shared with L (Lie) and three that were selected for Fs. Items were added to Fp-r that were found to improve the scale's ability to capture overreporting (Ben-Porath, 2012b; Tellegen & Ben-Porath, 2008/2011). The final scale includes items that are rarely endorsed by psychiatric patients, which is consistent with the rare symptoms detection strategy discussed by Rogers (2018). Similar to interpreting F-r, once non-content-based invalid responding has been ruled out (with Cannot Say [CNS], VRIN-r, TRIN-r), elevations on Fp-r are associated with a higher likelihood of overreporting of symptoms.

Wygant, Ben-Porath, and Arbisi (2004) developed the Fs scale by examining the response rates of every MMPI-2 item in several large samples of medical and chronic pain patients. Items were included in Fs if (a) they were endorsed in the keyed direction by less than 20 percent of the patients in each of the three samples, and (b) they described physical complaints and medical symptoms. The resulting 16-item scale is composed of items that describe physical health problems that are nevertheless rarely endorsed by medical patients.

The FBS-r is a revised version of the original FBS (Lees-Haley et al., 1991) and includes 30 of the 43 original items. FBS-r (like the original FBS) was designed to capture noncredible somatic and cognitive complaints in particular forensic contexts (e.g., personal injury, disability, forensic neuropsychological evaluations).

Finally, the RBS was developed by Gervais, Ben-Porath, Wygant, and Green (2007) to identify symptoms associated with poor performance (effort) on cognitive performance validity measures, such as the Test of Memory Malingering (Tombaugh, 1996) and Word Memory Test (Green, 2003). Employing an empirical keying approach, Gervais et al. (2007) identified 28 items that were significantly associated with failure on several cognitive Performance Validity Tests (PVTs) in a large sample of disability and personal injury litigants.

Content-Based Invalid Responding: Underreporting

The MMPI-2-RF includes two scales assessing underreporting or defensive responding: Uncommon Virtues (L-r) and Adjustment Validity (K-r). They function similarly to their MMPI and MMPI-2 counterparts, L and K (Correction).

L-r and K-r were developed by Ben-Porath and Tellegen (2008/2011) by factor analyzing the items from the MMPI-2 underreporting scales (L, K, and S [Superlative Self-Presentation]), as well as two earlier experimental MMPI scales designed to capture defensive responding: the Social Desirability Scale (Wiggins, 1959) and Positive Malingering Scale (Cofer, Chance, & Judson, 1949). Two factors emerged; the first of which included 11 items from L, 2 from the Social Desirability Scale, and 1 from the Positive Malingering Scale. These 14 items composing the L-r scale capture underreporting by the evaluee who presents himself or herself in an overly favorable light by denying minor faults that most people are willing to acknowledge (Ben-Porath & Tellegen, 2008/2011). The second factor, which became the K-r scale, is composed of 14 items from the K scale (five of which were also scored on S). This scale captures underreporting when the evaluee presents himself or herself as overly well adjusted (Ben-Porath, 2012b).

EFFECTIVENESS OF THE MMPI-2-RF VALIDITY SCALES

The general effectiveness of the MMPI-2-RF Validity Scales has been reviewed in other sources (Hoelzle et al., 2012; Sleep, Petty, & Wygant, 2015; Wygant et al., 2018). Additionally, two meta-analyses (Ingram & Ternes, 2016; Sharf, Rogers, Williams, & Henry, 2017) have examined the MMPI-2-RF overreporting Validity Scales. Both meta-analyses found general support for the scales as measures of response bias. Ingram and Ternes (2016) noted that across most studies, individuals in feigning or overreporting groups produced Validity Scale scores one standard deviation above the control group. Moreover, even after accounting for various moderators, such as study method and diagnostic comparisons, the MMPI-2-RF Validity Scales exhibited consistently large effect sizes. Sharf et al. (2017) stated that Fp-r was highly effective for discriminating feigned from genuine psychopathology. They noted that FBS-r produced a very large effect size in identifying feigned cognitive impairment. Fs had a large effect size in identifying feigned medical symptoms, but it was better at capturing feigned symptoms of psychopathology.

Several studies have focused on the ability of the MMPI-2-RF Validity Scales to detect overreported psychopathology (Goodwin, Sellbom, & Arbisi, 2013; Marion, Sellbom, & Bagby, 2011; Mason et al., 2013; Rogers et al., 2011; Sellbom & Bagby, 2010; Sellbom et al., 2010). Marion et al.

(2011) examined the ability of the Validity Scales to discriminate feigned major depressive disorder, schizophrenia, and posttraumatic stress disorder (PTSD) from genuine psychiatric patients. F-r and Fp-r both exhibited large effects in distinguishing between patient and feigning groups. Goodwin et al. (2013) found that the MMPI-2-RF Validity Scales were able to distinguish between veterans seeking disability compensation and mental health professionals who were asked to feign symptoms of PTSD. Sellbom and Bagby (2010) found that Fp-r best differentiated simulating participants from patient groups, even when they had been coached prior to completing the test. Finally, employing an analogue design, Mason et al. (2013) found that the Validity Scales could correctly classify 80 percent of the genuine PTSD patients and 73 percent of undergraduates feigning PTSD.

Two studies employed a criterion group design comparing those with genuine and those with feigned profiles on the Structured Interview of Reported Symptoms (SIRS) and SIRS-2. Both Sellbom et al. (2010), who examined a group of defendants undergoing competency and criminal responsibility evaluations, and Rogers et al. (2011), who examined civil litigants, found large effect sizes for F-r, Fp-r, and Fs in discriminating between those with genuine and feigning SIRS results. Similarly, Chmielewski, Zhu, Burchett, Bury, and Bagby (2017) found large effect sizes for F-r, Fs, and Fp-r in discriminating between disability litigants with passing and feigning scores on the Miller Forensic Assessment of Symptoms Test.

A number of studies support use of the MMPI-2-RF in the civil forensic arena (particularly disability and personal injury evaluations). RBS appears to be consistently correlated with performance on cognitive PVTs across numerous studies (e.g., Gervais, Ben-Porath, Wygant, & Sellbom, 2010; Gervais, Wygant, Sellbom, & Ben-Porath, 2011; Jones & Ingram, 2011; Jones, Ingram, & Ben-Porath, 2012; Wygant et al., 2010) and generally outperforms other MMPI-2-RF Validity Scales in this regard. Interestingly, McBride, Crighton, Wygant, and Granacher (2013) examined 92 litigants who completed MRI and computed tomography scans in order to document the presence of brain lesions. RBS scores (as well as cognitive PVTs) were not significantly associated with presence or location of a brain lesion.

Several studies have examined MMPI-2-RF Validity Scales among civil litigants in relation to structured malingering criteria developed by Slick, Sherman, and Iverson (1999) to detect malingering cognitive dysfunction (MND) and malingered pain disability (MPRD; Bianchini, Greve, & Glynn, 2005). These studies all highlight the utility of F-r, Fs, FBS-r, and RBS in capturing elements of malingering as operationalized by the MND and MPRD criteria (Nguyen, Green, & Barr, 2015; Schroeder et al., 2012; Tarescavage, Wygant, Gervais, & Ben-Porath, 2013; Wygant et al., 2011).

Four studies have examined the MMPI-2-RF Validity Scales in capturing overreporting of somatic and medical problems (Sellbom, Wygant, & Bagby, 2012; Wygant et al., 2009; 2011; Wygant, Arbisi, Bianchini, & Umlauf, 2017). Wygant et al. (2009) found large effect sizes for all of the overreporting Validity Scales in discriminating Veterans Administration medical patients instructed to feign medical symptoms (and their associated emotional symptoms) from medical (nonpsychiatric) patients who completed the test under standard instructions. Wygant et al. (2011) examined 251 personal injury and disability litigants who were evaluated with the MPRD criteria. They found that cut scores of 100T on F-r, 70T on Fp-r, 90T on Fs, 100T on FBS-r, and 100T on RBS yielded the best mix of sensitivity and specificity in the classification of MPRD. Sellbom et al. (2012) found that Fs had a large effect size discriminating undergraduates instructed to feign somatic symptoms from medical patients and disability litigants with genuine somatoform disorders. Finally, Wygant, Arbisi, et al. (2017) examined 230 outpatient chronic pain patients who completed the MMPI-2-RF and who were rated on Waddell's nonorganic signs. Fs had the largest effect size ($d = 1.31$) between patients with a Waddell score of 0 and those with scores above 2.

Fewer studies have examined the utility and classification accuracy of the underreporting scales. Sellbom and Bagby (2008) utilized an analogue design and found that both L-r and K-r yielded large effects in discriminating participants instructed to fake good from control groups, including child custody litigants, who theoretically already have a higher likelihood of minimizing problems on psychological testing. Bridges and Baum (2013) explored the potential of items on L-r to reflect traditional Christian beliefs rather than to indicate underreporting. They found that individuals espousing strong Christian beliefs tended to score significantly higher on several L-r items than those without those beliefs, thus noting this important factor that has to be considered in light of L-r elevations. Most recently, Crighton et al. (2015) employed an analogue design with a compliance check to ensure that faking instructions were followed. Participants who were compliant with the instructions produced larger effect sizes on L-r and K-r, with the overall findings replicating those of Sellbom and Bagby (2008). These few studies are promising in terms of the utility of L-r and K-r, but it should be noted that it is more difficult to identify underreporting than overreporting.

INTERPRETIVE STRATEGY FOR THE MMPI-2-RF VALIDITY SCALES

Similar to the interpretive strategy presented in Chapter 2, it is important for clinicians to strategize interpretation of the MMPI-2-RF Validity Scales. The basic steps for interpreting the scales are:

1. Review CNS to determine whether the evaluee responded to every item on the test. The *MMPI-2-RF Manual for Administration, Scoring, and Interpretation* states that a scale can be interpreted when at least 90 percent of its items have scorable responses. When greater than 10 percent of items on a particular scale are unscorable, it is possible that an unelevated scale simply reflects a lack of item responses rather than the absence of psychopathology. It is particularly important to check the response percentages for the Validity Scales to ensure that the evaluee has responded to enough of the items on the scales to interpret them. Case Example 3-1 illustrates the importance of this step.

2. Review VRIN-r and TRIN-r for evidence of inconsistent and fixed responding, respectively. Consistent with the *Manual for Administration, Scoring, and Interpretation,* T scores of 70 to 79 on either of these scales should begin to alert the clinician to potential inconsistent or fixed responding that could affect the overall scores on the test. If either of these scores is elevated above a cut score of 80T, the profile is considered to be invalid. Further interpretation of the remaining Validity Scales is not warranted, as these scores cannot be used to formulate impressions of overreporting or underreporting.

3. Review F-r and Fp-r for evidence of overreporting of psychopathology. Assuming that the evaluee has responded to enough items on the test (CNS) and did not evidence inconsistent (VRIN-r) or fixed (TRIN-r) responding, elevations on these two scales can be used to formulate impressions about overreporting of psychopathology. It is not uncommon for individuals with genuine psychopathology to have significant elevations on F-r. Although the *Manual for Administration, Scoring, and Interpretation* indicates concern about overreporting at a T score of 80, this cut score may lead to false positives, particularly if the evaluee has any history of psychopathology. We recommend that a cut score of 90T be used as a starting point for being concerned about possible overreporting, particularly if there is no evidence of psychopathology in the

evaluee's history. T scores of 100 on F-r are not uncommon among evaluees who have significant psychopathology (particularly psychotic and trauma-based disorders). Consistent with the manual, a cut score of 120T invalidates the profile. In reviewing available Validity Scale research, Wygant et al. (2018) noted that a cut score of 120T on F-r tends to result only in a 10 percent or less false positive rate in most feigning studies. In the presence of an elevated F-r score, one must review Fp-r, which is less susceptible to elevation owing to genuine psychopathology (Wygant et al., 2018). Thus, an elevation on F-r that is coupled with an elevation on Fp-r is substantially more likely to indicate feigning than F-r alone.

4. Consider Fp-r the primary Validity Scale in determining feigned psychopathology, especially severe forms of psychopathology, because it is more specific to overreporting. T scores above 90 on Fp-r should raise serious concerns about feigning, and scores above 100T appear to be quite specific to feigning.

5. Examine scores on Fs and FBS-r, both of which were designed to assess noncredible somatic reporting. These two scales will likely be particularly useful in civil lawsuit and disability evaluations, when litigants/claimants may report physical dysfunction in addition to emotional dysfunction. Fs appears to also show some utility in capturing severe psychopathology, similar to Fp-r (Wall, Wygant, & Gallagher, 2015). T scores of 80 on either of these scales should alert the clinician to the possibility that the evaluee overreported somatic symptoms on the test. T scores of 100 on these scales are associated with significant likelihood of feigning somatic symptoms. Elevations on these scales impact the potential interpretability of RC1 and the Somatic/Cognitive SP Scales. It is important to note that most of the empirical support for FBS-r is in the area of civil forensic assessment (e.g., disability, personal injury, forensic neuropsychological evaluations), whereas Fs is an assessment of somatic overreporting regardless of evaluation context.

6. Examine scores on RBS to assess for potential overreported cognitive complaints. If elevated (T scores above 80, with significant concern when scores are above 100T), one has less confidence that cognitive complaints (captured on the Cognitive Complaints [COG] scale) represent genuine impairment. If the evaluation includes intellectual or neuropsychological testing, one would definitely want to corroborate elevations on RBS with cognitive PVTs, such as the Word Memory Test or the Test of Memory Malingering. We do not recommend that RBS be used as a substitute

for cognitive PVTs in an evaluation. However, as noted by Wygant et al. (2018), the presence of failing scores on PVTs in conjunction with an elevated RBS score would enhance one's conclusion about feigned neurocognitive dysfunction.

7. Follow the interpretive guidelines in the *MMPI-2-RF Manual for Administration, Scoring, and Interpretation* (Ben-Porath & Tellegen, 2008/2011) with respect to underreporting. Scores above 65T on L-r should raise concerns that the evaluee underreported by presenting in an overly favorable and virtuous manner. Scores at or above 80T on L-r indicate significant likelihood of underreporting. Given the lower ceiling for scores on K-r, lower cutoffs are used for this scale. A T score of 60 on K-r should indicate concern about underreporting. As scores approach the ceiling on K-r (72T), underreporting is likely to be more pronounced. When L-r and K-r suggest the presence of underreporting, it is likely that the Substantive Scales will be suppressed. Therefore, one could not use the absence of such elevations to rule out the presence of psychopathology. However, it is important to note that any elevation is only a reflection of what the test-taker is willing to acknowledge and thus does not provide the full picture of personality and functioning.

Case Example 3-1

This case involved a 27-year-old Caucasian male who completed the MMPI-2-RF as part of his criminal responsibility evaluation. His MMPI-2-RF Validity Scale profile illustrates the importance of reviewing non-content-based invalid responding prior to interpreting overreporting indicators.

At first glance, the very elevated scores on F-r (115T), Fp-r (120T), and Fs (120T) are quite apparent. One might be tempted to conclude that this defendant overreported on the MMPI-2-RF, especially when the non-content-based invalid responding scales, VRIN-r and TRIN-r, are both below 70T. However, recall that the first step in the interpretive strategy for the Validity Scales is to check CNS, which in this case is 24T. The response percentage for each scale is presented right above CNS. The defendant in this case left a number of responses unscorable on the Validity Scales. Of most concern in this case, the defendant responded only to 82 percent of the items on the VRIN-r scale. Thus, although his score on VRIN-r is only 68T, it would take only three more raw-score points before he exceeded the cutoff of 80T.

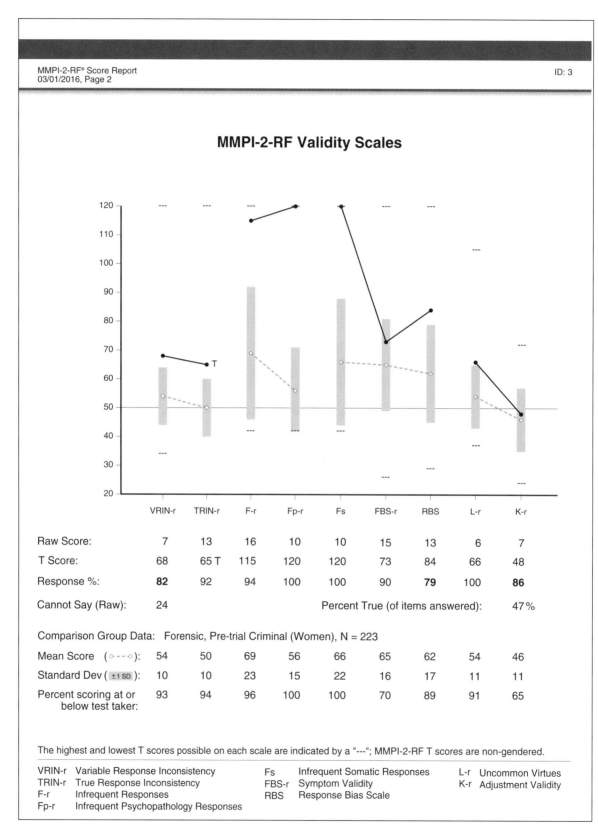

MMPI-2-RF Validity Scales

	VRIN-r	TRIN-r	F-r	Fp-r	Fs	FBS-r	RBS	L-r	K-r
Raw Score:	7	13	16	10	10	15	13	6	7
T Score:	68	65 T	115	120	120	73	84	66	48
Response %:	**82**	92	94	100	100	90	**79**	100	**86**

Cannot Say (Raw):   24   Percent True (of items answered):   47%

Comparison Group Data: Forensic, Pre-trial Criminal (Women), N = 223

Mean Score (◇---◇):	54	50	69	56	66	65	62	54	46
Standard Dev (±1 SD):	10	10	23	15	22	16	17	11	11
Percent scoring at or below test taker:	93	94	96	100	100	70	89	91	65

The highest and lowest T scores possible on each scale are indicated by a "---"; MMPI-2-RF T scores are non-gendered.

VRIN-r	Variable Response Inconsistency	Fs	Infrequent Somatic Responses	L-r	Uncommon Virtues
TRIN-r	True Response Inconsistency	FBS-r	Symptom Validity	K-r	Adjustment Validity
F-r	Infrequent Responses	RBS	Response Bias Scale		
Fp-r	Infrequent Psychopathology Responses				

FIGURE 3-1   Case Example 3-1: MMPI-2-RF Validity Scales Profile.

Therefore, we conclude that the profile is not interpretable owing to a large enough number of unscorable responses. We would not proceed to interpret the scores on F-r, Fp-r, and Fs as evidence of overreporting because we simply do not know whether he would have produced inconsistent results had he responded to more items on VRIN-r. This case illustrates the importance of ensuring that the evaluee responds to enough items on the test before proceeding to interpret the Validity Scales.

Case Example 3-2

This is the case of a 22-year-old Caucasian male who completed the MMPI-2-RF and other malingering measures as part of his competency to stand trial evaluation.

Starting with the CNS, we see that he left one item unanswered. This did not affect the Validity Scales. There was no substantial evidence of inconsistent (VRIN-r = 48T) or fixed (TRIN-r = 52T) responding. Turning to the overreporting scales, it is quite obvious that he evidenced substantial overreporting, as indicated by scoring at the ceiling of F-r and Fp-r (both at 120T). There is also some evidence of somatic overreporting, as indicated by his Fs score of 83T. Given these scores, we conclude that his MMPI-2-RF results are invalid for interpretation. It is interesting that he also produced an elevation on K-r (69T), suggesting possible underreporting or better adjustment. Although one would not interpret the Substantive Scales of his profile to form impressions of his psychological functioning, reviewing them still provides information. His H-O and RC profile illustrates a clear pattern of psychotic symptoms, with THD (100T), RC6 (98T), and RC8 (90T). None of the remaining H-O or RC Scales are in the elevated range, although RC4 (62T) is close. Although we would not conclude that these three elevations are indicative of psychotic symptomatology owing to his scores on the Validity Scales, it is illustrative of the types of symptoms that he was attempting to portray through his item endorsement pattern. Many of the Substantive Scales on the MMPI-2-RF include items that are quite face valid, thus making them susceptible to overreporting, a point that was examined empirically by Sellbom, Ben-Porath, Graham, Arbisi, and Bagby (2005) with the RC Scales.

The defendant's elevated score on K-r likely stemmed from his specific response pattern of not endorsing items reflecting other forms of

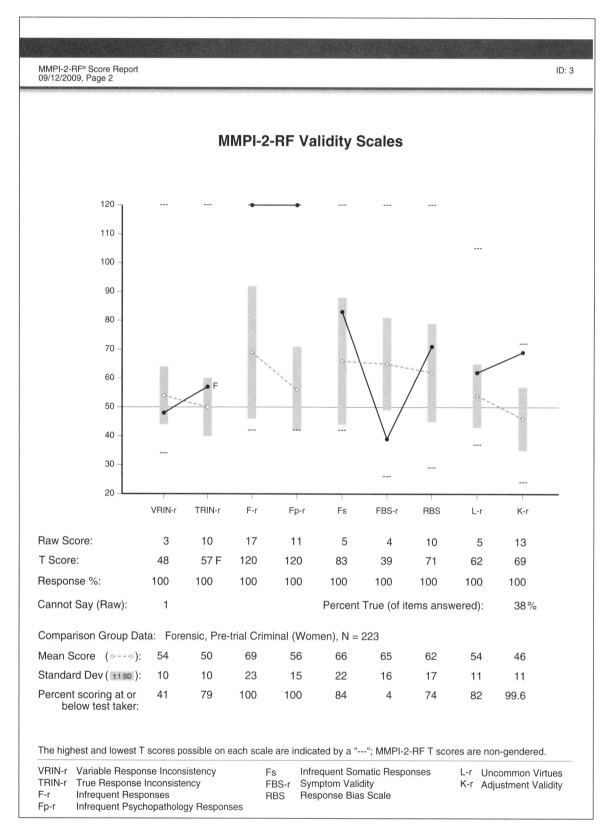

MMPI-2-RF Validity Scales

	VRIN-r	TRIN-r	F-r	Fp-r	Fs	FBS-r	RBS	L-r	K-r
Raw Score:	3	10	17	11	5	4	10	5	13
T Score:	48	57 F	120	120	83	39	71	62	69
Response %:	100	100	100	100	100	100	100	100	100

Cannot Say (Raw):   1   Percent True (of items answered):   38%

Comparison Group Data: Forensic, Pre-trial Criminal (Women), N = 223

	VRIN-r	TRIN-r	F-r	Fp-r	Fs	FBS-r	RBS	L-r	K-r
Mean Score (◇--◇):	54	50	69	56	66	65	62	54	46
Standard Dev (±1 SD):	10	10	23	15	22	16	17	11	11
Percent scoring at or below test taker:	41	79	100	100	84	4	74	82	99.6

The highest and lowest T scores possible on each scale are indicated by a "---"; MMPI-2-RF T scores are non-gendered.

VRIN-r	Variable Response Inconsistency	Fs	Infrequent Somatic Responses	L-r	Uncommon Virtues
TRIN-r	True Response Inconsistency	FBS-r	Symptom Validity	K-r	Adjustment Validity
F-r	Infrequent Responses	RBS	Response Bias Scale		
Fp-r	Infrequent Psychopathology Responses				

FIGURE 3-2 Case Example 3-2: MMPI-2-RF Validity, H-O, and RC Scales Profile, continued.

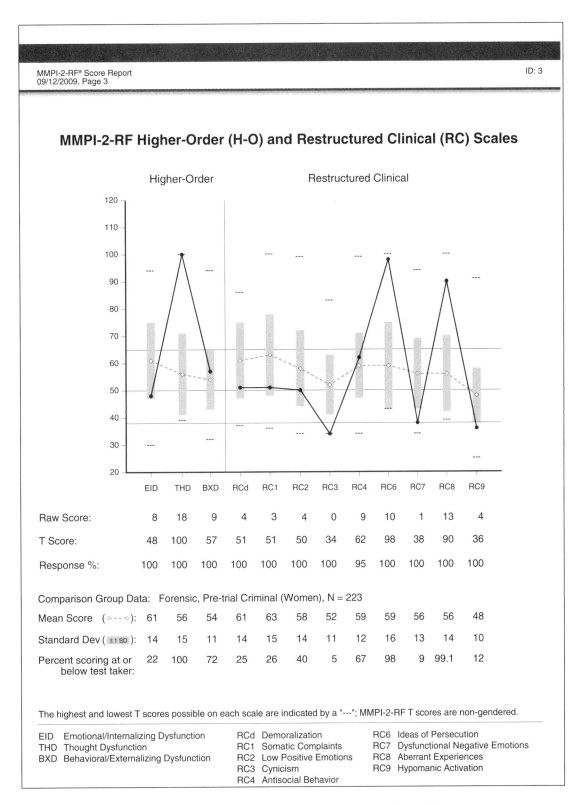

MMPI-2-RF Higher-Order (H-O) and Restructured Clinical (RC) Scales

Higher-Order   Restructured Clinical

	EID	THD	BXD	RCd	RC1	RC2	RC3	RC4	RC6	RC7	RC8	RC9
Raw Score:	8	18	9	4	3	4	0	9	10	1	13	4
T Score:	48	100	57	51	51	50	34	62	98	38	90	36
Response %:	100	100	100	100	100	100	100	95	100	100	100	100

Comparison Group Data: Forensic, Pre-trial Criminal (Women), N = 223

	EID	THD	BXD	RCd	RC1	RC2	RC3	RC4	RC6	RC7	RC8	RC9
Mean Score (◇--◇):	61	56	54	61	63	58	52	59	59	56	56	48
Standard Dev (±1 SD):	14	15	11	14	15	14	11	12	16	13	14	10
Percent scoring at or below test taker:	22	100	72	25	26	40	5	67	98	9	99.1	12

The highest and lowest T scores possible on each scale are indicated by a "---"; MMPI-2-RF T scores are non-gendered.

EID Emotional/Internalizing Dysfunction	RCd Demoralization	RC6 Ideas of Persecution
THD Thought Dysfunction	RC1 Somatic Complaints	RC7 Dysfunctional Negative Emotions
BXD Behavioral/Externalizing Dysfunction	RC2 Low Positive Emotions	RC8 Aberrant Experiences
	RC3 Cynicism	RC9 Hypomanic Activation
	RC4 Antisocial Behavior	

FIGURE 3-2   Case Example 3-2: MMPI-2-RF Validity, H-O, and RC Scales Profile.

45

psychopathology while focusing on the items that captured psychotic symptoms. His pattern of responses on the MMPI-2-RF suggested that he was attempting to feign specific psychotic symptoms in an effort to "act crazy." He was administered the SIRS (Rogers, Bagby, & Dickens, 1992) to corroborate the findings from his MMPI-2-RF. He produced a score in the definite feigning range on the Rare Symptoms and Selectivity of Symptoms scales, which yielded a definite feigning overall classification on the test. His scores on these two scales of the SIRS are conceptually related to the approach he utilized while completing the MMPI-2-RF, with Fp-r capturing rare symptoms (among psychiatric inpatients) and his distinct pattern of endorsing psychotic symptoms on THD, RC6, RC8, and PSYC-r. He was classified as malingering during evaluation and was ultimately ruled as competent to stand trial by the judge in his case.

CONCLUSIONS

The MMPI-2-RF Validity Scales play a vital role in the use of the test, particularly in forensic assessment, when evaluees have a higher motivation to distort their clinical presentation. The Validity Scales are effective in capturing forms of response bias consistent with the empirical literature on the strategies of such bias more generally. Moreover, a number of empirical studies can guide interpretation of the Validity Scales in forensic settings and give the clinician confidence in formulating opinions about the validity of the test results.

PART II

Criminal Forensic Applications of the MMPI-2-RF

Chapter 4

Competency to Stand Trial

Throughout the United States and most other developed countries, the criminal justice system is tasked with establishing criminal culpability through an adversarial process between the defendant charged with the offense and the state. Inherent in this system is the requirement that the defendant possess enough psychological and intellectual resources for self-defense with the aid of legal counsel. Rooted in English common law, the concept of trial competency espouses the ideals of fairness, accuracy, and dignity of court proceedings (Stafford & Sellbom, 2013). While competency to stand trial is the most common type of competency evaluation, several other competency issues are also raised, such as competence to waive an attorney and proceed *pro se*, competence to plead guilty, and competence to be executed. Competence to waive Miranda rights is also raised in some cases, but this type of referral involves a retrospective assessment of the defendant's competency to understand and voluntarily waive Miranda rights at the time of the arrest and when the defendant made statements to the police. In that respect, it is similar to an assessment of criminal responsibility (see Chapter 5).

In the United States, the standard for competency was formally established by the U.S. Supreme Court in *Dusky v. United States* (1960). The court opined:

> It is not enough for the district judge to find that "the defendant is oriented to time and place and has some recollection of events," but that the test must be whether he has sufficient present ability to consult with his lawyer with a reasonable degree of rational understanding - and whether he has a rational as well as factual understanding of the proceedings against him. (p. 402)

Most jurisdictions throughout the United States have adopted the language (or some variant) of the *Dusky* finding.

The issue of competency to stand trial is a present-focused and fluid construct, meaning that the issue of competency can be raised at any time during the proceedings. However, most requests for competency evaluations occur pretrial (Bonnie, 1992). Although the issue of competency can be raised by either side (prosecutor or defense counsel), or by the judge, the matter is most often raised by defense counsel if their client has a history of mental illness, intellectual disability, or if the defendant displays odd or bizarre behavior. Recent estimates indicate that approximately 50,000 to 60,000 competency evaluations are completed annually in the United States (Skeem & Golding, 1998) with approximately 30 percent resulting in a finding of incompetence (Nicholson & Kugler, 1991; Pirelli, Gottdiener, & Zapf (2011).

ASSESSING COMPETENCY TO STAND TRIAL

As noted, competency to stand trial evaluations are focused on present mental health functioning. Many jurisdictions require that the defendant show evidence of a mental condition, defect, or illness to be found incompetent to stand trial. The most recent comprehensive meta-analysis on competency to stand trial by Pirelli et al. (2011) found that defendants diagnosed with a psychotic disorder were nearly eight times more likely to be found incompetent to stand trial than were those without a psychotic disorder diagnosis. Other factors significantly related to findings of incompetence were unemployment and history of psychiatric hospitalization.

In addition to specific questions about legal issues (e.g., what is the role of a defense attorney), competency evaluations require a comprehensive examination of psychological functioning. This typically involves a thorough psychosocial history and mental status examination to formulate diagnostic and clinical impressions. Specific competency-related topics must also be assessed in this type of evaluation. This will often involve a discussion about the criminal charges. This is not done for purposes of establishing culpability, but rather to assess whether the defendant can describe the alleged instant offense in a clear, coherent, and sequential fashion. It is important to assess whether the defendant's account of the alleged offense appears to be influenced by symptoms of a mental disorder or cognitive dysfunction. Ultimately, the evaluator is determining whether the defendant can respond to questions about the circumstances surrounding the alleged instant offense in a manner that is likely to be meaningful and helpful to defense counsel. Competency evaluations also include a discussion of the roles of key individuals involved in the case (e.g., defendant, judge, jury, defense counsel, prosecutor, and witnesses). The evaluation also includes a discussion of various plea options and a plea-bargaining process. Finally, the evaluation includes an appraisal of the defendant's ability to maintain appropriate behavior during the course of a trial.

Bonnie (1992) wrote a seminal article on reformulating the theoretical foundations of competency to stand trial into two separate components: foundational competence and decisional competence. Foundational competence encompasses the minimum requirements for a defendant to participate in his/her defense and includes the capacity to understand the following (among others):

1. Criminal charge(s)
2. Purpose of the criminal process
3. Adversarial nature of proceedings
4. Position of being a defendant in the criminal proceedings
5. Capacity to relate pertinent information about his/her particular case to counsel

Decisional competence, on the other hand, involves the ability to make decisions in a rational manner. Rational legal participation requires the ability to reason through various issues that are likely to arise during a trial, such as deciding whether to take a plea bargain or proceed to trial. This type of decision requires reality-based, rational reasoning of issues such as understanding the strength of the evidence against the defendant and weighing and evaluating the likelihood of success for various defense strategies. This reasoning involves distinguishing more relevant from less relevant information, weighing and evaluating various legal options and their consequences, making comparisons, and providing reality-based justification for making particular case-specific decisions or drawing conclusions.

The interested reader can consult other, more comprehensive sources on conducting competency to stand trial evaluations, such as Zapf and Roesch (2009), Stafford and Sellbom (2013), and Grisso (2014).

CONSIDERATIONS FOR USING THE MMPI-2-RF IN COMPETENCY EVALUATIONS

As noted, competency to stand trial evaluations are focused on present functioning, and most jurisdictions include statutory language that requires the defendant to show evidence of a "mental condition" or "mental disease or defect" to be found incompetent. As such, the MMPI-2-RF can be quite useful in providing relevant information about current psychological status.

The MMPI-2-RF serves two primary purposes in a competency evaluation. First, the test has well-established indicators of response bias (Validity Scales) that will be useful in assessing the credibility of the responses to the test. (See Chapter 3 for a more detailed discussion of the MMPI-2-RF Validity Scales.) Two studies have examined the MMPI-2-RF Validity Scales among competency evaluees (Sellbom et al., 2010; Wygant et al., 2010) and found that the scales are effective in detecting overreporting in this setting.

The MMPI-2-RF can provide an overall impression of the defendant's psychological functioning. As noted, research suggests that most defendants ultimately found incompetent to stand trial have a psychiatric history and display psychotic symptoms (Pirelli et al., 2011). Lack of reality-based functioning has the potential to significantly limit the defendant's ability to rationally process information and make decisions in a rational fashion. The MMPI-2-RF has a set of scales specifically designed to assess psychotic symptomatology: THD, RC6, RC8, and PSYC-r. It is important to bear in mind that the content of some of these items, particularly those on RC6, may reflect a normal experience in the criminal justice system (e.g., items 194, 212, 233, 264, 310).[1] These items reflect content about self-referential experiences of persecution that could be interpreted by defendants as the prosecutor (or media) saying negative things about them. As such, endorsement of these items would not necessarily reflect delusional thinking. If all five of these items were endorsed in the keyed direction, the T score of 75 might mistakenly be interpreted as reflecting paranoid delusional thinking. Ultimately the evaluator must review the critical items at the end of the MMPI-2-RF results to determine whether they reflect psychopathology or the normal experience of going through the criminal justice system.

The score reports for the MMPI-2-RF provide the option of including various comparison groups (see Chapter 1 for more details). The Pretrial

Criminal comparison group is composed of 551 men and 223 women who were evaluated at a court clinic tasked with performing pretrial forensic psychological evaluations. Most of these evaluations involved assessing the issue of competency to stand trial and criminal responsibility. Thus, this comparison group is particularly useful in competency evaluations. To illustrate the utility of this comparison group, consider, for example, the mean T score on RC6 is 66 ($SD = 18$) for male defendants and 59 ($SD = 16$) for female defendants in those comparison groups. Those T scores roughly equate to a raw score of 2 to 3 on RC6. Thus, the evaluator may decide not to give serious consideration to scores on RC6 as reflecting psychopathological levels of paranoia or delusional symptomatology until they reach T scores of 80.

A number of scales will be particularly useful in assessing psychological functioning related to competency. As noted, THD, RC6, RC8, and PSYC-r Scales are useful in assessing psychotic symptoms. It is important to remember that additional scales, particularly those reflecting internalizing psychopathology, may be useful in ultimately forming diagnostic impressions. Other scales reflecting manic symptoms, such as RC9 or ACT, when coupled with RC8, could signal the presence of a schizoaffective condition.

Another area of concern in competency evaluations is whether the defendant is motivated to achieve the most desirable outcome. Rogers, Tillbrook, and Sewell (2004) noted the importance of assessing whether the defendant will engage in self-defeating behaviors to sabotage efforts by his or her attorney to achieve the most favorable outcome. To the degree that this might be impacted by depressive symptoms, scales such as RCd and HLP may be useful in identifying demoralized, depressive, and hopeless ideation in a defendant. The clinician should explore the extent to which any internalizing psychopathology would affect rational participation in the trial.

Finally, most competency evaluations include an assessment of behavioral functioning. MMPI-2-RF scales such as AGG and ANP can alert the clinician to the possibility that the defendant may be likely to exhibit sudden episodes of impulsive or aggressive behavior or angry verbal outbursts. If such concerns are present, the evaluator may request that the court consider having additional security measures in place during any court appearances.

CASE EXAMPLE 4-1

Case Background (2012 Evaluation)

The case examples in this chapter are unique because the examiner was requested by defense counsel to evaluate the competency of the defendant on two separate occasions, roughly three and a half years apart. The MMPI-2-RF was administered during each evaluation, which presents an opportunity to examine changes in the defendant's profiles across time.

During the initial evaluation in 2012, Mr. A, a white male in his 50s, was charged with terroristic threatening and harassing communications—both misdemeanor offenses. He was alleged to have contacted several individuals at a local university, expressing concerns that the school's administration should "gather all the homosexuals on campus and hide them because the Mexican Cartel and President were coming to kill all of them." After several phone calls, Mr. A was asked to have no contact with anyone working at the university. He was eventually arrested by the local authorities. During his booking in the county detention center, the defendant claimed that he was a "visionary prophet." He was appointed legal counsel through the local public defender's office.

Mr. A's lawyer requested a competency evaluation after receiving a series of letters and phone calls from her client. Consistent with his booking, the defendant wrote five letters to his attorney, referring to himself as a "visionary prophet" who "works with God to warn people of the end time terrors." He also expressed bizarre content in the letters, such as "I was visited by a holy angel that said the world is going to stop spinning on its axis and start spinning the other direction as it crosses over to the other side of the universe."

Given the nonviolent nature of the offenses, Mr. A was out of custody when the competency evaluation took place at his attorney's office. He presented as serious but amicable to the examiner and stated that he believed the "meeting was prophecy." While oriented to person, place, and time, his overall cognitive processes were highly reflective of thought disorder. He was tangential in his speech and frequently went off topic, displaying prominent bizarre delusions throughout the interview that focused on three primary themes: paranoia, grandiosity, and religion. He made numerous tangential statements that were connected to various verses in the Bible. He described an elaborate conspiracy that he believed included President Obama colluding with the "Mexican [drug] cartel" against Americans. The defendant stated that the president is "trying to take our guns" and "use AIDS against the people." He described himself as a prophet, which he believed "bestowed" him to be a "future fighter for Jesus against terrorists." The defendant expressed beliefs that the "end of the world is near" and that he would eventually "trigger the rapture by sitting on the mercy seat." He described perceptual experiences that appeared to be visual hallucinations, although he characterized them as "spiritual experiences" of seeing angels and the devil. He denied any symptoms of anxiety or depression, and he described his mood as "excited for the end of the world."

Mr. A's psychiatric history included two involuntary hospitalizations, one shortly after September 11, 2001, when he expressed to law enforcement officers that he was part of an "underground war movement" responsible for the 9/11 terrorist attacks.

Issues Pertaining to Competency

Consistent with many jurisdictions, Kentucky's competency stature defines incompetency "as a result of mental condition, lack of capacity to appreciate the nature and consequences of the proceedings against one or to participate rationally in one's own defense."

Mr. A's lawyer was concerned about his apparent unusual behavior and his contact with her via phone messages and letters. His presentation during the competency evaluation was consistent with a major mental illness, or "mental condition" as specified in the competency statute. The Miller Forensic Assessment of Symptoms Test (M-FAST; Miller, 2001) was used to screen for any evidence of symptom feigning. His Total Score of 3 fell below the measure's standard cutoff of 6 and was not reflective of any symptom exaggeration or feigning.

With respect to issues of competency, Mr. A believed that his attorney was "bestowed" to him by God. He believed the judge and prosecuting attorney were "colluding" and complicit with the university in allowing homosexual individuals to be harmed by the U.S. president and Mexican drug dealers. He also believed the prosecuting attorney would "stack the jury against me" with individuals "who want to silence me."

MMPI-2-RF Results from 2012 Evaluation

PROTOCOL VALIDITY

As can be seen in the defendant's initial MMPI-2-RF results (2012), Mr. A responded to each item (CNS = 0) and responded consistently to the items throughout the test (VRIN-r = 63, TRIN-r = 57F). There was no evidence of overreporting with respect to psychopathology (F-r, Fp-r) or somatic/cognitive symptoms (Fs, FBS-r, RBS), which is consistent with his low score on the M-FAST (Total Score = 3). Moreover, there was no evidence of underreporting on L-r or K-r. Consequently, the profile would be deemed valid for interpretation.

CLINICAL INTERPRETATION

Several clinical elevations in the profile provide some insight into Mr. A's psychological functioning and thus inform impressions about his competency to proceed to trial. Applying the interpretive strategy described in Chapter 1, we would begin by reviewing the scales in the thought dysfunction domain, since THD (67T) was the highest elevated H-O scale. Within this domain, we see that he had an elevation on RC6 (84T) and PSYC-r (66T), which suggests that he experiences poor reality testing. His score on RC6 is in the range that we would consider consistent with paranoid delusions, particularly since the critical items included some that were bizarre in content. His lower score on RC8 (59T) suggests that he is likely not experiencing significant hallucinations.

The next step in the interpretive strategy would be to examine the internalizing domain, since his score on EID was significantly low (36T). With the exception of SUI (66T), none of the internalizing RC or SP Scales were elevated. It is interesting that although his earlier results reflect significant thought dysfunction, he did not appear to be distressed about his current situation, which was consistent with his presentation during the clinical interview. His score on SUI is obviously important to consider from a risk perspective. Review of the item that he endorsed on this scale reflects a focus on death and life after death. Given that he believed that he was a prophet and that the end of the world was approaching, his endorsement of this item did not appear to be reflective of suicidal ideation, although this score prompted the examiner to explore this carefully in the evaluation. It is also worth noting that his score on NFC and STW were significantly low, indicating that

Minnesota Multiphasic
Personality Inventory-2
Restructured Form®

Score Report

MMPI-2-RF®

Minnesota Multiphasic Personality Inventory-2-Restructured Form®

Yossef S. Ben-Porath, PhD, & Auke Tellegen, PhD

Name:	Mr. A
ID Number:	4
Age:	50
Gender:	Male
Marital Status:	Divorced
Years of Education:	16
Date Assessed:	12/10/2012

ALWAYS LEARNING

PEARSON

FIGURE 4-1 Case Example 4-1: Mr. A's MMPI-2-RF Profile, continued.

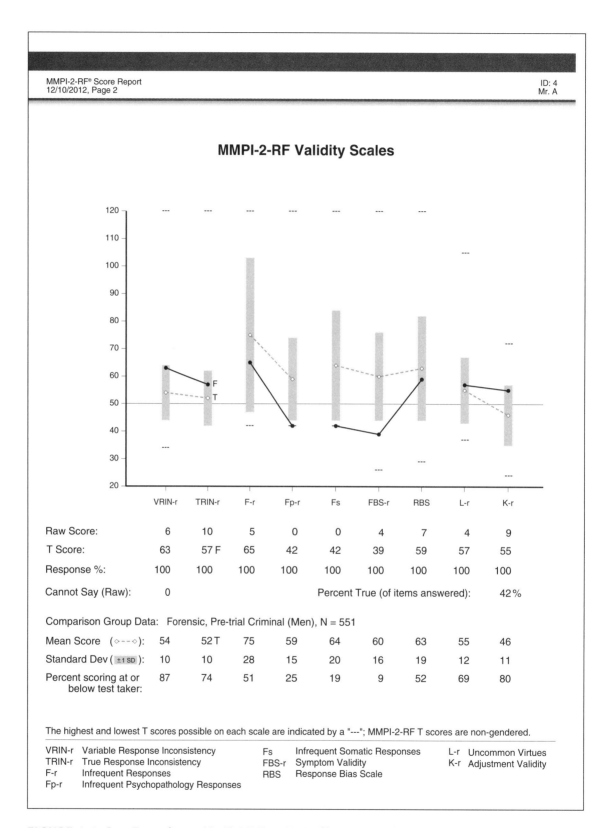

MMPI-2-RF Validity Scales

	VRIN-r	TRIN-r	F-r	Fp-r	Fs	FBS-r	RBS	L-r	K-r
Raw Score:	6	10	5	0	0	4	7	4	9
T Score:	63	57 F	65	42	42	39	59	57	55
Response %:	100	100	100	100	100	100	100	100	100

Cannot Say (Raw):   0   Percent True (of items answered):   42%

Comparison Group Data: Forensic, Pre-trial Criminal (Men), N = 551

	VRIN-r	TRIN-r	F-r	Fp-r	Fs	FBS-r	RBS	L-r	K-r
Mean Score (◇--◇):	54	52 T	75	59	64	60	63	55	46
Standard Dev (±1 SD):	10	10	28	15	20	16	19	12	11
Percent scoring at or below test taker:	87	74	51	25	19	9	52	69	80

The highest and lowest T scores possible on each scale are indicated by a "---"; MMPI-2-RF T scores are non-gendered.

VRIN-r	Variable Response Inconsistency	Fs	Infrequent Somatic Responses	L-r Uncommon Virtues
TRIN-r	True Response Inconsistency	FBS-r	Symptom Validity	K-r Adjustment Validity
F-r	Infrequent Responses	RBS	Response Bias Scale	
Fp-r	Infrequent Psychopathology Responses			

FIGURE 4-1 Case Example 4-1: Mr. A's MMPI-2-RF Profile, continued.

58

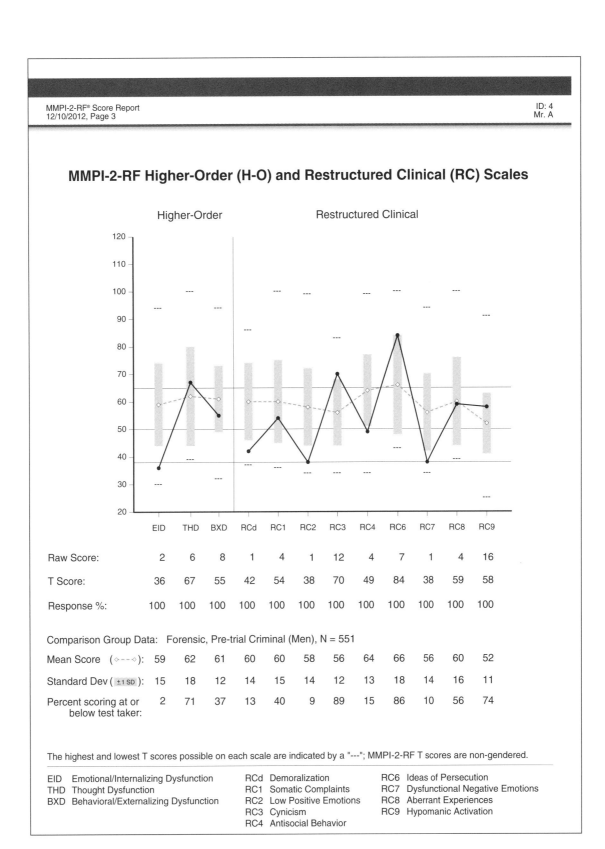

FIGURE 4-1 Case Example 4-1: Mr. A's MMPI-2-RF Profile, continued.

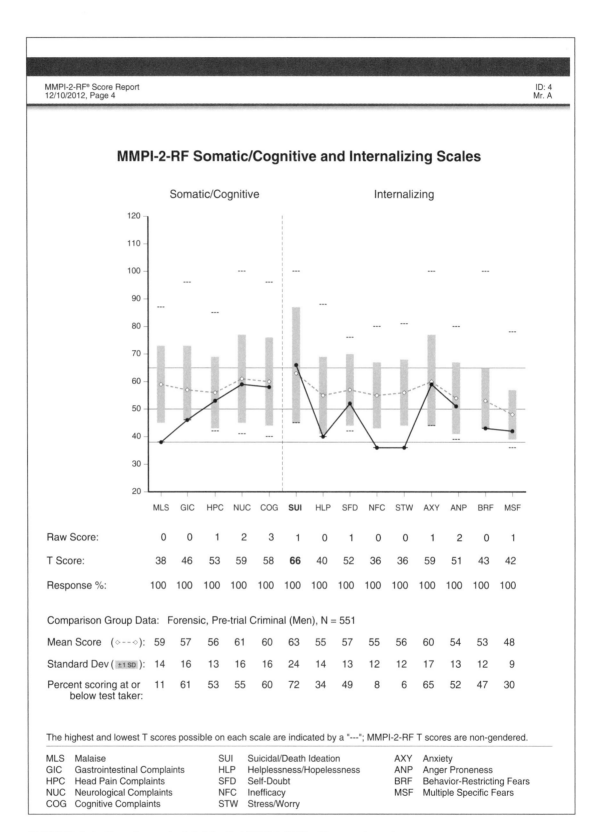

MMPI-2-RF Somatic/Cognitive and Internalizing Scales

Somatic/Cognitive | Internalizing

	MLS	GIC	HPC	NUC	COG	SUI	HLP	SFD	NFC	STW	AXY	ANP	BRF	MSF
Raw Score:	0	0	1	2	3	1	0	1	0	0	1	2	0	1
T Score:	38	46	53	59	58	**66**	40	52	36	36	59	51	43	42
Response %:	100	100	100	100	100	100	100	100	100	100	100	100	100	100

Comparison Group Data: Forensic, Pre-trial Criminal (Men), N = 551

	MLS	GIC	HPC	NUC	COG	SUI	HLP	SFD	NFC	STW	AXY	ANP	BRF	MSF
Mean Score (◇--◇):	59	57	56	61	60	63	55	57	55	56	60	54	53	48
Standard Dev (±1 SD):	14	16	13	16	16	24	14	13	12	12	17	13	12	9
Percent scoring at or below test taker:	11	61	53	55	60	72	34	49	8	6	65	52	47	30

The highest and lowest T scores possible on each scale are indicated by a "---"; MMPI-2-RF T scores are non-gendered.

MLS	Malaise	SUI	Suicidal/Death Ideation	AXY	Anxiety
GIC	Gastrointestinal Complaints	HLP	Helplessness/Hopelessness	ANP	Anger Proneness
HPC	Head Pain Complaints	SFD	Self-Doubt	BRF	Behavior-Restricting Fears
NUC	Neurological Complaints	NFC	Inefficacy	MSF	Multiple Specific Fears
COG	Cognitive Complaints	STW	Stress/Worry		

FIGURE 4-1 Case Example 4-1: Mr. A's MMPI-2-RF Profile, continued.

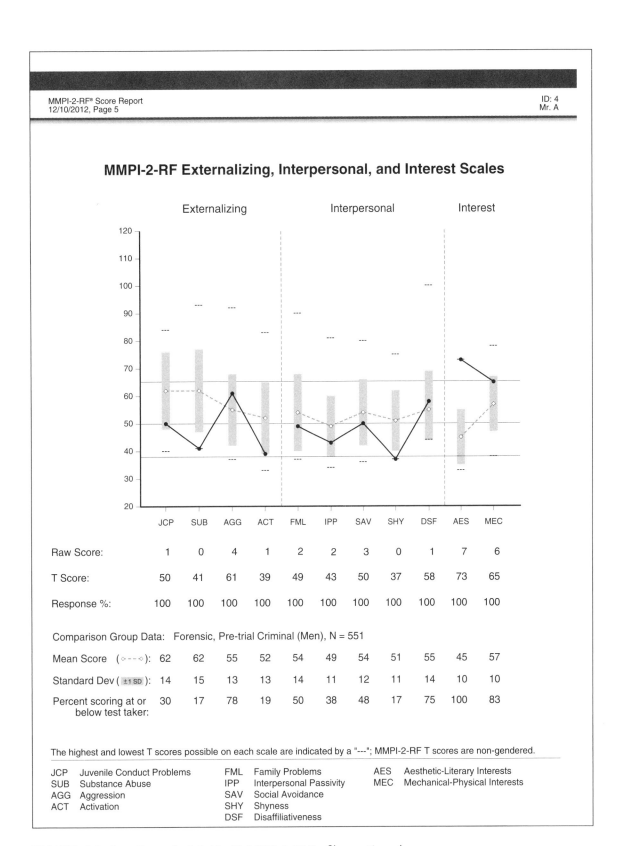

MMPI-2-RF Externalizing, Interpersonal, and Interest Scales

	JCP	SUB	AGG	ACT	FML	IPP	SAV	SHY	DSF	AES	MEC
Raw Score:	1	0	4	1	2	2	3	0	1	7	6
T Score:	50	41	61	39	49	43	50	37	58	73	65
Response %:	100	100	100	100	100	100	100	100	100	100	100

Comparison Group Data: Forensic, Pre-trial Criminal (Men), N = 551

	JCP	SUB	AGG	ACT	FML	IPP	SAV	SHY	DSF	AES	MEC
Mean Score (◇---◇):	62	62	55	52	54	49	54	51	55	45	57
Standard Dev (±1 SD):	14	15	13	13	14	11	12	11	14	10	10
Percent scoring at or below test taker:	30	17	78	19	50	38	48	17	75	100	83

The highest and lowest T scores possible on each scale are indicated by a "---"; MMPI-2-RF T scores are non-gendered.

JCP	Juvenile Conduct Problems	FML	Family Problems	AES	Aesthetic-Literary Interests
SUB	Substance Abuse	IPP	Interpersonal Passivity	MEC	Mechanical-Physical Interests
AGG	Aggression	SAV	Social Avoidance		
ACT	Activation	SHY	Shyness		
		DSF	Disaffiliativeness		

FIGURE 4-1 Case Example 4-1: Mr. A's MMPI-2-RF Profile, continued.

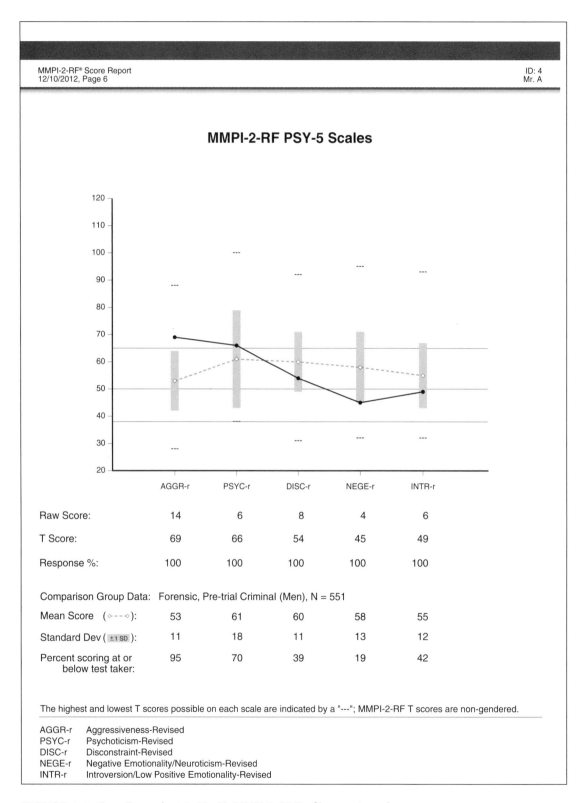

MMPI-2-RF PSY-5 Scales

	AGGR-r	PSYC-r	DISC-r	NEGE-r	INTR-r
Raw Score:	14	6	8	4	6
T Score:	69	66	54	45	49
Response %:	100	100	100	100	100

Comparison Group Data: Forensic, Pre-trial Criminal (Men), N = 551

Mean Score (◇- - -◇):	53	61	60	58	55
Standard Dev (±1 SD):	11	18	11	13	12
Percent scoring at or below test taker:	95	70	39	19	42

The highest and lowest T scores possible on each scale are indicated by a "---"; MMPI-2-RF T scores are non-gendered.

AGGR-r Aggressiveness-Revised
PSYC-r Psychoticism-Revised
DISC-r Disconstraint-Revised
NEGE-r Negative Emotionality/Neuroticism-Revised
INTR-r Introversion/Low Positive Emotionality-Revised

FIGURE 4-1 Case Example 4-1: Mr. A's MMPI-2-RF Profile, continued.

MMPI-2-RF T SCORES (BY DOMAIN)

PROTOCOL VALIDITY

Content Non-Responsiveness

0	63	57 F
CNS	VRIN-r	TRIN-r

Over-Reporting

65	42		42	39	59
F-r	Fp-r		Fs	FBS-r	RBS

Under-Reporting

57	55
L-r	K-r

SUBSTANTIVE SCALES

Somatic/Cognitive Dysfunction

54	38	46	53	59	58
RC1	MLS	GIC	HPC	NUC	COG

Emotional Dysfunction

36		42	66	40	52	36	
EID		RCd	SUI	HLP	SFD	NFC	

38	49
RC2	INTR-r

38	36	59	51	43	42	45
RC7	STW	AXY	ANP	BRF	MSF	NEGE-r

Thought Dysfunction

67		84
THD		RC6

59
RC8

66
PSYC-r

Behavioral Dysfunction

55		49	50	41
BXD		RC4	JCP	SUB

58	61	39	69	54
RC9	AGG	ACT	AGGR-r	DISC-r

Interpersonal Functioning

49	70	43	50	37	58
FML	RC3	IPP	SAV	SHY	DSF

Interests

73	65
AES	MEC

Note. This information is provided to facilitate interpretation following the recommended structure for MMPI-2-RF interpretation in Chapter 5 of the *MMPI-2-RF Manual for Administration, Scoring, and Interpretation*, which provides details in the text and an outline in Table 5-1.

FIGURE 4-1 Case Example 4-1: Mr. A's MMPI-2-RF Profile, continued.

ITEM-LEVEL INFORMATION

Unscorable Responses

The test taker produced scorable responses to all the MMPI-2-RF items.

Critical Responses

Seven MMPI-2-RF scales--Suicidal/Death Ideation (SUI), Helplessness/Hopelessness (HLP), Anxiety (AXY), Ideas of Persecution (RC6), Aberrant Experiences (RC8), Substance Abuse (SUB), and Aggression (AGG)--have been designated by the test authors as having critical item content that may require immediate attention and follow-up. Items answered by the individual in the keyed direction (True or False) on a critical scale are listed below if his T score on that scale is 65 or higher. The percentage of the MMPI-2-RF normative sample (NS) and of the Forensic, Pre-trial Criminal (Men) comparison group (CG) that answered each item in the keyed direction are provided in parentheses following the item content.

Suicidal/Death Ideation (SUI, T Score = 66)

334. Item Content Omitted. (True; NS 13.5%, CG 26.1%)

Ideas of Persecution (RC6, T Score = 84)

  34. Item Content Omitted. (True; NS 10.6%, CG 33.4%)
  92. Item Content Omitted. (True; NS 1.0%, CG 8.9%)
194. Item Content Omitted. (True; NS 17.1%, CG 42.5%)
212. Item Content Omitted. (False; NS 9.1%, CG 38.1%)
233. Item Content Omitted. (True; NS 5.5%, CG 32.3%)
287. Item Content Omitted. (True; NS 3.1%, CG 16.7%)
332. Item Content Omitted. (True; NS 3.2%, CG 21.1%)

User-Designated Item-Level Information

The following item-level information is based on the report user's selection of additional scales, and/or of lower cutoffs for the critical scales from the previous section. Items answered by the test taker in the keyed direction (True or False) on a selected scale are listed below if his T score on that scale is at the user-designated cutoff score or higher. The percentage of the MMPI-2-RF normative sample (NS) and of the Forensic, Pre-trial Criminal (Men) comparison group (CG) that answered each item in the keyed direction are provided in parentheses following the item content.

Thought Dysfunction (THD, T Score = 67)

  85. Item Content Omitted. (False; NS 17.1%, CG 39.6%)
  92. Item Content Omitted. (True; NS 1.0%, CG 8.9%)
212. Item Content Omitted. (False; NS 9.1%, CG 38.1%)
287. Item Content Omitted. (True; NS 3.1%, CG 16.7%)
330. Item Content Omitted. (True; NS 15.2%, CG 27.9%)

FIGURE 4-1 Case Example 4-1: Mr. A's MMPI-2-RF Profile, continued.

332. Item Content Omitted. (True; NS 3.2%, CG 21.1%), CG 21.1%

Cynicism (RC3, T Score = 70)

36. Item Content Omitted. (True; NS 58.3%, CG 60.6%)

55. Item Content Omitted. (True; NS 47.7%, CG 68.8%)

87. Item Content Omitted. (True; NS 39.7%, CG   46.6%)

99. Item Content Omitted. True; NS 53.6%, CG 68.1%)

121. Item Content Omitted. (True; NS 16.8%, CG 45.0%)

142. Item Content Omitted. (True; NS 22.0%, CG 45.6%)

171. Item Content Omitted. (True; NS 51.5%, CG 55.7%)

185. Item Content Omitted. (True; NS 29.3%, CG 51.4%

213. Item Content Omitted. (True; NS 71.4%, CG 78.6%)

238. Item Content Omitted. (True; NS 32.6%, CG 38.3%)

260. Item Content Omitted. (True; NS 36.2%, CG 48.3%)

304. Item Content Omitted. (True; NS 18.8%, CG 32.7%)

Hypomanic Activation (RC9, T Score = 58)

13. Item Content Omitted. (True; NS 40.9%, CG 41.4%)

26. Item Content Omitted. True; NS 19.9%, CG 27.0%)

39. Item Content Omitted. (True; NS 51.0%, CG 62.4%)

72. Item Content Omitted. (True; NS 81.5%, CG 75.7%)

97. Item Content Omitted. (True; NS 50.5%, CG 46.3%)

107. Item Content Omitted. (True; NS 47.3%, CG 40.1%)

118. Item Content Omitted. (True; NS 57.4%, CG 63.0%)

131. Item Content Omitted. (True; NS 43.3%, CG 43.0%)

155. Item Content Omitted. (True; NS 41.6%, CG 43.7%)

231. Item Content Omitted. (True; NS 6.3%, CG 10.9%)

244. Item Content Omitted. (True; NS 56.9%, CG 71.1%)

FIGURE 4-1 Case Example 4-1: Mr. A's MMPI-2-RF Profile, continued.

256. Item Content Omitted. (True; NS 65.7%, CG 63.5%)

292. Item Content Omitted. (True; NS 26.1%, CG 28.7%)
305. Item Content Omitted. (True; NS 37.6%, CG 39.9%)
316. Item Content Omitted. (True; NS 45.1%, CG 59.7%)

337. Item Content Omitted. (True; NS 50.2%, CG 55.2%)

Behavior-Restricting Fears (BRF, T Score = 43)
> No items that are scored on this scale were answered in the keyed direction.

Juvenile Conduct Problems (JCP, T Score = 50)
223. Item Content Omitted. (True; NS 12.3%, CG 50.1%)

Aggressiveness-Revised (AGGR-r, T Score = 69)
24. Item Content Omitted. (False; NS 74.6%, CG 69.9%)
26. Item Content Omitted. (True; NS 19.9%, CG 27.0%)

39. Item Content Omitted. (True; NS51.0%, CG 62.4%)

104. Item Content Omitted. (True; NS 67.1%, CG 68.4%)
147. Item Content Omitted. (True; NS 75.2%, CG 81.1%)
182. Item Content Omitted. (True; NS 33.6%, CG 38.5%)
197. Item Content Omitted. (True; NS 62.5%, CG 68.6%)

231. Item Content Omitted. (True; NS 6.3%, CG 10.9%)

239. Item Content Omitted. (True; NS 60.7%, CG 64.2%)

256. Item Content Omitted. (True; NS 65.7%, CG 63.5%)

276. Item Content Omitted. (True; NS 50.0%, CG 65.2%)

302. Item Content Omitted. (True; NS 67.9%, CG 57.9%)

316. Item Content Omitted. (True; NS 45.1%, CG 59.7%)

319. Item Content Omitted. (False; NS 64.7%, CG 62.4%)

Psychoticism-Revised (PSYC-r, T Score = 66)
34. Item Content Omitted. (True; NS 10.6%, CG 33.4%)
85. Item Content Omitted. (False; NS 17.1%, CG 39.6%)
92. Item Content Omitted. (True; NS 1.0%, CG 8.9%)
287. Item Content Omitted. (True; NS 3.1%, CG 16.7%)
330. Item Content Omitted. (True; NS 15.2%, CG 27.9%)

FIGURE 4-1 Case Example 4-1: Mr. A's MMPI-2-RF Profile, continued.

MMPI-2-RF® Score Report
12/10/2012, Page 11

ID: 4
Mr. A

332. Item Content Omitted. (True; NS 3.2%, CG 21.1%)

End of Report

This and previous pages of this report contain trade secrets and are not to be released in response to requests under HIPAA (or any other data disclosure law that exempts trade secret information from release). Further, release in response to litigation discovery demands should be made only in accordance with your profession's ethical guidelines and under an appropriate protective order.

FIGURE 4-1 Case Example 4-1: Mr. A's MMPI-2-RF Profile.

he experienced little to no stress or worry and did not perceive himself as having difficulty making decisions.

Next in the interpretive strategy we examine any remaining RC Scale elevations. We see that the defendant had an elevation on RC3 (70T). Consistent with his score on RC6, his elevation on RC3 suggests that he is likely to be quite cynical in his general outlook. He likely harbors intense hostility toward others and externalizes blame for his current situation. He is also likely to feel alienated from others (Sellbom & Ben-Porath, 2005) and to have difficulty forming trusting relationships. None of the specific problems on the Interpersonal Scales were elevated, but Shyness (SHY) was low, indicating a lack of social anxiety and feeling confident when interacting with others. His scores on the two Interest Scales were not considered to be clinically relevant in this case.

Although AGGR-r is listed in the externalizing domain, it also includes a prominent interpersonal component. The defendant's score on AGGR-r (69T) suggests that he is likely to be viewed by others as domineering and overly assertive in pushing his beliefs. This is consistent with the allegations pertaining to his current case. Recall that he was charged with repeatedly contacting a university library and insisting that the institution "gather all the homosexuals on campus" because the U.S. president and Mexican drug dealers would kill them. Since his score on AGG (61T) was not clinically elevated, his score on AGGR-r is more likely to reflect an aggressive interpersonal style and personality rather than a propensity to utilize physical aggression.

Aside from AGGR-r, none of the remaining externalizing scales were elevated. Neither BXD nor the RC Scales in this domain (RC4, RC9) were elevated, nor were any of the specific problems on the Externalizing Scales (JCP, SUB, AGG, ACT).

Case Conclusion (2012 Evaluation)

The competency evaluation revealed significant evidence of thought dysfunction that was indicative of schizophrenia. The evaluator opined that Mr. A's mental illness, substantiated in the clinical interview and MMPI-2-RF results, significantly impeded his rational appreciation of the nature and objectives of the court. Moreover, he was significantly compromised in his ability to adequately assist counsel in his defense. He viewed the authority of the court as inconsequential since he believed the world would end before his court date. The judge ultimately found him incompetent to stand trial and committed him to a state psychiatric facility for 1 month. His case was eventually dismissed by the state.

CASE EXAMPLE 4-2

2016 Competency Evaluation

Mr. A was indicted on similar charges in 2016. Once again, he was alleged to have committed two counts of terroristic threatening and three counts of harassing communications. The allegations were similar in nature to his charges in 2012. Since his previous court case, the defendant "mainly kept to myself," but once again he became increasingly preoccupied with his religious beliefs that he was a prophet. By 2016, he had not been taking any of his prescribed psychotropic medication for approximately one and a half years.

Mr. A presented as more psychiatrically impaired during the second evaluation, which took place in the local detention facility. His thoughts were more disjointed than the earlier evaluation and his speech was pressured at times.

The 2016 evaluation included administration of the Evaluation of Competency to Stand Trial-Revised (Rogers et al., 2004), which is a semistructured interview designed to assess the dimensions of competency to stand trial. His scores on this measure revealed significant difficulties in consulting with counsel, as well as limited rational understanding of the proceedings. His score on the M-FAST (Total Score of 4) was, once again, not indicative of feigning or exaggeration.

MMPI-2-RF Results from 2016 Evaluation

Mr. A's 2016 MMPI-2-RF Validity Scales results[2] included higher scores on F-r and Fp-r than on the earlier administration. Nevertheless, his results were deemed valid for interpretation because of his significant psychiatric history (which appeared to have gotten worse since 2012, and, thus, could lead to higher overreporting scale scores), credible presentation during the evaluation, and score on the M-FAST was not indicative of overreporting.

His clinical profile was once again characterized by thought dysfunction, although the severity of these symptoms was substantially worse in 2016

Minnesota Multiphasic
Personality Inventory-2
Restructured Form®

Score Report

MMPI-2-RF®

Minnesota Multiphasic Personality Inventory-2-Restructured Form®

Yossef S. Ben-Porath, PhD, & Auke Tellegen, PhD

Name:	Mr. A
ID Number:	4
Age:	53
Gender:	Male
Marital Status:	Divorced
Years of Education:	13
Date Assessed:	05/31/2016

ALWAYS LEARNING

PEARSON

FIGURE 4-2 Case Example 4-2: Mr. A's MMPI-2-RF Profile, continued.

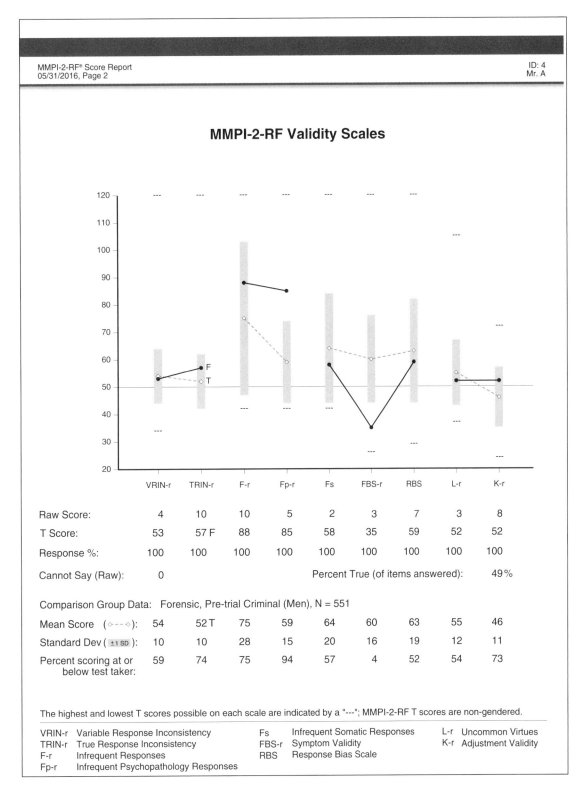

MMPI-2-RF Validity Scales

	VRIN-r	TRIN-r	F-r	Fp-r	Fs	FBS-r	RBS	L-r	K-r
Raw Score:	4	10	10	5	2	3	7	3	8
T Score:	53	57 F	88	85	58	35	59	52	52
Response %:	100	100	100	100	100	100	100	100	100

Cannot Say (Raw):   0   Percent True (of items answered):   49%

Comparison Group Data: Forensic, Pre-trial Criminal (Men), N = 551

	VRIN-r	TRIN-r	F-r	Fp-r	Fs	FBS-r	RBS	L-r	K-r
Mean Score (◇---◇):	54	52 T	75	59	64	60	63	55	46
Standard Dev (±1 SD):	10	10	28	15	20	16	19	12	11
Percent scoring at or below test taker:	59	74	75	94	57	4	52	54	73

The highest and lowest T scores possible on each scale are indicated by a "---"; MMPI-2-RF T scores are non-gendered.

VRIN-r	Variable Response Inconsistency	Fs	Infrequent Somatic Responses
TRIN-r	True Response Inconsistency	FBS-r	Symptom Validity
F-r	Infrequent Responses	RBS	Response Bias Scale
Fp-r	Infrequent Psychopathology Responses		

L-r	Uncommon Virtues
K-r	Adjustment Validity

FIGURE 4-2 Case Example 4-2: Mr. A's MMPI-2-RF Profile, continued.

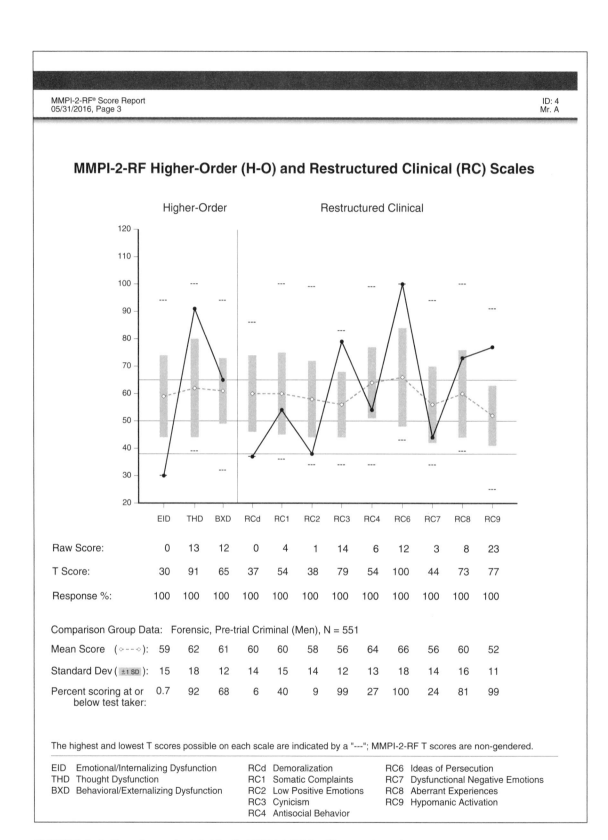

MMPI-2-RF Higher-Order (H-O) and Restructured Clinical (RC) Scales

	EID	THD	BXD	RCd	RC1	RC2	RC3	RC4	RC6	RC7	RC8	RC9
Raw Score:	0	13	12	0	4	1	14	6	12	3	8	23
T Score:	30	91	65	37	54	38	79	54	100	44	73	77
Response %:	100	100	100	100	100	100	100	100	100	100	100	100

Comparison Group Data: Forensic, Pre-trial Criminal (Men), N = 551

	EID	THD	BXD	RCd	RC1	RC2	RC3	RC4	RC6	RC7	RC8	RC9
Mean Score (◇- - -◇):	59	62	61	60	60	58	56	64	66	56	60	52
Standard Dev (±1 SD):	15	18	12	14	15	14	12	13	18	14	16	11
Percent scoring at or below test taker:	0.7	92	68	6	40	9	99	27	100	24	81	99

The highest and lowest T scores possible on each scale are indicated by a "---"; MMPI-2-RF T scores are non-gendered.

EID	Emotional/Internalizing Dysfunction
THD	Thought Dysfunction
BXD	Behavioral/Externalizing Dysfunction

RCd	Demoralization
RC1	Somatic Complaints
RC2	Low Positive Emotions
RC3	Cynicism
RC4	Antisocial Behavior

RC6	Ideas of Persecution
RC7	Dysfunctional Negative Emotions
RC8	Aberrant Experiences
RC9	Hypomanic Activation

FIGURE 4-2 Case Example 4-2: Mr. A's MMPI-2-RF Profile, continued.

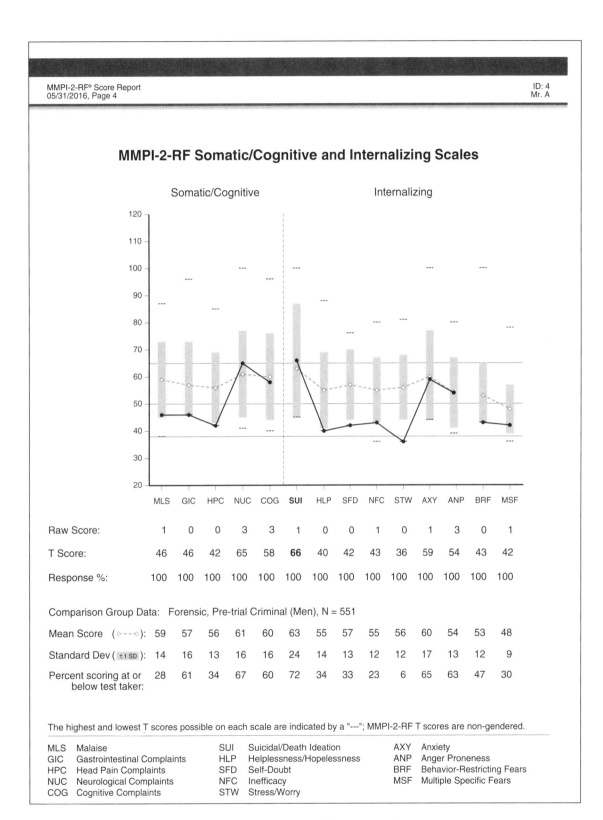

MMPI-2-RF Somatic/Cognitive and Internalizing Scales

Somatic/Cognitive   Internalizing

	MLS	GIC	HPC	NUC	COG	SUI	HLP	SFD	NFC	STW	AXY	ANP	BRF	MSF
Raw Score:	1	0	0	3	3	1	0	0	1	0	1	3	0	1
T Score:	46	46	42	65	58	**66**	40	42	43	36	59	54	43	42
Response %:	100	100	100	100	100	100	100	100	100	100	100	100	100	100

Comparison Group Data: Forensic, Pre-trial Criminal (Men), N = 551

	MLS	GIC	HPC	NUC	COG	SUI	HLP	SFD	NFC	STW	AXY	ANP	BRF	MSF
Mean Score (◇---◇):	59	57	56	61	60	63	55	57	55	56	60	54	53	48
Standard Dev (±1 SD):	14	16	13	16	16	24	14	13	12	12	17	13	12	9
Percent scoring at or below test taker:	28	61	34	67	60	72	34	33	23	6	65	63	47	30

The highest and lowest T scores possible on each scale are indicated by a "---"; MMPI-2-RF T scores are non-gendered.

MLS	Malaise	SUI	Suicidal/Death Ideation	AXY	Anxiety
GIC	Gastrointestinal Complaints	HLP	Helplessness/Hopelessness	ANP	Anger Proneness
HPC	Head Pain Complaints	SFD	Self-Doubt	BRF	Behavior-Restricting Fears
NUC	Neurological Complaints	NFC	Inefficacy	MSF	Multiple Specific Fears
COG	Cognitive Complaints	STW	Stress/Worry		

FIGURE 4-2 Case Example 4-2: Mr. A's MMPI-2-RF Profile, continued.

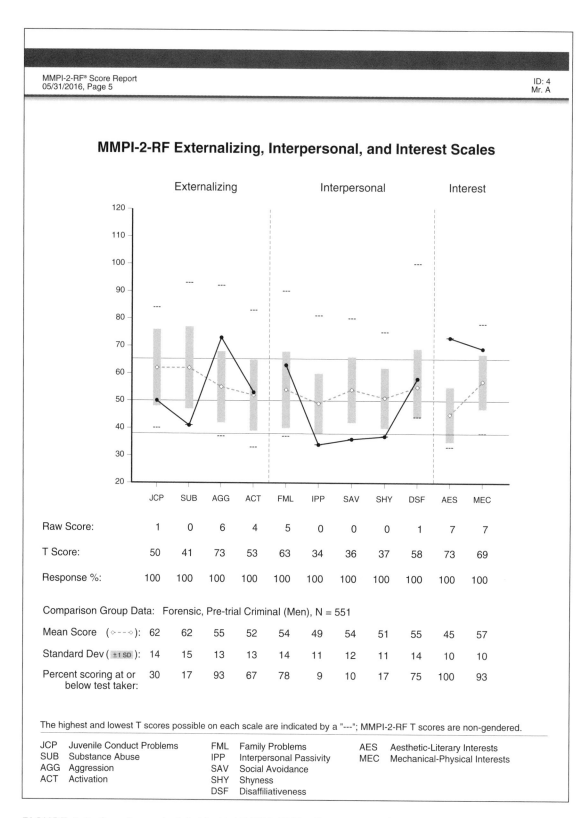

MMPI-2-RF Externalizing, Interpersonal, and Interest Scales

	Externalizing				Interpersonal				Interest	
	JCP	SUB	AGG	ACT	FML	IPP	SAV	SHY	DSF	AES	MEC
Raw Score:	1	0	6	4	5	0	0	0	1	7	7
T Score:	50	41	73	53	63	34	36	37	58	73	69
Response %:	100	100	100	100	100	100	100	100	100	100	100

Comparison Group Data: Forensic, Pre-trial Criminal (Men), N = 551

Mean Score (◇--◇):	62	62	55	52	54	49	54	51	55	45	57
Standard Dev (±1 SD):	14	15	13	13	14	11	12	11	14	10	10
Percent scoring at or below test taker:	30	17	93	67	78	9	10	17	75	100	93

The highest and lowest T scores possible on each scale are indicated by a "---"; MMPI-2-RF T scores are non-gendered.

JCP	Juvenile Conduct Problems	FML	Family Problems	AES	Aesthetic-Literary Interests
SUB	Substance Abuse	IPP	Interpersonal Passivity	MEC	Mechanical-Physical Interests
AGG	Aggression	SAV	Social Avoidance		
ACT	Activation	SHY	Shyness		
		DSF	Disaffiliativeness		

FIGURE 4-2 Case Example 4-2: Mr. A's MMPI-2-RF Profile, continued.

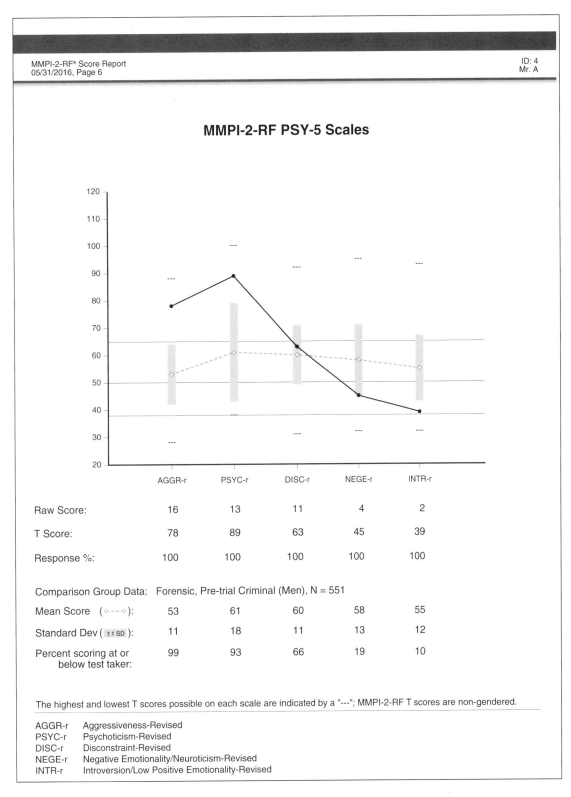

MMPI-2-RF PSY-5 Scales

	AGGR-r	PSYC-r	DISC-r	NEGE-r	INTR-r
Raw Score:	16	13	11	4	2
T Score:	78	89	63	45	39
Response %:	100	100	100	100	100

Comparison Group Data: Forensic, Pre-trial Criminal (Men), N = 551

	AGGR-r	PSYC-r	DISC-r	NEGE-r	INTR-r
Mean Score (◇--◇):	53	61	60	58	55
Standard Dev (±1 SD):	11	18	11	13	12
Percent scoring at or below test taker:	99	93	66	19	10

The highest and lowest T scores possible on each scale are indicated by a "---"; MMPI-2-RF T scores are non-gendered.

AGGR-r	Aggressiveness-Revised
PSYC-r	Psychoticism-Revised
DISC-r	Disconstraint-Revised
NEGE-r	Negative Emotionality/Neuroticism-Revised
INTR-r	Introversion/Low Positive Emotionality-Revised

FIGURE 4-2 Case Example 4-2: Mr. A's MMPI-2-RF Profile, continued.

MMPI-2-RF T SCORES (BY DOMAIN)

PROTOCOL VALIDITY

Content Non-Responsiveness

0	53	57 F
CNS	VRIN-r	TRIN-r

Over-Reporting

88	85		58	35	59
F-r	Fp-r		Fs	FBS-r	RBS

Under-Reporting

52	52
L-r	K-r

SUBSTANTIVE SCALES

Somatic/Cognitive Dysfunction

54	46	46	42	65	58
RC1	MLS	GIC	HPC	NUC	COG

Emotional Dysfunction

30					
EID					

37	66	40	42	43
RCd	SUI	HLP	SFD	NFC

38	39
RC2	INTR-r

44	36	59	54	43	42	45
RC7	STW	AXY	ANP	BRF	MSF	NEGE-r

Thought Dysfunction

91
THD

100
RC6

73
RC8

89
PSYC-r

Behavioral Dysfunction

65
BXD

54	50	41
RC4	JCP	SUB

77	73	53	78	63
RC9	AGG	ACT	AGGR-r	DISC-r

Interpersonal Functioning

63	79	34	36	37	58
FML	RC3	IPP	SAV	SHY	DSF

Interests

73	69
AES	MEC

Note. This information is provided to facilitate interpretation following the recommended structure for MMPI-2-RF interpretation in Chapter 5 of the *MMPI-2-RF Manual for Administration, Scoring, and Interpretation*, which provides details in the text and an outline in Table 5-1.

FIGURE 4-2 Case Example 4-2: Mr. A's MMPI-2-RF Profile, continued.

ITEM-LEVEL INFORMATION

Unscorable Responses

The test taker produced scorable responses to all the MMPI-2-RF items.

Critical Responses

Seven MMPI-2-RF scales--Suicidal/Death Ideation (SUI), Helplessness/Hopelessness (HLP), Anxiety (AXY), Ideas of Persecution (RC6), Aberrant Experiences (RC8), Substance Abuse (SUB), and Aggression (AGG)--have been designated by the test authors as having critical item content that may require immediate attention and follow-up. Items answered by the individual in the keyed direction (True or False) on a critical scale are listed below if his T score on that scale is 65 or higher. The percentage of the MMPI-2-RF normative sample (NS) and of the Forensic, Pre-trial Criminal (Men) comparison group (CG) that answered each item in the keyed direction are provided in parentheses following the item content.

Suicidal/Death Ideation (SUI, T Score = 66)

   334. Item Content Omitted. (True; NS 13.5%, CG 26.1%)

Ideas of Persecution (RC6, T Score = 100)

   34. Item Content Omitted. (True; NS 10.6%, CG 33.4%)
   71. Item Content Omitted. (True; NS 2.0%, CG 23.4%)
   92. Item Content Omitted. (True; NS 1.0%, CG 8.9%)
  129. Item Content Omitted. (True; NS 0.5%, CG 2.0%)
  150. Item Content Omitted. (True; NS 2.0%, CG 7.8%)
  168. Item Content Omitted. (True; NS 2.8%, CG 7.6%)
  194. Item Content Omitted. (True; NS 17.1%, CG 42.5%)
  212. Item Content Omitted. (False; NS 9.1%, CG 38.1%)
  233. Item Content Omitted. (True; NS 5.5%, CG 32.3%)
  264. Item Content Omitted. (True; NS 5.3%, CG 28.5%)
  287. Item Content Omitted. (True; NS 3.1%, CG 16.7%)
  310. Item Content Omitted. (True; NS 3.0%, CG 18.3%)

Aberrant Experiences (RC8, T Score = 73)

   32. Item Content Omitted. (True; NS 21.1%, CG 57.4%)
   85. Item Content Omitted. (False; NS 17.1%, CG 39.6%)
  106. Item Content Omitted. (True; NS 8.7%, CG 42.8%)
  179. Item Content Omitted. (True; NS 12.6%, CG 26.9%)
  203. Item Content Omitted. (True; NS 4.5%, CG 13.8%)
  257. Item Content Omitted. (True; NS 12.4%, CG 32.1%)
  294. Item Content Omitted. (True; NS 7.1%, CG 12.9%)
  330. Item Content Omitted. (True; NS 15.2%, CG 27.9%)

FIGURE 4-2 Case Example 4-2: Mr. A's MMPI-2-RF Profile, continued.

Aggression (AGG, T Score = 73)

23. Item Content Omitted. (True; NS 39.0%, CG 43.6%)
26. Item Content Omitted.
    (True; NS 19.9%, CG 27.0%)
41. Item Content Omitted. (True; NS 5.0%, CG 3.6%)
231. Item Content Omitted. (True; NS 6.3%,
    CG 10.9%)
316. Item Content Omitted. (True; NS 45.1%, CG
    59.7%)
337. Item Content Omitted. (True; NS 50.2%,
    CG 55.2%)

User-Designated Item-Level Information

The following item-level information is based on the report user's selection of additional scales, and/or of lower cutoffs for the critical scales from the previous section. Items answered by the test taker in the keyed direction (True or False) on a selected scale are listed below if his T score on that scale is at the user-designated cutoff score or higher. The percentage of the MMPI-2-RF normative sample (NS) and of the Forensic, Pre-trial Criminal (Men) comparison group (CG) that answered each item in the keyed direction are provided in parentheses following the item content.

Thought Dysfunction (THD, T Score = 91)

71. Item Content Omitted. (True; NS 2.0%, CG 23.4%)
85. Item Content Omitted. (False; NS 17.1%, CG 39.6%)
92. Item Content Omitted. (True; NS 1.0%, CG 8.9%)
129. Item Content Omitted. (True; NS 0.5%, CG 2.0%)
150. Item Content Omitted. (True; NS 2.0%, CG 7.8%)
168. Item Content Omitted. (True; NS 2.8%, CG 7.6%)
179. Item Content Omitted. (True; NS 12.6%, CG
    26.9%)
203. Item Content Omitted. (True; NS 4.5%, CG 13.8%)
212. Item Content Omitted. (False; NS 9.1%, CG 38.1%)
264. Item Content Omitted. (True; NS 5.3%, CG 28.5%)
287. Item Content Omitted. (True; NS 3.1%, CG 16.7%)
294. Item Content Omitted. (True; NS 7.1%, CG 12.9%)
330. Item Content Omitted. (True; NS 15.2%, CG 27.9%)

Behavioral/Externalizing Dysfunction (BXD, T Score = 65)

61. Item Content Omitted. (False; NS 61.6%, CG 67.9%)
96. Item Content Omitted. (True; NS 18.8%, CG
    49.4%)
107. Item Content Omitted. (True; NS 47.3%, CG 40.1%)
131. Item Content Omitted. (True; NS 43.3%, CG 43.0%)
156. Item Content Omitted. (True; NS 59.8%, CG 61.2%)
190. Item Content Omitted. (False; NS 28.6%, CG 85.8%)

FIGURE 4-2 Case Example 4-2: Mr. A's MMPI-2-RF Profile, continued.

193. Item Content Omitted.
     (True; NS 32.8%, CG 30.7%)
226. Item Content Omitted. (True; NS 21.5%, CG 42.6%)
231. Item Content Omitted. (True; NS 6.3%,
     CG 10.9%)
248. Item Content Omitted. (True; NS 16.1%, CG 34.3%)
292. Item Content Omitted. (True; NS 26.1%, CG 28.7%)
316. Item Content Omitted. (True; NS 45.1%, CG
     59.7%)

Cynicism (RC3, T Score = 79)

36. Item Content Omitted.
    (True; NS 58.3%, CG 60.6%)
55. Item Content Omitted. (True; NS 47.7%, CG 68.8%)
87. Item Content Omitted. (True; NS 39.7%, CG
    46.6%)
99. Item Content Omitted.
    (True; NS 53.6%, CG 68.1%)
121. Item Content Omitted. (True; NS 16.8%, CG 45.0%)
142. Item Content Omitted. (True; NS 22.0%, CG
     45.6%)
171. Item Content Omitted. (True; NS 51.5%, CG 55.7%)
185. Item Content Omitted. (True; NS 29.3%, CG
     51.4%)
213. Item Content Omitted.
     (True; NS 71.4%, CG 78.6%)
238. Item Content Omitted. (True; NS
     32.6%, CG 38.3%)
260. Item Content Omitted.
     (True; NS 36.2%, CG 48.3%)

279. Item Content Omitted. (True; NS 39.1%, CG 51.2%)
304. Item Content Omitted. (True; NS 18.8%, CG 32.7%)
326. Item Content Omitted. (True; NS 28.8%, CG 27.9%)

Hypomanic Activation (RC9, T Score = 77)

13. Item Content Omitted. (True; NS 40.9%, CG
    41.4%)
26. Item Content Omitted.
    (True; NS 19.9%, CG 27.0%)
39. Item Content Omitted. (True; NS
    51.0%, CG 62.4%)
47. Item Content Omitted. (True; NS 42.7%, CG
    46.1%)
61. Item Content Omitted. (False; NS 61.6%, CG 67.9%)

FIGURE 4-2 Case Example 4-2: Mr. A's MMPI-2-RF Profile, continued.

72. Item Content Omitted. (True; NS 81.5%, CG
   75.7%)
97. IItem Content Omitted. (True; NS 50.5%, CG
   46.3%)
107. Item Content Omitted. (True; NS 47.3%, CG 40.1%)
118. Item Content Omitted. (True; NS 57.4%, CG 63.0%)
131. Item Content Omitted. (True; NS 43.3%, CG 43.0%)
155. Item Content Omitted. (True; NS 41.6%, CG 43.7%)
166. Item Content Omitted.
   (True; NS 38.9%, CG 39.2%)
181. Item Content Omitted. (True; NS 35.3%, CG 39.2%)
193. Item Content Omitted.
   (True; NS 32.8%, CG 30.7%)
231. Item Content Omitted. (True; NS 6.3%,
   CG 10.9%)
244. Item Content Omitted. (True; NS
   56.9%, CG 71.1%)
248. Item Content Omitted. (True; NS 16.1%, CG 34.3%)
256. Item Content Omitted. (True; NS
   65.7%, CG 63.5%)
292. Item Content Omitted. (True; NS 26.1%, CG 28.7%)
305. Item Content Omitted. (True; NS 37.6%, CG 39.9%)
316. Item Content Omitted. (True; NS 45.1%, CG
   59.7%)
327. Item Content Omitted.
   (True; NS 41.7%, CG 47.2%)
337. Item Content Omitted. (True; NS 50.2%,
   CG 55.2%)

Behavior-Restricting Fears (BRF, T Score = 43)

No items that are scored on this scale were answered in the keyed direction.

Juvenile Conduct Problems (JCP, T Score = 50)

96. Item Content Omitted. (True; NS 18.8%, CG
   49.4%)

Aggressiveness-Revised (AGGR-r, T Score = 78)

24. Item Content Omitted. (False; NS 74.6%, CG 69.9%)
26. Item Content Omitted.
   (True; NS 19.9%, CG 27.0%)
39. Item Content Omitted. (True; NS
   51.0%, CG 62.4%)
104. Item Content Omitted. (True; NS 67.1%, CG 68.4%)
147. Item Content Omitted. (True; NS 75.2%, CG 81.1%)
182. Item Content Omitted. (True; NS 33.6%, CG 38.5%)

FIGURE 4-2 Case Example 4-2: Mr. A's MMPI-2-RF Profile, continued.

197. Item Content Omitted. (True; NS 62.5%, CG
    68.6%)
231. Item Content Omitted. (True; NS 6.3%,
    CG 10.9%)
239. Item Content Omitted. (True; NS 60.7%, CG 64.2%)
256. Item Content Omitted. (True; NS
    65.7%, CG 63.5%)
276. Item Content Omitted. (True; NS
    50.0%, CG 65.2%)
302. Item Content Omitted. (True; NS 67.9%, CG 57.9%)
316. Item Content Omitted. (True; NS 45.1%, CG
    59.7%)
319. Item Content Omitted. (False; NS 64.7%,
    CG 62.4%)
321. Item Content Omitted. (True; NS 31.3%, CG 40.1%)
327. Item Content Omitted.
    (True; NS 41.7%, CG 47.2%)

Psychoticism-Revised (PSYC-r, T Score = 89)
    34. Item Content Omitted. (True; NS 10.6%, CG 33.4%)
    71. Item Content Omitted. (True; NS 2.0%, CG 23.4%)
    85. Item Content Omitted. (False; NS 17.1%, CG 39.6%)
    92. Item Content Omitted. (True; NS 1.0%, CG 8.9%)
    129. Item Content Omitted. (True; NS 0.5%, CG 2.0%)
    150. Item Content Omitted. (True; NS 2.0%, CG 7.8%)
    168. Item Content Omitted. (True; NS 2.8%, CG 7.6%)
    179. Item Content Omitted. (True; NS 12.6%, CG
        26.9%)
    203. Item Content Omitted. (True; NS 4.5%, CG 13.8%)
    264. Item Content Omitted. (True; NS 5.3%, CG 28.5%)
    287. Item Content Omitted. (True; NS 3.1%, CG 16.7%)
    294. Item Content Omitted. (True; NS 7.1%, CG 12.9%)
    330. Item Content Omitted. (True; NS 15.2%, CG 27.9%)

End of Report

FIGURE 4-2 Case Example 4-2: Mr. A's MMPI-2-RF Profile.

than in his earlier evaluation. In 2016, his score on RC6 increased to 100T from 84T, and his score on RC8 increased to 73T from 59T. Consistent with his clinical presentation, this suggests that the defendant has become more psychiatrically unstable, with an endorsement of significant psychosis involving bizarre sensory experiences and thought broadcasting, in addition to paranoid and persecutory ideation. Although his score on RC9 (77T) is now in the elevated range, this is likely owing to an increase in his overall level of aggression (AGG = 73T) and not manic symptoms (ACT = 53T).

Other points of interest in the defendant's 2016 MMPI-2-RF results include an elevation on Neurological Complaints (NUC) (65T), which suggests the possibility of sensory problems. His medical history was free of any head trauma or neurological problems, so this score may reflect aspects of his psychosis. The defendant once again endorsed the SUI item reflecting an interest in death and life after death. He also elevated both AGG (73T) and AGGR-r (78T), versus just elevating AGGR-r in 2012, which suggests a greater concern about his aggressive personality. Also, it suggests that he may be at a higher risk to engage in physical violence (Tarescavage, Glassmire, et al., 2016). Finally, his scores on EID and RCd are even lower in 2016, suggesting that he is not experiencing any distress and may in fact be even more used to his current psychological functioning.

Mr. A was once again diagnosed with schizophrenia and the examiner opined that he was significantly impeded in his rational appreciation of the nature and objectives of the court, as well as in his ability to adequately assist counsel in his defense. The judge once again found him incompetent to stand trial, dismissed his case, and filed a mental inquest warrant for his transfer to a state psychiatric facility. Unfortunately, the defendant was inadvertently released from jail before he could be transferred to the hospital.

CONCLUSIONS

The MMPI-2-RF is a useful measure in a competency evaluation, which is focused on current psychological functioning. The test has well-established Validity Scales that can capture the types of symptoms that are likely to be exaggerated in this setting. Moreover, the test can identify an array of psychopathological symptoms, particularly psychosis and thought dysfunction, which are common among defendants found incompetent to stand trial.

Chapter 5

Criminal Responsibility

The consideration of "criminal responsibility," or the degree to which a person should be held accountable for his or her offending behavior, has been in existence for as long as systematic legal codes have been in place (e.g., the Code of Hammurabi from 1754 B.C.). Modern considerations of acquittal from offending conduct owing to mental impairment ("insanity") have evolved through English common law, with *M'Naghten*'s case from 1843 setting the stage for contemporary standards (Goldstein, Morse, & Packer, 2013). Daniel M'Naghten was a delusional man who believed that the governing party at the time was plotting to kill him. In an effort to defend himself, he traveled to London to kill the prime minister, Sir Robert Peel. He mistook Edward Drummond, the prime minister's secretary, for Sir Peel and killed him instead. During trial, M'Naghten's defense argued that he should not be held accountable owing to severe mental illness and, as a result, not knowing right from wrong. M'Naghten was eventually acquitted owing to insanity (Moran, 1981). This case was not the only such insanity case at the time, but became the most influential of its kind because of the public outcry (as well as concerns raised by the queen) following the decision. The British House of Lords considered the case and ultimately developed the M'Naghten rules for insanity (Goldstein et al., 2013). The M'Naghten rules have been highly influential in shaping insanity defense standards in the United States and commonwealth countries. In the United States in particular, a number of legal tests for insanity have been proposed (e.g., irresistible impulse test, Durham rule, substantial capacity test), but a review of these tests is beyond the scope of this chapter (see e.g., Goldstein et al., 2013, for a review).

The legal tests for insanity concern mens rea, which is the mental state element of a criminal offense. More specifically, in most jurisdictions a person must have the ability to form some purpose, intent, and/or exhibit knowledge about the wrongfulness of the conduct, to be held accountable for criminal conduct. In most jurisdictions, the insanity defense is an affirmative defense, which means the burden is on the defendant to prove insanity at the time of the offense. There are generally two major prongs to the legal insanity test (Goldstein et al., 2013; Zapf, Golding, Roesch, & Pirelli, 2013):

(a) the person must exhibit mental impairment (often considered as severe mental illness or neurological condition), and,

(b) the mental impairment must affect the person's ability to reason rationally, understand the nature and quality of conduct, be able to know (or appreciate) the wrongfulness of the conduct, and/or be able to exhibit volitional control of the conduct.

Jurisdictions within the United States, as well as across most Western countries, typically differ in their definitions in the various prongs. For instance, the M'Naghten rule is a very cognitive test that requires the presence of a mental disease or defect that prevents the individual from knowing right from wrong, whereas the American Law Institute's substantial capacity test requires mental impairment that substantially affects the ability to appreciate the wrongfulness of the conduct, or to conform to the conduct of the law (Goldstein et al., 2013). It is important for forensic examiners to fully understand the definition of insanity as worded in the particular jurisdiction within which he or she practices, since it equates to different operationalizations of the psycho-legal question.

Jurisdictions also have exclusionary criteria for the insanity defense. The most common one refers to voluntary intoxication. If an individual was substantially affected by an intoxicating agent (e.g., alcohol or drugs), which was administered under voluntary control (e.g., the person chose to consume it), then he or she is usually disqualified from the insanity defense regardless of current mental impairment. In some jurisdictions, if the defendant can clearly disentangle the effects of mental impairment from voluntary intoxication and prove that the former independently affected mens rea to the degree required by the insanity standard, then it would still apply.

Furthermore, there are also other aspects of criminal responsibility that do not fully excuse the behavior from a legal perspective, such as diminished capacity or responsibility, guilty but mentally ill, provocation/passion, and imperfect self-defense. These defenses might mitigate or attenuate responsibility, but the person is still held criminally accountable. As such, these considerations are typically applied for sentencing purposes rather than for conviction and are not considered further in this chapter.

ASSESSING CRIMINAL RESPONSIBILITY

The assessment of criminal responsibility refers to a person's mental state at the time of the offense (MSO) and is therefore retrospective in nature. The forensic examiner may evaluate the defendant weeks, months, or (on rare occasions) years after the alleged criminal conduct. This process is therefore challenging, as there is often no direct evidence about the person's exact mental state (beyond possibly self-report, which needs to be viewed in its self-serving light). Consequently, the forensic examiner must examine as much evidence as possible, from multiple sources, to triangulate the defendant's mental state at the time.

A second challenge to MSO evaluations is malingering. As with other forensic evaluations, individuals undergoing them have significant incentive to misrepresent themselves, and this incentive is arguably the highest (at least in criminal proceedings) for an MSO evaluation, where the possibility of acquittal is at stake. In the retrospective context, malingering also becomes more difficult to assess, especially as psychological instruments designed to assess malingering and response bias typically focus on current rather than past functioning.

Typically, MSO evaluations focus on three major (and critical) components: clinical interview, third-party information (e.g., collateral interviews, various records), and psychological testing. An exhaustive review of these evaluations is beyond the scope of this chapter (readers are referred to Goldstein et al., 2013; Melton, Petrila, Poythress, & Slobogin, 2007; Zapf et al., 2013, for comprehensive reviews). In brief, the goal of the clinical interview is to gather a historical context for the defendant's mental health functioning, including the success of any interventions, as well as the person's subjective MSO and present mental functioning. The mental impairments that typically qualify for the insanity defense are chronic, disabling conditions rather than temporary or transient ones that only appeared at the time of the offense (with involuntary intoxication being one salient exception). As such, past and current functioning (considered in light of any ongoing treatment) has substantial implications for the possibility that the reported subjective MSO is credible. For instance, an individual with no documented past mental health history who does not exhibit symptoms of mental impairment at the time of the evaluation (and is not being treated for such problems) is highly unlikely to have exhibited such impairment at the time of the offense.

Third party information is critical to determine MSO. Collateral interviews, police reports, witness statements, jail intake records, and possible hospital admissions close to the time of the offense can be very useful in this regard. For instance, relatives and/or friends can describe the defendant's presentation in the time leading up to (and the day of) the offense. Police and jail staff often record observable mental health symptoms or atypical behavior. If the police transported the defendant to a hospital for psychiatric emergency services rather than to jail, this would likely be an indication of significant mental health problems at the time of the offense.

Finally, psychological testing can be very useful in articulating current functioning, including chronic mental states. For instance, if intellectual disability is suspected, the Wechsler Adult Intelligence Scale, Fourth Edition or Stanford-Binet, Fifth Edition would estimate current intellectual functioning, which, barring any brain trauma subsequent to the offense, would be indicative of intellectual ability at the time as well. Multiscale personality inventories measure psychotic symptoms and other thought pathology that is often chronic in nature. Some (e.g., Melton et al., 2007) have questioned the utility of psychological test instruments in MSO evaluations in light of their retrospective nature and advocate more strongly for forensic assessment instruments (e.g., Rogers's Criminal Responsibility Assessment Scales) and tests that inform about potential malingering. Nevertheless, we believe that the MMPI-2-RF can be useful in these evaluations.

CONSIDERATIONS FOR USING THE MMPI-2-RF IN CRIMINAL RESPONSIBILITY EVALUATIONS

Because the determination of legal sanity requires answering specific questions regarding an individual's mental state at the time of the offense, the MMPI-2-RF and similar tests have more limited utility in MSO evaluations than in the case of competency to stand trial evaluations. Moreover, there is little research to support MMPI-2-RF use in answering legal questions directly related to insanity. For example, Rogers and McKee (1995) did not find that defendants adjudicated not guilty by reason of insanity (insane defendants) scored differently from sane defendants on the MMPI-2, with the exception of the antisocial behavior scales (e.g., Scale 4, Antisocial Practices) on which insane defendants scored lower than did those adjudicated sane. Barendregt, Muller, Nijman, and de Beuers (2008) replicated this finding in a Dutch sample of defendants undergoing criminal responsibility evaluations, indicating that experts who use MMPI-2 results were less likely to opine insanity in cases where individuals exhibit personality disorders, particularly of an antisocial or psychopathic nature. A recent study on the MMPI-2-RF showed that those defendants opined to be insane scored lower on externalizing scales than sane defendants (Sellbom, in press).

Despite the questionable utility of MMPI-2-RF scores in these evaluations, Lally (2003) reported that the majority of the diplomate forensic examiners in his study recommended using the MMPI-2 for criminal responsibility evaluations. There is no reason to believe that such recommendations would not extend to the MMPI-2-RF today. Moreover, Neal and Grisso (2014) found that MMPI instruments (which included the MMPI-2-RF to an unspecified degree) were the most frequently used psychological assessment tool of any kind in insanity evaluations. This finding is likely because tests like the MMPI-2-RF generate information that is relevant to the evaluation even though it does not directly address the psycho-legal question. The MMPI-2-RF Validity Scales can assist in the identification of current attempts to malinger psychopathology. This is noteworthy because if a defendant attempts to malinger psychopathology in the course of an MSO evaluation, it occurs at the time of the evaluation, not at the time of the alleged crime. In addition, individuals who are found not guilty by reason of insanity are likely to have chronic and severe disorders that would likely be reflected in a current MMPI-2-RF protocol unless evidence for current, successful intervention is apparent. Finally, such defendants have sometimes had prior contact with the mental health system, and preoffense MMPI-2-RF protocols may exist that can be compared with a current protocol to further establish the presence or absence of a severe disorder prior to an alleged offense.

CASE EXAMPLE 5-1

Case Background

Ms. B is a 33-year-old Caucasian woman from Canberra, Australia. She has pleaded not guilty by reason of mental impairment to common assault with intent to cause grievous bodily harm; this offense allegedly occurred approximately 4 months prior to the evaluation. Ms. B has a lengthy history of behavioral, mental health, and substance abuse difficulties. As a child, she experienced sexual abuse by her older brother at 5 years of age. She reported a history of behavioral problems in school and was expelled twice for violent behavior. She left school in the 10th grade. Her difficulties adjusting to reasonable expectations during childhood intensified during adolescence and following the death of her mother when she was 17. Ms. B never married and had no children. She had numerous unstable relationships with men and was reportedly obsessed with an ex-boyfriend for whom she created a tombstone on a social media page.

Ms. B has had extensive involvement with the legal system since early adolescence, which included numerous theft-related charges as an adult as well as drug-related charges. She also has a significant history of substance abuse, which includes alcohol, marijuana, methamphetamine, and cocaine abuse, with medical records indicating positive drug screens 1 month prior to the evaluation. Ms. B had been employed as an exotic dancer for numerous years since the age of 18, in addition to collecting Social Security for mental disability (bipolar disorder). Furthermore, Ms. B has been hospitalized numerous times since adolescence (first for hyperactivity) as well as an adult (for mania, suicide threats/attempts, and/or violence). She had repeatedly been diagnosed with bipolar disorder, substance use disorders, and several personality disorders across these hospitalizations, but had not been consistently compliant with treatment in the community.

Ms. B was referred for a criminal responsibility evaluation because of her history of mental illness and possible manic state at the time of the offense. According to both official and defendant accounts of the offense, she had sought employment at a gentlemen's club as an exotic dancer. After an interview with the club owner, she was observed pouring a beer bottle out on the floor, breaking it on the edge of the bar while walking up to the victim and swinging it at him. A witness stated that she had heard the victim ask the defendant to leave, since he was not going to hire her to dance. Ms. B made no attempt to escape the scene. While in police custody in the back of a police cruiser, she told the officers that the owner (the victim) told her to go to a back room with him to talk about a job. Once in the room, the owner told her to "suck his dick." She said, "I'd rather suck on a fish." When she refused, she said the victim grabbed her head and forced it "down there." She grabbed a beer bottle and hit him with it, but she did not mean for it to break.

Issues Pertaining to MSO

The Australian Capital Territory's standard for the insanity defense is rooted in *M'Naghten* and the irresistible impulse defense. More specifically, a person is not held criminally responsible for an offense if he or she was suffering from a mental impairment at the time of the offense. In addition, the impairment must have directly resulted in the person (a) not knowing the nature and quality of the conduct; (b) not knowing that the conduct was wrong (the person does not know that the conduct is wrong if the person cannot reason with a moderate degree of sense and composure about whether the conduct, as seen by a reasonable person, is wrong); or (c) not able to control his or her conduct.

As discussed earlier, the key issue in addressing this psycho-legal question is whether the person was mentally impaired at the time of the offense. There is certainly reason to believe that this might have been the case with Ms. B, if one examines the evidence surrounding the time of this incident. For instance, 16 days before the offense, she was admitted for involuntary hospitalization. She had been "shooting at the first floor in her apartment" and was described by witnesses as threatening. Upon admission, she was described as "psychotic" and "hypomanic" by staff, and displayed flight of ideas, mood lability, and the volume of her voice was loud. She was diagnosed with bipolar disorder; her most recent episode was determined to be manic; and she was prescribed medication. She was discharged 4 days later and did not follow up with outpatient care; her boyfriend at the time also informed the examiner that she stopped taking her medication immediately upon release and became progressively worse. Moreover, jail mental health records indicated that Ms. B was described as manic, disorganized, and demanding following her arrest in this matter.

The second part of an insanity defense is whether she knew the nature and quality of her conduct, knew it was wrong, or could not control it. Corroborative evidence is key in this determination. Ms. B explained in the interview that she was a "vigilante" and had been highly preoccupied with the Internet and finding sexual predators and perverts whom she would want to turn over to the police. She did not sleep much at all and had spent entire nights searching for sexual predators online. She added, "I was losing control; I thought I could be an angel. I had been reading about The Punisher. He was a comic book vigilante. . . . I wanted to be that . . . . I guess I wasn't right." On the night of the alleged offense, she had gone to the club looking for potential employment. During her interview, the owner asked her to perform oral sex on him and was fondling her. She explained, "I was pushed over the edge. While he was grabbing me, I hit him with a beer bottle." She denied knowing the wrongfulness of this act at the time, stating "I thought I was a vigilante . . . a martyr for females and I was gonna free them [referring to other dancers at the bar], but these whores just wanted to smoke crack and have big daddy [referring to the owner] take care of them." Her (now ex-) boyfriend corroborated her cognitive state at the time, indicating that she indeed was referring to herself as a vigilante and that she felt that she and women in society had been wronged. He also stated that she had become obsessive with obtaining weapons and crossbows, to be "like the Punisher." He also told this examiner that she committed the offenses because the victim solicited oral sex from her and she "assaulted him to show that he was wrong and to protect all other people he had wronged."

MMPI-2-RF Results

PROTOCOL VALIDITY

One of the most useful ways in which MMPI-2-RF information[1] can be used in MSO evaluations is to determine how to best approach the evaluation and provide evidence to rule out malingering. As can be seen in Ms. B's MMPI-2-RF results, she responded to each item (CNS = 0) and responded consistently to the items throughout the test (VRIN-r = 58, TRIN-r = 57F). There was no evidence of overreporting with respect to psychopathology (F-r, Fp-r) or somatic/cognitive symptoms (Fs, FBS-r, RBS). It should be noted that her Fp-r score is atypical for individuals undergoing pretrial evaluations, but it is not in the range in which protocol validity would be of significant concern, especially in light of her serious psychopathology. Moreover, there was no evidence of underreporting on L-r or K-r. Consequently, the profile would be deemed valid for interpretation. The defendant has also been administered the M-FAST (see Chapter 4) and obtained a score of 4. As such, it was determined that it was highly unlikely that she was attempting to malinger psychopathology during the evaluation.

Minnesota Multiphasic
Personality Inventory-2
Restructured Form®

Score Report

MMPI-2-RF®

Minnesota Multiphasic Personality Inventory-2-Restructured Form®

Yossef S. Ben-Porath, PhD, & Auke Tellegen, PhD

Name:	Ms. B
ID Number:	5
Age:	33
Gender:	Female
Marital Status:	Never Married
Years of Education:	10
Date Assessed:	02/15/2008

ALWAYS LEARNING   PEARSON

FIGURE 5-1 Case Example 5-1: Ms. B's MMPI-2-RF Profile, continued.

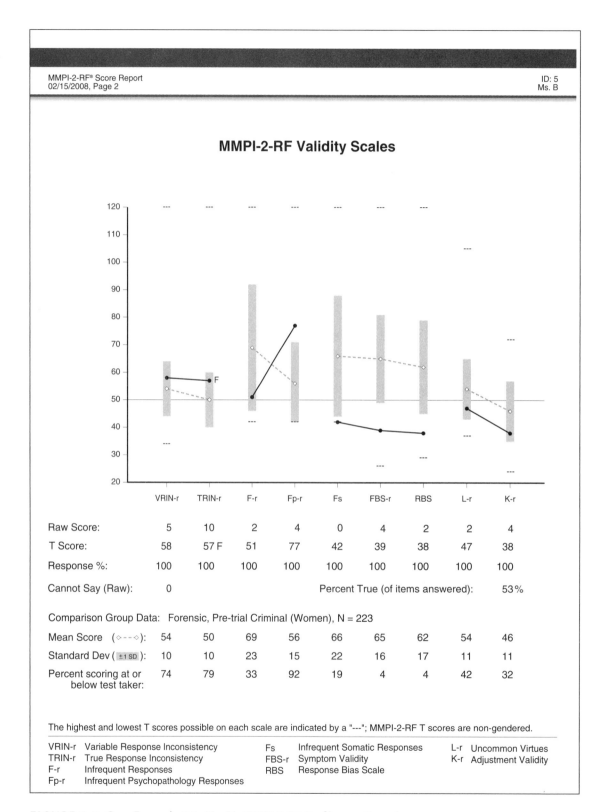

MMPI-2-RF Validity Scales

	VRIN-r	TRIN-r	F-r	Fp-r	Fs	FBS-r	RBS	L-r	K-r
Raw Score:	5	10	2	4	0	4	2	2	4
T Score:	58	57 F	51	77	42	39	38	47	38
Response %:	100	100	100	100	100	100	100	100	100

Cannot Say (Raw):　0　　　　　　　　　　Percent True (of items answered):　53%

Comparison Group Data:　Forensic, Pre-trial Criminal (Women), N = 223

	VRIN-r	TRIN-r	F-r	Fp-r	Fs	FBS-r	RBS	L-r	K-r
Mean Score (◇---◇):	54	50	69	56	66	65	62	54	46
Standard Dev (±1 SD):	10	10	23	15	22	16	17	11	11
Percent scoring at or below test taker:	74	79	33	92	19	4	4	42	32

The highest and lowest T scores possible on each scale are indicated by a "---"; MMPI-2-RF T scores are non-gendered.

VRIN-r	Variable Response Inconsistency	Fs	Infrequent Somatic Responses	L-r	Uncommon Virtues
TRIN-r	True Response Inconsistency	FBS-r	Symptom Validity	K-r	Adjustment Validity
F-r	Infrequent Responses	RBS	Response Bias Scale		
Fp-r	Infrequent Psychopathology Responses				

FIGURE 5-1　Case Example 5-1: Ms. B's MMPI-2-RF Profile, continued.

MMPI-2-RF Higher-Order (H-O) and Restructured Clinical (RC) Scales

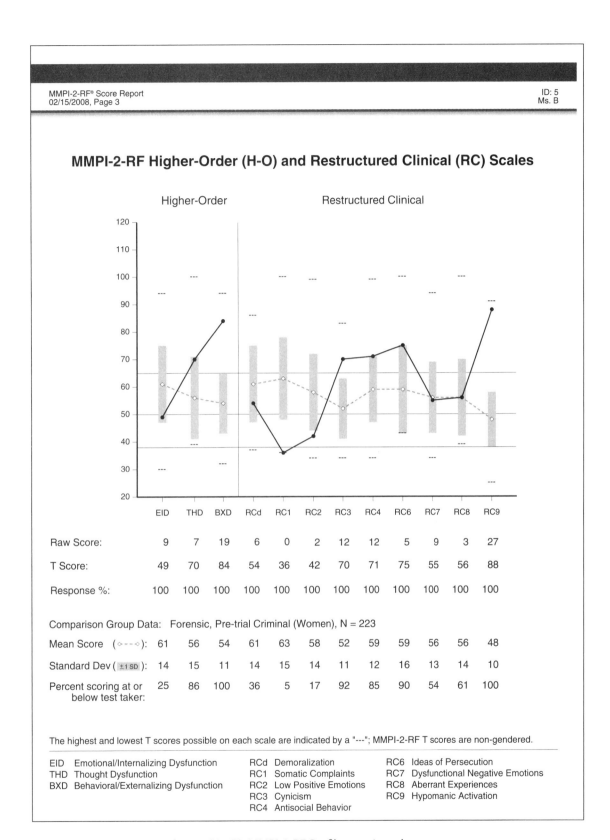

	EID	THD	BXD	RCd	RC1	RC2	RC3	RC4	RC6	RC7	RC8	RC9
Raw Score:	9	7	19	6	0	2	12	12	5	9	3	27
T Score:	49	70	84	54	36	42	70	71	75	55	56	88
Response %:	100	100	100	100	100	100	100	100	100	100	100	100

Comparison Group Data: Forensic, Pre-trial Criminal (Women), N = 223

	EID	THD	BXD	RCd	RC1	RC2	RC3	RC4	RC6	RC7	RC8	RC9
Mean Score (◇- - -◇):	61	56	54	61	63	58	52	59	59	56	56	48
Standard Dev (±1 SD):	14	15	11	14	15	14	11	12	16	13	14	10
Percent scoring at or below test taker:	25	86	100	36	5	17	92	85	90	54	61	100

The highest and lowest T scores possible on each scale are indicated by a "---"; MMPI-2-RF T scores are non-gendered.

EID	Emotional/Internalizing Dysfunction	RCd	Demoralization	RC6 Ideas of Persecution
THD	Thought Dysfunction	RC1	Somatic Complaints	RC7 Dysfunctional Negative Emotions
BXD	Behavioral/Externalizing Dysfunction	RC2	Low Positive Emotions	RC8 Aberrant Experiences
		RC3	Cynicism	RC9 Hypomanic Activation
		RC4	Antisocial Behavior	

FIGURE 5-1 Case Example 5-1: Ms. B's MMPI-2-RF Profile, continued.

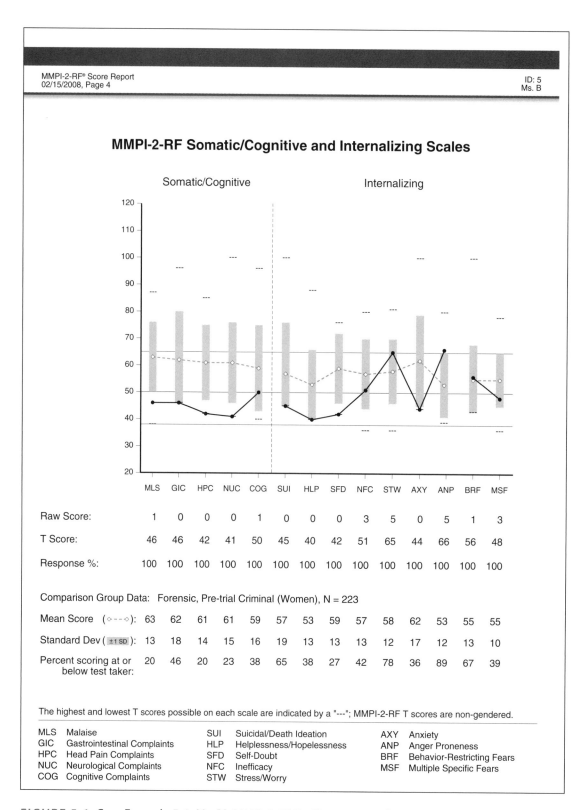

MMPI-2-RF Somatic/Cognitive and Internalizing Scales

	MLS	GIC	HPC	NUC	COG	SUI	HLP	SFD	NFC	STW	AXY	ANP	BRF	MSF
Raw Score:	1	0	0	0	1	0	0	0	3	5	0	5	1	3
T Score:	46	46	42	41	50	45	40	42	51	65	44	66	56	48
Response %:	100	100	100	100	100	100	100	100	100	100	100	100	100	100

Comparison Group Data: Forensic, Pre-trial Criminal (Women), N = 223

	MLS	GIC	HPC	NUC	COG	SUI	HLP	SFD	NFC	STW	AXY	ANP	BRF	MSF
Mean Score (◇--◇):	63	62	61	61	59	57	53	59	57	58	62	53	55	55
Standard Dev (±1 SD):	13	18	14	15	16	19	13	13	13	12	17	12	13	10
Percent scoring at or below test taker:	20	46	20	23	38	65	38	27	42	78	36	89	67	39

The highest and lowest T scores possible on each scale are indicated by a "---"; MMPI-2-RF T scores are non-gendered.

MLS	Malaise	SUI	Suicidal/Death Ideation	AXY	Anxiety
GIC	Gastrointestinal Complaints	HLP	Helplessness/Hopelessness	ANP	Anger Proneness
HPC	Head Pain Complaints	SFD	Self-Doubt	BRF	Behavior-Restricting Fears
NUC	Neurological Complaints	NFC	Inefficacy	MSF	Multiple Specific Fears
COG	Cognitive Complaints	STW	Stress/Worry		

FIGURE 5-1 Case Example 5-1: Ms. B's MMPI-2-RF Profile, continued.

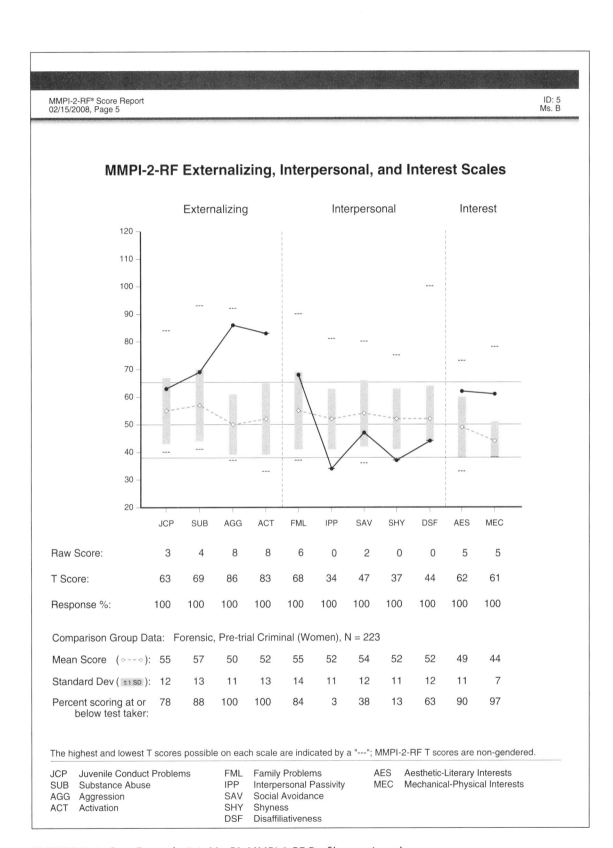

MMPI-2-RF Externalizing, Interpersonal, and Interest Scales

	JCP	SUB	AGG	ACT	FML	IPP	SAV	SHY	DSF	AES	MEC
Raw Score:	3	4	8	8	6	0	2	0	0	5	5
T Score:	63	69	86	83	68	34	47	37	44	62	61
Response %:	100	100	100	100	100	100	100	100	100	100	100

Comparison Group Data: Forensic, Pre-trial Criminal (Women), N = 223

Mean Score (◇--◇):	55	57	50	52	55	52	54	52	52	49	44
Standard Dev (±1 SD):	12	13	11	13	14	11	12	11	12	11	7
Percent scoring at or below test taker:	78	88	100	100	84	3	38	13	63	90	97

The highest and lowest T scores possible on each scale are indicated by a "---"; MMPI-2-RF T scores are non-gendered.

JCP	Juvenile Conduct Problems	FML	Family Problems
SUB	Substance Abuse	IPP	Interpersonal Passivity
AGG	Aggression	SAV	Social Avoidance
ACT	Activation	SHY	Shyness
		DSF	Disaffiliativeness

AES Aesthetic-Literary Interests
MEC Mechanical-Physical Interests

FIGURE 5-1 Case Example 5-1: Ms. B's MMPI-2-RF Profile, continued.

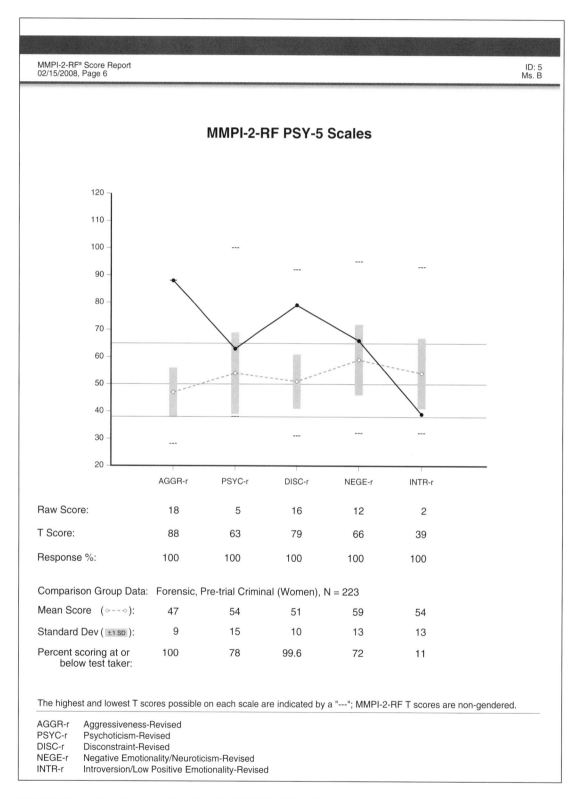

MMPI-2-RF PSY-5 Scales

	AGGR-r	PSYC-r	DISC-r	NEGE-r	INTR-r
Raw Score:	18	5	16	12	2
T Score:	88	63	79	66	39
Response %:	100	100	100	100	100

Comparison Group Data: Forensic, Pre-trial Criminal (Women), N = 223

	AGGR-r	PSYC-r	DISC-r	NEGE-r	INTR-r
Mean Score (◇--◇):	47	54	51	59	54
Standard Dev (±1 SD):	9	15	10	13	13
Percent scoring at or below test taker:	100	78	99.6	72	11

The highest and lowest T scores possible on each scale are indicated by a "---"; MMPI-2-RF T scores are non-gendered.

AGGR-r Aggressiveness-Revised
PSYC-r Psychoticism-Revised
DISC-r Disconstraint-Revised
NEGE-r Negative Emotionality/Neuroticism-Revised
INTR-r Introversion/Low Positive Emotionality-Revised

FIGURE 5-1 Case Example 5-1: Ms. B's MMPI-2-RF Profile, continued.

MMPI-2-RF T SCORES (BY DOMAIN)

PROTOCOL VALIDITY

Content Non-Responsiveness

0	58	57 F
CNS	VRIN-r	TRIN-r

Over-Reporting

51	77		42	39	38
F-r	Fp-r		Fs	FBS-r	RBS

Under-Reporting

47	38
L-r	K-r

SUBSTANTIVE SCALES

Somatic/Cognitive Dysfunction

36	46	46	42	41	50
RC1	MLS	GIC	HPC	NUC	COG

Emotional Dysfunction

49		54	45	40	42	51
EID		RCd	SUI	HLP	SFD	NFC

42	39
RC2	INTR-r

55	65	44	66	56	48	66
RC7	STW	AXY	ANP	BRF	MSF	NEGE-r

Thought Dysfunction

70		75
THD		RC6

56
RC8

63
PSYC-r

Behavioral Dysfunction

84		71	63	69
BXD		RC4	JCP	SUB

88	86	83	88	79
RC9	AGG	ACT	AGGR-r	DISC-r

Interpersonal Functioning

68	70	34	47	37	44
FML	RC3	IPP	SAV	SHY	DSF

Interests

62	61
AES	MEC

Note. This information is provided to facilitate interpretation following the recommended structure for MMPI-2-RF interpretation in Chapter 5 of the *MMPI-2-RF Manual for Administration, Scoring, and Interpretation*, which provides details in the text and an outline in Table 5-1.

FIGURE 5-1 Case Example 5-1: Ms. B's MMPI-2-RF Profile, continued.

ITEM-LEVEL INFORMATION

Unscorable Responses

The test taker produced scorable responses to all the MMPI-2-RF items.

Critical Responses

Seven MMPI-2-RF scales--Suicidal/Death Ideation (SUI), Helplessness/Hopelessness (HLP), Anxiety (AXY), Ideas of Persecution (RC6), Aberrant Experiences (RC8), Substance Abuse (SUB), and Aggression (AGG)--have been designated by the test authors as having critical item content that may require immediate attention and follow-up. Items answered by the individual in the keyed direction (True or False) on a critical scale are listed below if her T score on that scale is 65 or higher. The percentage of the MMPI-2-RF normative sample (NS) and of the Forensic, Pre-trial Criminal (Women) comparison group (CG) that answered each item in the keyed direction are provided in parentheses following the item content.

Ideas of Persecution (RC6, T Score = 75)

    110. Item Content Omitted. (True; NS 9.9%, CG 33.2%)
    150. Item Content Omitted. (True; NS 2.0%, CG 6.7%)
    168. Item Content Omitted. (True; NS 2.8%, CG 4.5%)
    194. Item Content Omitted. (True; NS 17.1%, CG 31.8%)
    212. Item Content Omitted. (False; NS 9.1%, CG 26.5%)

Substance Abuse (SUB, T Score = 69)

    49. Item Content Omitted. (True; NS 29.6%, CG 35.9%)
    237. Item Content Omitted. (False; NS 27.4%, CG 57.0%)
    266. Item Content Omitted. (True; NS 5.0%, CG 55.6%)
    297. Item Content Omitted. (True; NS 14.4%, CG 18.4%)

Aggression (AGG, T Score = 86)

    23. Item Content Omitted. (True; NS 39.0%, CG 36.3%)
    26. Item Content Omitted.
       (True; NS 19.9%, CG 12.1%)
    84. Item Content Omitted. (True; NS 12.1%, CG 8.5%)
    231. Item Content Omitted. (True; NS 6.3%,
       CG 7.6%)
    312. Item Content Omitted. (True; NS 5.5%, CG
       18.8%)
    316. Item Content Omitted. (True; NS 45.1%, CG
       39.5%)
    329. Item Content Omitted. (True; NS 12.7%, CG
       16.1%)
    337. IItem Content Omitted. (True; NS 50.2%,
       CG 52.0%)

FIGURE 5-1 Case Example 5-1: Ms. B's MMPI-2-RF Profile, continued.

User-Designated Item-Level Information

The following item-level information is based on the report user's selection of additional scales, and/or of lower cutoffs for the critical scales from the previous section. Items answered by the test taker in the keyed direction (True or False) on a selected scale are listed below if her T score on that scale is at the user-designated cutoff score or higher. The percentage of the MMPI-2-RF normative sample (NS) and of the Forensic, Pre-trial Criminal (Women) comparison group (CG) that answered each item in the keyed direction are provided in parentheses following the item content.

Thought Dysfunction (THD, T Score = 70)

   85. Item Content Omitted. (False; NS 17.1%, CG 30.5%)
110. Item Content Omitted. (True; NS 9.9%, CG 33.2%)
150. Item Content Omitted. (True; NS 2.0%, CG 6.7%)
168. Item Content Omitted. (True; NS 2.8%, CG 4.5%)
212. Item Content Omitted. (False; NS 9.1%, CG 26.5%)
311. Item Content Omitted. (True; NS 32.4%, CG
    27.8%)
330. Item Content Omitted. (True; NS 15.2%, CG 16.1%)

Behavioral/Externalizing Dysfunction (BXD, T Score = 84)

   21. Item Content Omitted. (True; NS 47.1%, CG 46.2%)
   49. Item Content Omitted. (True; NS 29.6%, CG 35.9%)
   61. Item Content Omitted. (False; NS 61.6%, CG 48.0%)
   66. Item Content Omitted. (True; NS 20.3%, CG 28.7%)
   84. Item Content Omitted. (True; NS 12.1%, CG 8.5%)
107. Item Content Omitted. (True; NS 47.3%, CG 26.0%)
131. Item Content Omitted. (True; NS 43.3%, CG 37.7%)
156. Item Content Omitted. (True; NS 59.8%, CG 64.6%)
190. Item Content Omitted. (False; NS 28.6%, CG 83.4%)
193. Item Content Omitted.
    (True; NS 32.8%, CG 13.9%)
205. Item Content Omitted. (True; NS 13.0%,
    CG 32.7%)
231. Item Content Omitted. (True; NS 6.3%,
    CG 7.6%)
237. Item Content Omitted. (False; NS 27.4%, CG 57.0%) 248. I am often said to be hotheaded.
    (True; NS 16.1%, CG 24.2%)
266. Item Content Omitted. (True; NS 5.0%, CG 55.6%)
292. Item Content Omitted. (True; NS 26.1%, CG 22.0%)
312. Item Content. (True; NS 5.5%, CG
    18.8%)
316. Item Content Omitted. (True; NS 45.1%, CG
    39.5%)
329. Item Content Omitted. (True; NS 12.7%, CG
    16.1%)

FIGURE 5-1 Case Example 5-1: Ms. B's MMPI-2-RF Profile, continued.

Cynicism (RC3, T Score = 70)

    10. Item Content Omitted. (True; NS 35.9%, CG 35.9%)
    36. Item Content Omitted.
       (True; NS 58.3%, CG 50.2%)
    55. Item Content Omitted. (True; NS 47.7%, CG 57.8%)
    99. Item Content Omitted.
       (True; NS 53.6%, CG 53.8%)
   121. Item Content Omitted. (True; NS 16.8%, CG 33.6%)
   142. Item Content Omitted. (True; NS 22.0%, CG
       25.6%)
   171. Item Content Omitted. (True; NS 51.5%, CG 44.8%)
   185. Item Content Omitted. (True; NS 29.3%, CG
       45.3%)
   213. Item Content Omitted.
       (True; NS 71.4%, CG 71.3%)
   238. Item Content Omitted. (True; NS
       32.6%, CG 40.8%)
   260. Item Content Omitted.
       (True; NS 36.2%, CG
       39.9%)
   279. Item Content Omitted. (True; NS 39.1%, CG 52.0%)

Antisocial Behavior (RC4, T Score = 71)

     5. Item Content Omitted. (True; NS 36.7%, CG 55.6%)
    21. Item Content Omitted. (True; NS 47.1%, CG 46.2%)
    49. Item Content Omitted. (True; NS 29.6%, CG 35.9%)
    66. Item Content Omitted. (True; NS 20.3%, CG 28.7%)
   156. Item Content Omitted. (True; NS 59.8%, CG 64.6%)
   190. Item Content Omitted. (False; NS 28.6%, CG 83.4%)
   205. Item Content Omitted. (True; NS 13.0%,
       CG 32.7%)
   237. Item Content Omitted. (False; NS 27.4%, CG 57.0%)
   266. Item Content Omitted. (True; NS 5.0%, CG 55.6%)
   297. Item Content Omitted. (True; NS 14.4%, CG 18.4%)
   312. Item Content Omitted. (True; NS 5.5%, CG
       18.8%)
   329. Item Content Omitted. (True; NS 12.7%, CG
       16.1%)

Hypomanic Activation (RC9, T Score = 88)

    13. Item Content Omitted. (True; NS 40.9%, CG
       35.4%)
    26. Item Content Omitted.
       (True; NS 19.9%, CG 12.1%)
    39. Item Content Omitted. (True; NS
       51.0%, CG 53.4%)

FIGURE 5-1 Case Example 5-1: Ms. B's MMPI-2-RF Profile, continued.

61. Item Content Omitted. (False; NS 61.6%, CG 48.0%)
72. Item Content Omitted. (True; NS 81.5%, CG
    73.1%)
84. Item Content Omitted. (True; NS 12.1%, CG 8.5%)
97. Item Content Omitted. (True; NS 50.5%, CG
    39.9%)
107. Item Content Omitted. (True; NS 47.3%, CG 26.0%)
118. Item Content Omitted. (True; NS 57.4%, CG 54.3%)
131. Item Content Omitted. (True; NS 43.3%, CG 37.7%)
143. Item Content Omitted.
     (True; NS 27.5%, CG 30.0%)
155. Item Content Omitted. (True; NS 41.6%, CG 39.5%)
166. Item Content Omitted.
     (True; NS 38.9%, CG 38.1%)
181. Item Content Omitted. (True; NS 35.3%, CG 38.6%)
193. Item Content Omitted.
     (True; NS 32.8%, CG 13.9%)
207. Item Content Omitted. (True; NS 66.9%,
     CG 56.1%)
219. Item Content Omitted. (True; NS 51.5%, CG 55.2%)
231. Item Content Omitted. (True; NS 6.3%,
     CG 7.6%)
244. Item Content Omitted. (True; NS
     56.9%, CG 66.8%)
248. Item Content Omitted. (True; NS 16.1%, CG 24.2%)
256. Item Content Omitted. (True; NS
     65.7%, CG 60.5%)
267. Item Content Omitted.
     (True; NS 12.9%, CG 21.5%)
292. Item Content Omitted. (True; NS 26.1%, CG 22.0%)
305. Item Content Omitted. (True; NS 37.6%, CG 21.5%)
316. Item Content Omitted. (True; NS 45.1%, CG
     39.5%)
327. Item Content Omitted.
     (True; NS 41.7%, CG 33.6%)
337. Item Content Omitted. (True; NS 50.2%,
     CG 52.0%)

Anger Proneness (ANP, T Score = 66)
134. Item Content Omitted. (False; NS 32.5%, CG 38.6%)
155. Item Content Omitted. (True; NS 41.6%, CG 39.5%)
248. Item Content Omitted. (True; NS 16.1%, CG 24.2%)
303. Item Content Omitted. (True; NS 28.6%, CG 33.6%)
318. Item Content Omitted. (True; NS 19.9%, CG
     33.2%)

FIGURE 5-1 Case Example 5-1: Ms. B's MMPI-2-RF Profile, continued.

Behavior-Restricting Fears (BRF, T Score = 56)
 165. Item Content Omitted. (True; NS 11.9%, CG 18.8%)

Juvenile Conduct Problems (JCP, T Score = 63)

 21. Item Content Omitted. (True; NS 47.1%, CG 46.2%)
 66. Item Content Omitted. (True; NS 20.3%, CG 28.7%)
 205. Item Content Omitted. (True; NS 13.0%,
   CG 32.7%)

Activation (ACT, T Score = 83)

 72. Item Content Omitted. (True; NS 81.5%, CG
   73.1%)
 81. Item Content Omitted. (True; NS 12.1%, CG 37.7%)
 166. Item Content Omitted.
   (True; NS 38.9%, CG 38.1%)
 181. Item Content Omitted. (True; NS 35.3%, CG 38.6%)
 207. Item Content Omitted. (True; NS 66.9%,
   CG 56.1%)
 219. Item Content Omitted. (True; NS 51.5%, CG 55.2%)
 267. Item Content Omitted.
   (True; NS 12.9%, CG 21.5%)
 285. Item Content Omitted. (True; NS 21.9%, CG 33.6%)

Aggressiveness-Revised (AGGR-r, T Score = 88)

 24. Item Content Omitted. (False; NS 74.6%, CG 61.9%)
 26. Item Content Omitted.
   (True; NS 19.9%, CG 12.1%)
 39. Item Content Omitted. (True; NS
   51.0%, CG 53.4%)
 84. Item Content Omitted. (True; NS 12.1%, CG 8.5%)
 104. Item Content Omitted. (True; NS 67.1%, CG 62.8%)
 147. Item Content Omitted. (True; NS 75.2%, CG 78.0%)
 182. Item Content Omitted. (True; NS 33.6%, CG 22.4%)
 197. Item Content Omitted. (True; NS 62.5%, CG
   57.4%)
 231. Item Content Omitted. (True; NS 6.3%,
   CG 7.6%)
 239. Item Content Omitted. (True; NS 60.7%, CG 50.7%)
 256. Item Content Omitted. (True; NS
   65.7%, CG 60.5%)
 276. Item Content Omitted. (True; NS
   50.0%, CG 57.4%)
 302. Item Content Omitted. (True; NS 67.9%, CG 43.0%)
 316. Item Content Omitted. (True; NS 45.1%, CG
   39.5%)

FIGURE 5-1 Case Example 5-1: Ms. B's MMPI-2-RF Profile, continued.

319. Item Content Omitted. (False; NS 64.7%,
     CG 58.7%)
321. Item Content Omitted. (True; NS 31.3%, CG 23.8%)
327. Item Content Omitted.
     (True; NS 41.7%, CG 33.6%)
329. Item Content Omitted. (True; NS 12.7%, CG
     16.1%)

Disconstraint-Revised (DISC-r, T Score = 79)

21. Item Content Omitted. (True; NS 47.1%, CG 46.2%)
42. Item Content Omitted. (True; NS 10.3%, CG 4.0%)
49. Item Content Omitted. (True; NS 29.6%, CG 35.9%)
61. Item Content Omitted. (False; NS 61.6%, CG 48.0%)
66. Item Content Omitted. (True; NS 20.3%, CG 28.7%)
107. Item Content Omitted. (True; NS 47.3%, CG 26.0%)
115. Item Content Omitted. (True; NS 55.0%, CG 33.6%)
131. Item Content Omitted. (True; NS 43.3%, CG 37.7%)
156. Item Content Omitted. (True; NS 59.8%, CG 64.6%)
190. Item Content Omitted. (False; NS 28.6%, CG 83.4%)
193. Item Content Omitted.
     (True; NS 32.8%, CG 13.9%)
205. Item Content Omitted. (True; NS 13.0%,
     CG 32.7%)
237. Item Content Omitted. (False; NS 27.4%, CG 57.0%)
292. Item Content Omitted. (True; NS 26.1%, CG 22.0%)
297. Item Content Omitted. (True; NS 14.4%, CG 18.4%)
300. Item Content Omitted. (True; NS 26.5%, CG 13.5%)

Negative Emotionality/Neuroticism-Revised (NEGE-r, T Score = 66)

9. Item Content Omitted. (True;
   NS 13.4%, CG 13.5%)
23. Item Content Omitted. (True; NS 39.0%, CG 36.3%)
29. Item Content Omitted. (True; NS
    29.6%, CG 40.4%)
73. Item Content Omitted. (False; NS 16.6%, CG 51.1%)
116. Item Content Omitted. (True; NS 40.0%, CG 62.3%)
123. Item Content Omitted. (True; NS 28.0%, CG 45.7%)
134. Item Content Omitted. (False; NS 32.5%, CG 38.6%)
155. Item Content Omitted. (True; NS 41.6%, CG 39.5%)
209. Item Content Omitted. (True; NS 32.5%, CG 78.5%)
234. Item Content Omitted. (False; NS 53.9%, CG 87.4%)
263. Item Content Omitted.
     (True; NS 64.0%, CG 62.8%)
309. Item Content Omitted. (True; NS 34.0%, CG 59.6%)

FIGURE 5-1 Case Example 5-1: Ms. B's MMPI-2-RF Profile, continued.

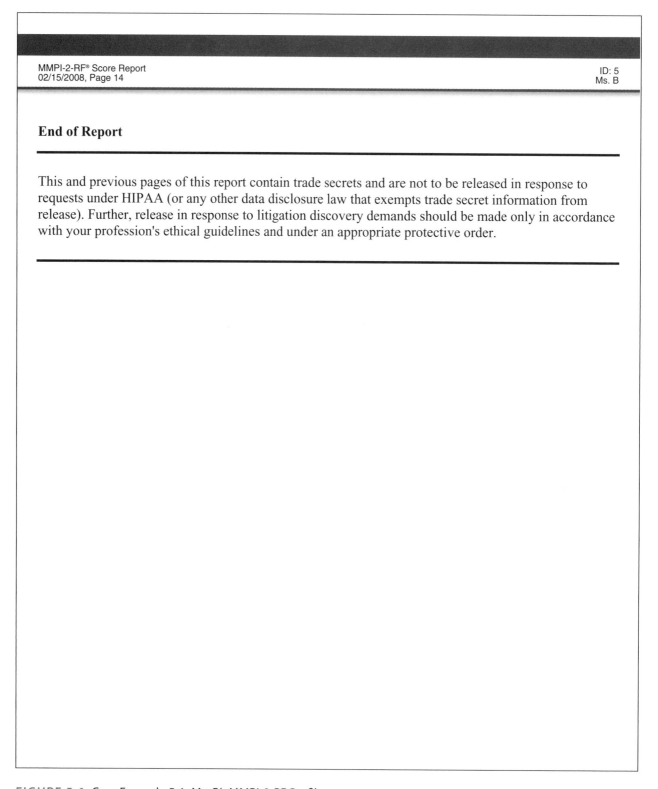

End of Report

This and previous pages of this report contain trade secrets and are not to be released in response to requests under HIPAA (or any other data disclosure law that exempts trade secret information from release). Further, release in response to litigation discovery demands should be made only in accordance with your profession's ethical guidelines and under an appropriate protective order.

FIGURE 5-1 Case Example 5-1: Ms. B's MMPI-2-RF Profile.

CLINICAL INTERPRETATION

As described in Chapter 1, the place to start the interpretation is to consult the H-O scales. In Ms. B's profile, BXD is the highest of the Higher Order scales (84T), which indicates a range of externalizing behaviors. The other elevated scales within this domain (RC4, RC9, SUB, AGG, ACT, AGGR-r, DISC-r) further clarify her behavioral dysfunction. RC9 is extremely elevated and near the ceiling in terms of scores (88T), which is possibly reflected in manic symptoms such as excessive energy, euphoria, racing thoughts, grandiosity, irritability, and aggressive tendencies. It is noteworthy that ACT is at the ceiling (83T), which is the best scale on the test in differentiating bipolar mood disorder from unipolar mood disorder (e.g., Sellbom, Bagby, et al., 2012; Watson et al., 2011). Such symptoms would also be quite consistent with both her presentation during the interview as well as her general mental health history. Moreover, her scores indicate significant social deviance, impulse control problems, substance abuse, and aggressive behavior, which is consistent with her history. However, it is important to consider that many of these behaviors are consistent with a manic episode, and the degree to which some of these scales (in particular AGGR-r and DISC-r) signal personality pathology would need to be examined when manic symptoms are actively treated.

The second elevated H-O scale in this profile is THD (70T), which indicates the possibility for significant thought disorder. These symptoms are best clarified in light of RC6 (75T) being the only elevated scale in this domain. This elevation is consistent with her self-reported and observed (by her ex-boyfriend) extreme paranoia about men violating women, including herself. What is also noteworthy in this context is her elevated RC3 scale (70T), which reflects non-self-referential cynical beliefs about the world. Indeed, Ms. B was obsessed about sexual predators victimizing women in general.

Additional scales that have not yet been interpreted come from the emotional dysfunction domain (NEGE-r, STW, and ANP). It is possible that Ms. B has a dispositional propensity toward emotional instability, anxiety, obsessive ruminatory thinking, as well as anger dyscontrol. Certainly, these symptoms would all be consistent with her current manic manifestation, but as just mentioned, the degree to which they reflect personality proclivities needs to be evaluated when she is not in a manic state.

Finally, the interpersonal functioning scales should be interpreted. We just considered RC3, admittedly out of order, in the context of her paranoid ideation. FML is also elevated, which is not surprising in light of her family history, which included childhood sexual abuse.

Case Conclusion

The criminal responsibility evaluation led the forensic examiner to opine the following. First, there was sufficient evidence to indicate that, at the time of the offense, Ms. B met criteria for mental impairment. She met diagnostic criteria for bipolar disorder, most recent episode manic, with psychotic features. Records indicate hospitalization leading up to the offense; her boyfriend gave evidence of treatment noncompliance as well as a symptom description consistent with other information; and the MMPI-2-RF supported the presence of current manic symptoms. Second, there was deemed sufficient evidence to support that, as a result of her mental impairment, Ms. B lacked sufficient knowledge of her wrongdoing, and she was unable to control her conduct. She believed that she was a vigilante on a crusade, was obsessing about sexual predators, and had developed delusional thoughts about the victim in the current offense. Ultimately, the judge found her not guilty by reason of mental impairment and adjudicated the least restrictive environment for her and the community's needs, which was hospitalization in a secure unit.

CONCLUSIONS

The MMPI-2-RF is a useful measure in a criminal responsibility evaluation. Although it does not directly yield information about MSO, its indirect utility is sufficiently worthwhile to warrant its administration. In the case example, the MMPI-2-RF Validity Scales were useful in ruling out malingering during the evaluation. Moreover, the Substantive Scales provided a clear picture of severe manic symptoms, obsessive thinking, general social deviance, and substance abuse. This profile was highly consistent with her history and functioning at the time of the offense as evidenced by collateral reports and records.

Chapter 6

Violence Risk Assessment

Violence risk assessment is typically defined as the prediction of future dangerousness toward oneself or others.[1] Although the role of mental health professionals in this venture has been controversial (Melton et al., 2007), in the United States, landmark Supreme Court cases such as *Barefoot v. Estrelle* (1983) and *Schall v. Martin* (1984) have not only supported their involvement but also encouraged it. The main goals of risk assessments are typically two-fold: (a) determine the level of care and intervention for the person under evaluation to attenuate future risk to the extent possible and (b) protect the community. Furthermore, one of the main criticisms of risk assessment (and its research) is the lack of careful consideration of the actual outcome (Mulvey & Lidz, 1985). In other words, what are we trying to predict? Obviously, the careful delineation of such outcomes would be imperative as the field determines the best predictors of violence. A careful review of the risk assessment literature, and its evolution, is well beyond the scope of this chapter, but readers are referred to Douglas, Hart, Groscup, and Litwack (2013) and Melton et al. (2007) for discussion. Currently, violence is viewed as "actual, attempted, or threatened physical harm that is deliberate and nonconsenting" (Hart, 2005, p. 4, as cited in Huss, 2013), and risk is viewed as a multifaceted hazard typically operationalized by its nature, severity, frequency, imminence, escalation, and specificity (Douglas, Cox, & Webster, 1999).

Scholars in this field have indicated that a variety of factors should be considered when making a dangerousness prediction (e.g., Conroy & Murrie, 2007; Heilbrun & Heilbrun, 1995; Monahan, 2013). These can be grouped broadly into static and dynamic factors (Douglas & Skeem, 2005). The static factors refer to those historical and demographic factors that are unchangeable, including gender, age, arrest history, juvenile delinquency, number of past violent offenses, age at first violent offense, and psychopathic personality, to mention a few. Dynamic risk factors are those clinical and risk management factors that are amenable to treatment, and thus changeable in each individual, and arguably more interesting and useful from a clinical perspective (Douglas & Skeem, 2005). After all, clinicians are interested in the prevention of violence (Hart, 1998). These include clinical risk factors, exemplified by active symptoms of mental illness, substance abuse, negative affectivity (especially anger), interpersonal difficulties, antisocial attitudes, and negative treatment attitudes (Douglas & Skeem, 2005). They also comprise future risk management (including contextual) factors, such as availability of weapons and victims, social support, and treatment monitoring (Monahan, 2013; Webster & Hucker, 2007). Given that most conceptual and measurement models of violence risk assessment now incorporate both static and dynamic risk factor domains (e.g., Monahan, 2013; Douglas, Hart, Webster, & Belfrage, 2013), many of which consider both psychopathology symptoms and maladaptive personality traits, there is clearly a role for considering omnibus personality inventories in the assessment and formulation of risk (e.g., Neal & Grisso, 2014; Tarescavage, Glassmire et al., 2016; Wygant et al., 2015). First, however, we consider the assessment process of violence risk more generally.

ASSESSING VIOLENCE RISK

There are three major paradigms that currently dominate the field of violence risk assessment: unstructured clinical judgment, actuarial approaches, and structured professional judgment (SPJ) (e.g., Monahan, 2013). Unstructured assessments rely on the expertise and clinical judgment of the evaluator, with little standardization in terms of the data that are collected, the assessment approach, and the integration of the data into a risk estimate. This approach is considered to be unreliable and of questionable validity in the risk assessment literature (Conroy & Witt, 2013; Witt, Dattilio, & Bradford, 2011).

Actuarial approaches are based on mathematical algorithms that calculate scores based on empirically identified static variables (e.g., age of perpetrator, history of violence or delinquency) that have been found to optimize the prediction of violence risk across settings. Every item in the actuarial approach is assigned a weighted value and the sum of all of the items yields a total score that falls into a broad risk category (e.g., high, moderate, low) with respect to a specified time frame (e.g., 10 years). The most frequently used actuarial tool for violence risk assessment is the Violence Risk Appraisal Guide (Quinsey, Harris, Rice, & Cormier, 1998; see Archer, Buffington-Vollum, Stredny, & Handel, 2006; Neal & Grisso, 2014). These tools are frequently viewed as superior to clinical judgment in predicting violence risk and are therefore often preferred for such evaluations (Quinsey, Jones, Book, & Barr, 2006).

On the other hand, SPJs are indeed clinical judgments, but with the assistance of a structural approach that is based on the consideration of an empirically validated set of risk factors. SPJs are viewed as more flexible, and in some cases superior, to actuarial approaches (Douglas, Ogloff, & Hart, 2003). Because actuarial approaches rely on static and mostly historical variables, there is a much lesser role for personality assessment instruments in violence risk assessments that predominantly rely on such factors. Therefore, our focus in this chapter will be on SPJs, which are more flexible and rely on multiple sources of information.

SPJs provide the clinician with empirically supported static and dynamic risk variables that should be considered during the assessment, such as violence history, history of mental illness, personality disorder diagnosis, impulsivity, emotional instability, treatment attitudes, etc. Rather than quantitatively arriving at a risk score, SPJ measures often provide a categorical descriptor of risk (e.g., low, moderate, high). This approach often guides the assessment in terms of identifying risk management strategies.

The most frequently used SPJ in violence risk assessments is the Historical Clinical Risk Management-20, Version 3 (HCR-20-V3; Douglas, Hart, Webster, et al., 2013; see Neal & Grisso, 2014). The HCR-20-V3 can be used with civil and forensic psychiatric clients as well as criminal offenders to formulate risk conceptualizations and ratings as well as generate intervention and rehabilitation plans to mitigate future risk. It incorporates 20 empirically validated risk factors drawn from existing research and professional literature on violence and aggression. The first part consists of 10 historical indicators of violence risk (e.g., history of violence, substance use, and history of mental illness and personality disorder). These are "static" risk factors, which will never change regardless of rehabilitation. The second part consists of five present-oriented clinical risk factors (e.g., poor insight, violent thoughts, instability), whereas a third part incorporates five future-oriented risk management factors that have been found to mitigate an individual's risk for violence (e.g., a good rehabilitation plan, strong social support, and stress and coping skills). Both the clinical and risk management factors are considered dynamic in nature and are amenable to change via rehabilitation and improvement in release plans.

CONSIDERATIONS FOR USING THE MMPI-2-RF IN VIOLENCE RISK EVALUATIONS

The MMPI-2-RF scale scores are likely of limited utility in directly predicting who will be violent in the future, but they can provide useful information that can aid such predictions both with regard to static and dynamic risk factors. There are two published reviews on how the MMPI-2-RF can map onto the HCR-20 model (Tarescavage, Glassmire, et al., 2016; Wygant et al., 2015), which has partly (albeit not completely) inspired the considerations that follow. We recommend that readers using the MMPI-2-RF in a violence risk assessment consult these sources as well.

More specifically, in terms of historical/static risk factors, including history of violence, antisocial behavior, relationship difficulties, substance abuse, trauma, and violent attitudes, a number of MMPI-2-RF scales can provide direct information. For instance, MMPI-2-RF SP Scales, such as AGG, JCP, FML, SUB, AXY, and AGGR-r, address some of these respective factors directly. Broader risk factors, such as history of mental illness and personality disorder, would rely on multiple scale elevations that are specific to the pathology at hand (e.g., RC9, ACT for bipolar disorder, see Chapter 5; or THD, RC6, and RC9 for psychosis) though it is important to consider that it is not always possible to clearly disentangle historical presence of psychopathology from current functioning on the basis of these scales alone (with the main exception being JCP).

Personality disorders, and psychopathy in particular, are often considered a historical/static risk factor, though such a dogmatic view might be overly narrow (e.g., Leichsenring & Leibing, 2003; Salekin, 2002; Salekin, Worley, & Grimes, 2010). The MMPI-2-RF has shown significant utility in the assessment of personality pathology more broadly, both from the traditional perspective of the DSM-5 (see e.g., Anderson, Sellbom, Pymont, et al., 2015; Finn, Arbisi, Erbes, Polusny, & Thuras, 2014; Sellbom & Smith, 2017; Sellbom et al., 2014) and from the alternative dimensional trait perspective (Anderson, Sellbom, Ayearst, et al., 2015; Anderson et al., 2013; Sellbom,

Anderson, & Bagby, 2013). A full review is well beyond the scope of this chapter, but this body of work has indicated that different MMPI-2-RF scale scores can be mapped onto different personality disorders in clear ways. For instance, antisocial personality disorder is clearly linked to BXD, RC4, ANP, JCP, SUB, AGG, AGGR-r, and DISC-r.

Psychopathic personality disorder frequently emerges as a potent risk factor in the literature and is often embedded within various violent risk assessment tools (e.g., Violence Risk Appraisal Guide, HCR-20-V3). As described in Chapter 2, the MMPI-2-RF has demonstrated utility in capturing psychopathic personality traits, with standard scales (e.g., Kastner, Sellbom, & Lilienfeld, 2012; Sellbom, Ben-Porath, et al., 2005; Sellbom, Ben-Porath, & Stafford, 2007; Wygant & Sellbom, 2012) as well as with psychopathy-specific indices and scales (Kutchen et al., 2017; Phillips et al., 2014; Sellbom et al., 2012; Sellbom et al., 2016). This research by and large demonstrates that the scales listed earlier for antisocial personality disorder, along with low scores on fearfulness scales (BRF, MSF), interpersonal scales (Interpersonal Passivity [IPP], Social Avoidance [SAV], SHY) and high Disaffiliativeness (DSF) is indicative of primary psychopathic personality traits. Research has supported Sellbom et al.'s (2012) psychopathic indices as predictive of poor treatment outcome and future reoffending in male domestic violence offenders (Rock et al., 2013), risky sexual behavior (Kastner & Sellbom, 2012), and aggression in a psychiatric hospital (Grossi et al., 2015).

We believe that the MMPI-2-RF likely has the greatest utility in providing information about dynamic risk factors that are amenable to intervention. In terms of active symptoms of major mental illness, THD, RC6, RC8, PSYC, and RC9, along with ACT, would provide direct information about this risk factor. Severe depression, which indicates risk for self-harm, is readily measured by MMPI-2-RF scales as well (EID, RCd, RC2, SUI, HLP). Moreover, several scales provide broad-based measurement of negative affectivity, including RC7 and NEGE-r, which constitutes an important dynamic risk factor (Douglas & Skeem, 2005). More specifically, the MMPI-2-RF SP Scales provide more fine-tuned assessment of specific negative emotions, including ANP, which is an important dynamic risk factor (Douglas & Skeem, 2005; Monahan, 2013). In terms of behavioral instability/impulsivity, DISC-r is a direct marker of poor impulse control, and AGG is a marker of aggressive behavior (Tarescavage, Glassmire, et al., 2016). Furthermore, antisocial cognitions are often referred to as one of the big four risk factors (Andrews & Bonta, 2010) and appear as violent ideation or intent on the MMPI-2-RF.

AGG and AGGR-r provide the best assessment of proactive and behavioral violence. Another important dynamic risk factor is insight (Douglas, Hart, Webster, et al., 2013). Tarescavage, Glassmire, et al. (2016) hypothesized that the underreporting scales L-r and K-r would potentially represent indirect measures of poor insight, that RC6 could represent poor insight into psychosis, and RC1 of the psychological factors underlying medically unexplained symptoms.

The HCR-20-V3 includes five risk management factors that are important in generating optimal release plans. The MMPI-2-RF has no scales that can directly inform such risk factors, though Tarescavage, Glassmire, et al. (2016) provided some tentative recommendations. The interpersonal scales could provide an indication of the degree to which an individual would avail himself or herself of social support. They also cited research that consistently supports BXD, THD, RC4, RC8, JCP, AGG, and DISC-r as predictors of poor treatment outcome in forensic contexts (Mattson et al., 2012; Sellbom et al., 2008; Tarescavage et al., 2014), which might inform future treatment or supervision response.

There is limited research on the predictive validity of MMPI-2-RF scale scores in terms of violence risk. Sellbom et al. (2008) published a study that used the RC Scales in the prediction of violent recidivism among offenders undergoing treatment in a domestic violence treatment program. RC4 and RC9 were the main predictors of recidivism even after both historical (e.g., arrest history) and demographic (e.g., age, income) variables had been accounted for. Rock et al. (2013) used the same sample and outcome variables and found that psychopathic personality traits, as measured by the MMPI-2-RF, were predictive of recidivism. The disinhibitory traits (impulsive-antisociality) were the primary predictors, which mirror the RC4 and RC9 scale findings.

Glassmire et al. (2016) examined the utility of the SUI scale in predicting future suicidal attempts within 1 year in 229 forensic psychiatric inpatients. They found that this scale evidenced a small-to-moderate correlation ($r = .28$) with future attempts. They also showed that this effect remained statistically significant after historical attempts and current suicidal ideation were accounted for. The SUI scale also outperformed scales reflective of depressive symptoms more generally (RCd and RC2) in these predictions.

Most recently, Tarescavage, Glassmire, et al. (2016) tested their HCR-20-V3 mapping of MMPI-2-RF scales on an external criterion of future violent acts in a forensic psychiatric hospital. The sample consisted of 303 patients who had been administered the MMPI-2-RF. They found that externalizing scales only were predictive of total amount of institutional violence; specifically, BXD, RC4, RC9, ANP, JCP, AGG, AGGR-r, and DISC-r. No other scales augmented these predictors. Tarescavage, Glassmire, et al. proposed that a possible explanation for other symptom-based scales being nonpredictive was likely owing to them being treated in a controlled environment. In a different study, Grossi et al. (2015) found that thought dysfunction scales were the strongest predictors of concurrent ratings of aggression.

CASE EXAMPLE 6-1

Case Background

Mr. C is a 40-year-old man of New Zealand Māori descent. He was referred by his lawyer for a violence risk assessment pursuant to an application for parole into the community. He was originally convicted of murder and aggravated robbery with a firearm during which he shot a clerk in cold blood during the robbery of a liquor store. One of his codefendants testified in court that there was no need to shoot the victim, as he was cooperating fully, but the defendant did so anyway "with a smile on his face." He was sentenced to life imprisonment, which, in New Zealand, automatically comes with eligibility for parole consideration after 10 years. Subsequent to this eligibility, the parole board denied him conditional release six previous times, and he had now been continuously incarcerated for 19 years.

The defendant had a poor upbringing in a gang-infested neighborhood of Wellington, New Zealand. His parents were alcoholics and extremely neglectful, leading him and his younger siblings to fend for themselves. He would frequently shoplift for food and other necessities. By age 10, he and his friends were drinking alcohol regularly, as it was freely available at home. He and his siblings were removed several times from their home by the Department of Social Services and placed in foster care, but they frequently ran away. Mr. C was expelled from two different schools, once at age 11, for hitting another student in the head with a cricket bat. He left school after year 9. At age 13, he helped start a neighborhood gang to protect the neighborhood from rivals, as well as engage in a diverse range of criminality such as car theft, burglary, assaults, and weapon possession. By age 17, he was the clear leader and primary enforcer. Mr. C had an extensive juvenile delinquency legal history. As an adolescent, he was convicted numerous times for theft, burglary, unlawful taking of cars and motorcycles, and common assault. At 17 years old, he was briefly incarcerated in adult prison for disqualified driving, burglary, and assaults. As an adult, Mr. C continued on a similar trajectory with theft, burglary, disqualified driving, common assaults, and possession of weapons. These charges accumulated on a regular basis, and he was incarcerated twice briefly, prior to his arrest in the current case.

During his incarceration, he initially adjusted quite poorly from a behavioral perspective. In his first 5 years, he had over 30 proven misconducts—many of a violent nature. He would intimidate and assault other offenders, intimidate and threaten staff, and possess a number of disallowed items (e.g., cell phones, cannabis). Over time, his number of sustained misconducts gradually decreased, though he continued to be the subject of numerous investigations every year. He completed a mandatory serious violent offender treatment program as well as substance abuse programming in his first 10 years. After being denied parole, he began taking a number of courses on self-improvement, including national certificates for high school education equivalence. For the last 5 years leading up to the evaluation, his number of proven misconducts had dramatically decreased, though prison staff continued to comment on his extremely entitled attitude, manipulativeness, and poor anger control. Nevertheless, he had been employed on the grounds crew for the year leading up to the current evaluation, though he recently lost this job subsequent to threatening his grounds supervisor.

Issues Pertaining to Violence Risk

Mr. C was administered the *Psychopathy Checklist: Screening Version* (Hart, Cox, & Hare, 1995) as part of the evaluation, and his risk evaluation was organized using the HCR-20-V3. Mr. C exhibited a number of historical (static) risk factors that indicated high risk for future reoffending. He had an early and diverse history of violent behavior in the past. He had engaged in a wide range of nonviolent antisocial acts, as is evident from his criminal record and his own admission. He had an unstable relationship history, characterized by at least one act of perpetrated violence against a former partner. Mr. C also met diagnostic criteria for antisocial personality disorder in light of his past behavior and personality traits. He also had a history of alcohol abuse as a teenager and young adult. Moreover, Mr. C exhibited a range of violence-oriented attitudes, as is evident from his justification of violent acts for personal benefit (including status and power) and to protect his neighborhood from rival gangs, associations with like-minded antisocial peers, and general disregard for others' rights. As an adolescent and young adult, these attitudes intensified over time. Furthermore, Mr. C also reported significant traumatic experiences as a child, including an extremely unstable home environment, being the victim of physical and emotional abuse and neglect, and witnessing domestic violence in the home. Finally, although he has generally been described as having a positive attitude and being motivated in past treatment efforts, he had an escape charge on his record, which is noteworthy.

The most significant dynamic risk factor present was his instability with behavior, emotion, and cognitions, in that he was prone to frustration intolerance. He had a temper and sudden outbursts of anger, sometimes acted in an impulsive manner, continued to exhibit a tendency toward blaming others, and exhibited self-entitlement. However, the behavioral manifestation of these tendencies had become milder. Moreover, previous psychological evaluations had commented on his lack of insight, but this risk factor appeared to have somewhat attenuated over time. He clearly seemed to have developed an understanding of what contributed to his acting out. For instance, on his own volition, he was able to discuss how his communication difficulties contribute to misunderstandings and increased frustration; the role of antisocial associations in triggering violence and other misconduct; and what contexts were most likely to serve as violence triggers. He continued to need to improve his insight into his entitled/demanding attitude, and this was identified as a future target for intervention. Finally, he continued to exhibit a hostile attribution bias ("violent ideation" risk factor), but to his credit, he had developed some insight that he had a tendency to read into situations incorrectly and had been working to improve in this regard. In terms of the remaining clinical risk factors, Mr. C was not deemed to suffer from symptoms of a major mental illness, nor was he judged to exhibit poor treatment or supervision response.

MMPI-2-RF Results

PROTOCOL VALIDITY

First, we look at the Validity Scales. It is important to keep in mind the type of response style that is incentivized for a particular type of evaluation. For a risk assessment, where an individual typically wants to be released from prison or a hospital, the most likely response style would be underreporting. Mr. C responded to all of the items and there was no evidence of inconsistent (VRIN-r), fixed indiscriminant (TRIN-r), or overreported (F-r, Fp-r, Fs, FBS-r, and RBS) responding. He did score substantially higher than what would be expected of a prison inmate on Fp-r, but this score (77T) was not in the range where actual overreporting is of significant concern. Mr. C did, however, produce an elevated score on L-r (66T), but not K-r (55T), which indicates the potential for attempting to appear as an overly virtuous person (L-r), but not necessarily appearing to be better psychologically adjusted than is the case. The hypothesis that L-r might be a reflection of poor insight is a good one here, particularly as it would be consistent with clinical impressions.

CLINICAL INTERPRETATION

As noted, the H-O scales are the first point of consultation to anchor the interpretation. The pattern of H-O Scales is somewhat unusual, since it includes both an extremely elevated scale (BXD, 89T) and a scale with a low score (EID). We start with the behavioral dysfunction domain. RC4, JCP, SUB, AGG, AGGR-r, and DISC-r are all elevated to very high degrees, which indicates a significant and pervasive dysfunction manifested in nonadherence to social norms and standards, rejection of authority, impulsivity, irresponsibility, alcohol and drug abuse, sensation-seeking, thrill-seeking, interpersonal antagonism, grandiosity, and possibly callousness. It is noteworthy when examining the prison inmate comparison group (a group already more prone to externalizing than the average person) that over 90 percent of inmates score lower than Mr. C on these scales. This combination of scales is highly consistent with an antisocial personality pattern, and the scales were also the most potent predictors of violent risk in the literature reviewed earlier (e.g., Sellbom et al., 2008; Tarescavage, Glassmire, et al., 2016). They are also consistent with the current (dynamic) risk factors of behavioral instability and potential proviolence attitudes.

Next, we choose to interpret the emotional dysfunction domain in light of the low score on EID. Consistent with this domain, Mr. C scored quite low on most internalizing scales, expressing a disavowal of emotional problems. In other words, he is communicating that he is not demoralized or depressed, and he does not exhibit anxiety or fear. The latter is often viewed

Minnesota Multiphasic
Personality Inventory-2
Restructured Form®

Score Report

MMPI-2-RF®

Minnesota Multiphasic Personality Inventory-2-Restructured Form®

Yossef S. Ben-Porath, PhD, & Auke Tellegen, PhD

Name:	Mr. C
ID Number:	6
Age:	40
Gender:	Male
Marital Status:	Never Married
Years of Education:	12
Date Assessed:	03/10/2009

ALWAYS LEARNING

PEARSON

FIGURE 6-1 Case Example 6-1: Mr. C's MMPI-2-RF Profile, continued.

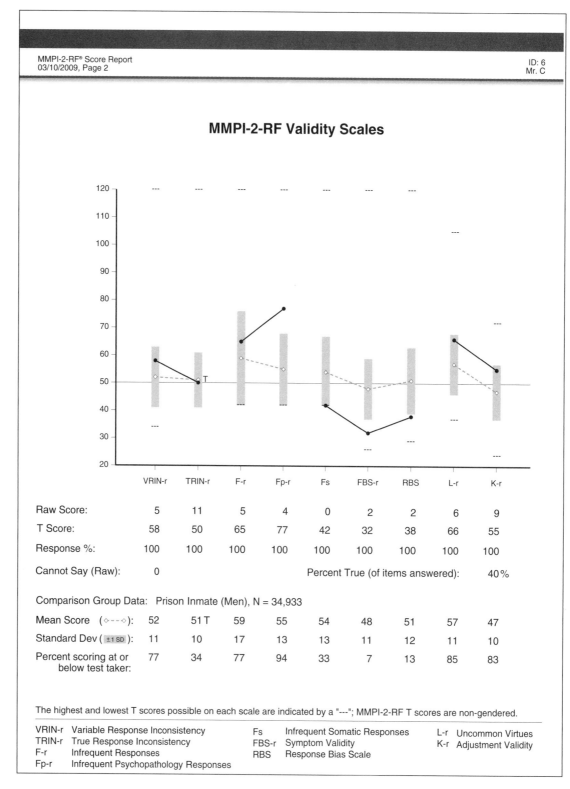

FIGURE 6-1 Case Example 6-1: Mr. C's MMPI-2-RF Profile, continued.

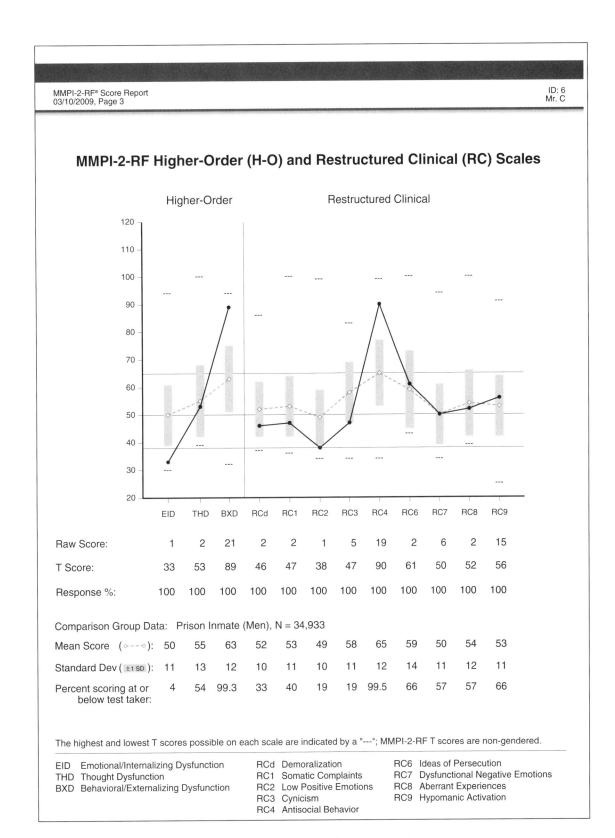

MMPI-2-RF Higher-Order (H-O) and Restructured Clinical (RC) Scales

	EID	THD	BXD	RCd	RC1	RC2	RC3	RC4	RC6	RC7	RC8	RC9
Raw Score:	1	2	21	2	2	1	5	19	2	6	2	15
T Score:	33	53	89	46	47	38	47	90	61	50	52	56
Response %:	100	100	100	100	100	100	100	100	100	100	100	100

Comparison Group Data: Prison Inmate (Men), N = 34,933

	EID	THD	BXD	RCd	RC1	RC2	RC3	RC4	RC6	RC7	RC8	RC9
Mean Score (◇- - -◇):	50	55	63	52	53	49	58	65	59	50	54	53
Standard Dev (±1 SD):	11	13	12	10	11	10	11	12	14	11	12	11
Percent scoring at or below test taker:	4	54	99.3	33	40	19	19	99.5	66	57	57	66

The highest and lowest T scores possible on each scale are indicated by a "---"; MMPI-2-RF T scores are non-gendered.

EID Emotional/Internalizing Dysfunction	RCd Demoralization	RC6 Ideas of Persecution
THD Thought Dysfunction	RC1 Somatic Complaints	RC7 Dysfunctional Negative Emotions
BXD Behavioral/Externalizing Dysfunction	RC2 Low Positive Emotions	RC8 Aberrant Experiences
	RC3 Cynicism	RC9 Hypomanic Activation
	RC4 Antisocial Behavior	

FIGURE 6-1 Case Example 6-1: Mr. C's MMPI-2-RF Profile, continued.

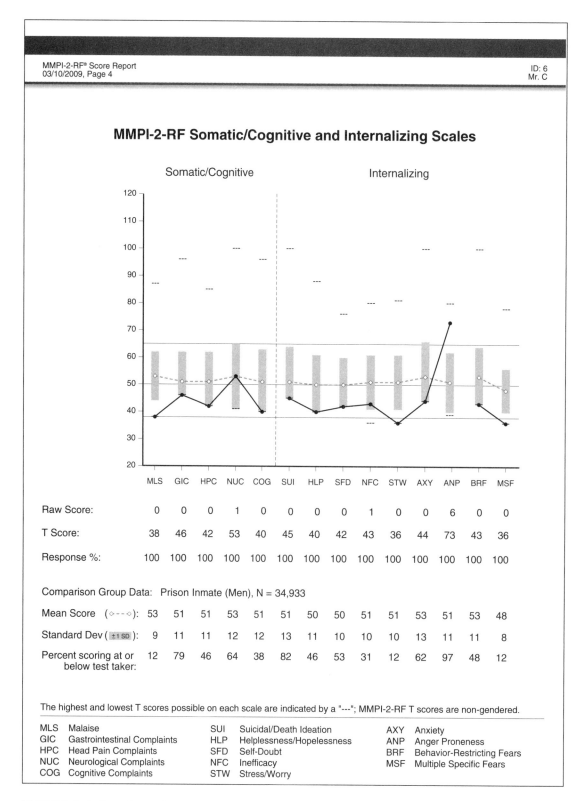

FIGURE 6-1 Case Example 6-1: Mr. C's MMPI-2-RF Profile, continued.

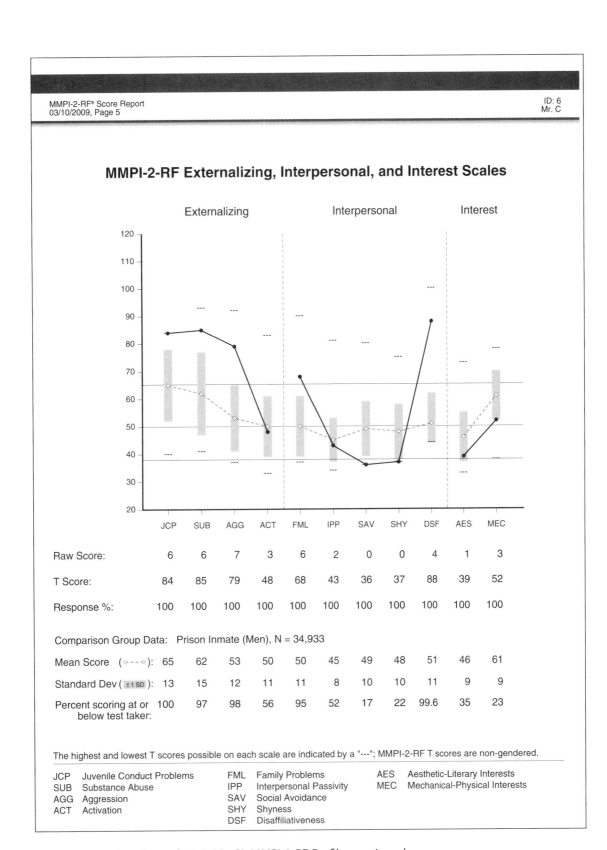

MMPI-2-RF Externalizing, Interpersonal, and Interest Scales

	JCP	SUB	AGG	ACT	FML	IPP	SAV	SHY	DSF	AES	MEC
Raw Score:	6	6	7	3	6	2	0	0	4	1	3
T Score:	84	85	79	48	68	43	36	37	88	39	52
Response %:	100	100	100	100	100	100	100	100	100	100	100

Comparison Group Data: Prison Inmate (Men), N = 34,933

	JCP	SUB	AGG	ACT	FML	IPP	SAV	SHY	DSF	AES	MEC
Mean Score (◇---◇):	65	62	53	50	50	45	49	48	51	46	61
Standard Dev (±1 SD):	13	15	12	11	11	8	10	10	11	9	9
Percent scoring at or below test taker:	100	97	98	56	95	52	17	22	99.6	35	23

The highest and lowest T scores possible on each scale are indicated by a "---"; MMPI-2-RF T scores are non-gendered.

JCP	Juvenile Conduct Problems	FML	Family Problems	AES	Aesthetic-Literary Interests
SUB	Substance Abuse	IPP	Interpersonal Passivity	MEC	Mechanical-Physical Interests
AGG	Aggression	SAV	Social Avoidance		
ACT	Activation	SHY	Shyness		
		DSF	Disaffiliativeness		

FIGURE 6-1 Case Example 6-1: Mr. C's MMPI-2-RF Profile, continued.

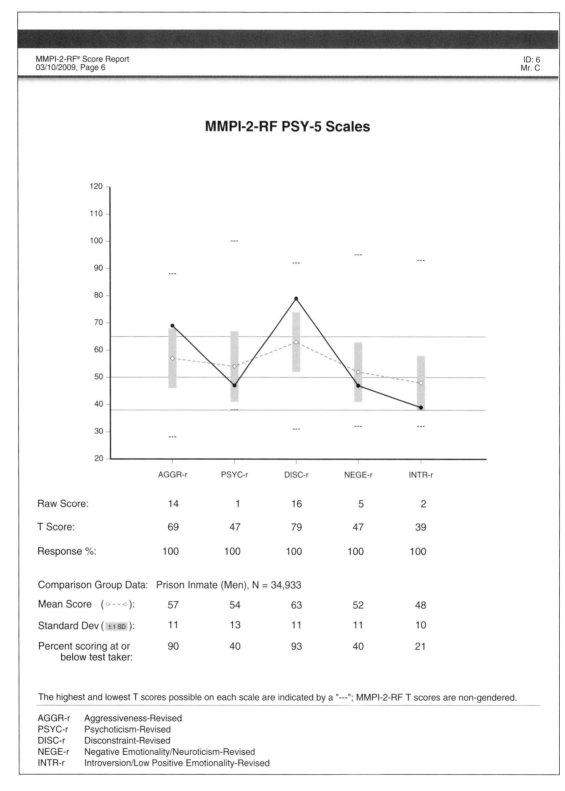

MMPI-2-RF PSY-5 Scales

	AGGR-r	PSYC-r	DISC-r	NEGE-r	INTR-r
Raw Score:	14	1	16	5	2
T Score:	69	47	79	47	39
Response %:	100	100	100	100	100

Comparison Group Data: Prison Inmate (Men), N = 34,933

	AGGR-r	PSYC-r	DISC-r	NEGE-r	INTR-r
Mean Score (◇---◇):	57	54	63	52	48
Standard Dev (±1 SD):	11	13	11	11	10
Percent scoring at or below test taker:	90	40	93	40	21

The highest and lowest T scores possible on each scale are indicated by a "---"; MMPI-2-RF T scores are non-gendered.

AGGR-r Aggressiveness-Revised
PSYC-r Psychoticism-Revised
DISC-r Disconstraint-Revised
NEGE-r Negative Emotionality/Neuroticism-Revised
INTR-r Introversion/Low Positive Emotionality-Revised

FIGURE 6-1 Case Example 6-1: Mr. C's MMPI-2-RF Profile, continued.

MMPI-2-RF T SCORES (BY DOMAIN)

PROTOCOL VALIDITY

Content Non-Responsiveness

0	58	50
CNS	VRIN-r	TRIN-r

Over-Reporting

65	77		42	32	38
F-r	Fp-r		Fs	FBS-r	RBS

Under-Reporting

66	55
L-r	K-r

SUBSTANTIVE SCALES

Somatic/Cognitive Dysfunction

47	38	46	42	53	40
RC1	MLS	GIC	HPC	NUC	COG

Emotional Dysfunction

33
EID

46	45	40	42	43
RCd	SUI	HLP	SFD	NFC

38	39
RC2	INTR-r

50	36	44	73	43	36	47
RC7	STW	AXY	ANP	BRF	MSF	NEGE-r

Thought Dysfunction

53
THD

61
RC6

52
RC8

47
PSYC-r

Behavioral Dysfunction

89
BXD

90	84	85
RC4	JCP	SUB

56	79	48	69	79
RC9	AGG	ACT	AGGR-r	DISC-r

Interpersonal Functioning

68	47	43	36	37	88
FML	RC3	IPP	SAV	SHY	DSF

Interests

39	52
AES	MEC

Note. This information is provided to facilitate interpretation following the recommended structure for MMPI-2-RF interpretation in Chapter 5 of the *MMPI-2-RF Manual for Administration, Scoring, and Interpretation*, which provides details in the text and an outline in Table 5-1.

FIGURE 6-1 Case Example 6-1: Mr. C's MMPI-2-RF Profile, continued.

ITEM-LEVEL INFORMATION

Unscorable Responses

The test taker produced scorable responses to all the MMPI-2-RF items.

Critical Responses

Seven MMPI-2-RF scales--Suicidal/Death Ideation (SUI), Helplessness/Hopelessness (HLP), Anxiety (AXY), Ideas of Persecution (RC6), Aberrant Experiences (RC8), Substance Abuse (SUB), and Aggression (AGG)--have been designated by the test authors as having critical item content that may require immediate attention and follow-up. Items answered by the individual in the keyed direction (True or False) on a critical scale are listed below if his T score on that scale is 65 or higher. The percentage of the MMPI-2-RF normative sample (NS) and of the Prison Inmate (Men) comparison group (CG) that answered each item in the keyed direction are provided in parentheses following the item content.

Substance Abuse (SUB, T Score = 85)

    49. Item Content Omitted. (True; NS 29.6%, CG 55.7%)
   141. Item Content Omitted. (True; NS 34.2%, CG 49.2%)
   192. Item Content Omitted. (True; NS 11.2%, CG 28.3%)
   237. Item Content Omitted. (False; NS 27.4%, CG 59.0%)
   266. Item Content Omitted. (True; NS 5.0%, CG 43.4%)
   297. Item Content Omitted. (True; NS 14.4%, CG 45.0%)

Aggression (AGG, T Score = 79)

   23. Item Content Omitted. (True; NS 39.0%, CG 29.1%)
   84. Item Content Omitted. (True; NS 12.1%, CG 14.6%)
  231. Item Content Omitted. (True; NS 6.3%,
     CG 10.0%)
  312. Item Content Omitted. (True; NS 5.5%, CG
     25.6%)
  316. Item Content Omitted. (True; NS 45.1%, CG
     62.3%)
  329. Item Content Omitted. (True; NS 12.7%, CG
     33.5%)
  337. Item Content Omitted. (True; NS 50.2%,
     CG 43.9%)

FIGURE 6-1 Case Example 6-1: Mr. C's MMPI-2-RF Profile, continued.

User-Designated Item-Level Information

The following item-level information is based on the report user's selection of additional scales, and/or of lower cutoffs for the critical scales from the previous section. Items answered by the test taker in the keyed direction (True or False) on a selected scale are listed below if his T score on that scale is at the user-designated cutoff score or higher. The percentage of the MMPI-2-RF normative sample (NS) and of the Prison Inmate (Men) comparison group (CG) that answered each item in the keyed direction are provided in parentheses following the item content.

Behavioral/Externalizing Dysfunction (BXD, T Score = 89)
- 21. Item Content Omitted. (True; NS 47.1%, CG 72.3%)
- 49. Item Content Omitted. (True; NS 29.6%, CG 55.7%)
- 61. Item Content Omitted. (False; NS 61.6%, CG 61.2%)
- 66. Item Content Omitted. (True; NS 20.3%, CG 68.4%)
- 84. Item Content Omitted. (True; NS 12.1%, CG 14.6%)
- 96. Item Content Omitted. (True; NS 18.8%, CG 61.3%)
- 131. Item Content Omitted. (True; NS 43.3%, CG 50.6%)
- 156. Item Content Omitted. (True; NS 59.8%, CG 72.0%)
- 190. Item Content Omitted. (False; NS 28.6%, CG 92.0%)
- 193. Item Content Omitted. (True; NS 32.8%, CG 41.2%)
- 205. Item Content Omitted. (True; NS 13.0%, CG 46.3%)
- 223. Item Content Omitted. (True; NS 12.3%, CG 61.1%)
- 231. Item Content Omitted. (True; NS 6.3%, CG 10.0%)
- 237. Item Content Omitted. (False; NS 27.4%, CG 59.0%)
- 248. Item Content Omitted. (True; NS 16.1%, CG 30.4%)
- 253. Item Content Omitted. (True; NS 5.8%, CG 24.3%)
- 266. Item Content Omitted. (True; NS 5.0%, CG 43.4%)
- 292. Item Content Omitted. (True; NS 26.1%, CG 40.3%)
- 312. Item Content Omitted. (True; NS 5.5%, CG 25.6%)
- 316. Item Content Omitted. (True; NS 45.1%, CG 62.3%)
- 329. Item Content Omitted. (True; NS 12.7%, CG 33.5%)

Antisocial Behavior (RC4, T Score = 90)
- 5. Item Content Omitted. (True; NS 36.7%, CG 44.9%)
- 19. Item Content Omitted. (False; NS 17.0%, CG 17.4%)
- 21. Item Content Omitted. (True; NS 47.1%, CG 72.3%)
- 49. Item Content Omitted. (True; NS 29.6%, CG 55.7%)

FIGURE 6-1 Case Example 6-1: Mr. C's MMPI-2-RF Profile, continued.

66. Item Content Omitted. (True; NS 20.3%, CG 68.4%)
80. Item Content Omitted. (False; NS 21.2%, CG 22.3%)
96. Item Content Omitted. (True; NS 18.8%, CG
    61.3%)
141. Item Content Omitted. (True; NS 34.2%, CG 49.2%)
156. Item Content Omitted. (True; NS 59.8%, CG 72.0%)
173. Item Content Omitted. (True; NS 13.4%, CG 27.9%)
190. Item Content Omitted. (False; NS 28.6%, CG 92.0%)
205. Item Content Omitted. (True; NS 13.0%,
     CG 46.3%)
223. Item Content Omitted. (True; NS 12.3%, CG 61.1%)
237. Item Content Omitted. (False; NS 27.4%, CG 59.0%)
253. Item Content Omitted. (True; NS 5.8%, CG
     24.3%)
266. Item Content Omitted. (True; NS 5.0%, CG 43.4%)
297. Item Content Omitted. (True; NS 14.4%, CG 45.0%)
312. Item Content Omitted. (True; NS 5.5%, CG
     25.6%)
329. Item Content Omitted. (True; NS 12.7%, CG
     33.5%)

Ideas of Persecution (RC6, T Score = 61)

212. Item Content Omitted. (False; NS 9.1%, CG 34.4%)
233. Item Content Omitted. (True; NS 5.5%, CG 23.3%)

Hypomanic Activation (RC9, T Score = 56)

47. Item Content Omitted. (True; NS 42.7%, CG
    64.5%)
61. Item Content Omitted. (False; NS 61.6%, CG 61.2%)
84. Item Content Omitted. (True; NS 12.1%, CG 14.6%)
118. Item Content Omitted. (True; NS 57.4%, CG 71.7%)
131. Item Content Omitted. (True; NS 43.3%, CG 50.6%)
155. Item Content Omitted. (True; NS 41.6%, CG 45.9%)
181. Item Content Omitted. (True; NS 35.3%, CG 38.2%)
193. Item Content Omitted.
     (True; NS 32.8%, CG 41.2%)
231. Item Content Omitted. (True; NS 6.3%,
     CG 10.0%)
248. Item Content Omitted. (True; NS 16.1%, CG 30.4%)
256. Item Content Omitted. (True; NS
     65.7%, CG 71.8%)
292. Item Content Omitted. (True; NS 26.1%, CG 40.3%)
316. Item Content Omitted. (True; NS 45.1%, CG
     62.3%)
327. Item Content Omitted.
     (True; NS 41.7%, CG 47.4%)

FIGURE 6-1 Case Example 6-1: Mr. C's MMPI-2-RF Profile, continued.

337. Item Content Omitted. (True; NS 50.2%,
CG 43.9%)

Anger Proneness (ANP, T Score = 73)

119. Item Content Omitted. (True; NS 39.5%, CG 30.6%)
134. Item Content Omitted. (False; NS 32.5%, CG 28.0%)
155. Item Content Omitted. (True; NS 41.6%, CG 45.9%)
248. Item Content Omitted. (True; NS 16.1%, CG 30.4%)
303. Item Content Omitted. (True; NS 28.6%, CG 37.3%)
318. Item Content Omitted. (True; NS 19.9%, CG
27.0%)

Behavior-Restricting Fears (BRF, T Score = 43)

No items that are scored on this scale were answered in the keyed direction.

Juvenile Conduct Problems (JCP, T Score = 84)

21. Item Content Omitted. (True; NS 47.1%, CG 72.3%)
66. Item Content Omitted. (True; NS 20.3%, CG 68.4%)
96. Item Content Omitted. (True; NS 18.8%, CG
61.3%)
205. Item Content Omitted. (True; NS 13.0%,
CG 46.3%)
223. Item Content Omitted. (True; NS 12.3%, CG 61.1%)
253. Item Content Omitted. (True; NS 5.8%, CG
24.3%)

Aggressiveness-Revised (AGGR-r, T Score = 69)

24. Item Content Omitted. (False; NS 74.6%, CG 83.3%)
84. Item Content Omitted. (True; NS 12.1%, CG 14.6%)
104. Item Content Omitted. (True; NS 67.1%, CG 70.7%)
147. Item Content Omitted. (True; NS 75.2%, CG 88.3%)
182. Item Content Omitted. (True; NS 33.6%, CG 63.0%)
197. Item Content Omitted. (True; NS 62.5%, CG
76.2%)
231. Item Content Omitted. (True; NS 6.3%,
CG 10.0%)
256. Item Content Omitted. (True; NS
65.7%, CG 71.8%)
276. Item Content Omitted. (True; NS
50.0%, CG 72.1%)
316. Item Content Omitted. (True; NS 45.1%, CG
62.3%)
319. Item Content Omitted. (False; NS 64.7%,
CG 74.0%)
321. Item Content Omitted. (True; NS 31.3%, CG 47.4%)

FIGURE 6-1 Case Example 6-1: Mr. C's MMPI-2-RF Profile, continued.

327. Item Content Omitted.
     (True; NS 41.7%, CG 47.4%)
329. Item Content Omitted. (True; NS 12.7%, CG
     33.5%)

Disconstraint-Revised (DISC-r, T Score = 79)
 21. Item Content Omitted. (True; NS 47.1%, CG 72.3%)
 49. Item Content Omitted. (True; NS 29.6%, CG 55.7%)
 61. Item Content Omitted. (False; NS 61.6%, CG 61.2%)
 66. Item Content Omitted. (True; NS 20.3%, CG 68.4%)
115. Item Content Omitted. (True; NS 55.0%, CG 55.1%)
131. Item Content Omitted. (True; NS 43.3%, CG 50.6%)
156. Item Content Omitted. (True; NS 59.8%, CG 72.0%)
190. Item Content Omitted. (False; NS 28.6%, CG 92.0%)
193. Item Content Omitted.
     (True; NS 32.8%, CG 41.2%)
205. Item Content Omitted. (True; NS 13.0%,
     CG 46.3%)
223. Item Content Omitted. (True; NS 12.3%, CG 61.1%)
237. Item Content Omitted. (False; NS 27.4%, CG 59.0%)
253. Item Content Omitted. (True; NS 5.8%, CG
     24.3%)
292. Item Content Omitted. (True; NS 26.1%, CG 40.3%)
297. Item Content Omitted. (True; NS 14.4%, CG 45.0%)
300. Item Content Omitted. (True; NS 26.5%, CG 69.3%)

End of Report

FIGURE 6-1 Case Example 6-1: Mr. C's MMPI-2-RF Profile.

as a core of primary psychopathy (e.g., Lykken, 1995). However, there is one emotion that he does experience to a clinically meaningful degree, which is anger (ANP = 73T). He is likely to have poor frustration tolerance, be irritable, and be impatient with others. It is also noteworthy that ANP is an independent predictor for future violence (Tarescavage, Glassmire, et al., 2016).

The final domain with interpretable scores is the interpersonal domain, which also shows an interesting pattern of elevations versus low scores. FML is elevated (68T), suggesting significant familial alienation and discord, which is not surprising given his history. SAV and SHY are both low, indicating gregariousness and lacking in social anxiety; thus, Mr. C likely has little difficulty navigating the social landscape and can do so with ease. On the other hand, the very elevated DSF score indicates a substantial lack of desire (or even ability) for connecting with other people, as well as significant misanthropic beliefs. The MMPI-2-RF psychopathy research reviewed earlier revealed that the externalizing pattern, coupled with low fear and the interpersonal scale constellation just observed, were highly indicative of the presence of psychopathic personality traits.

Case Conclusion

Mr. C clearly exhibits a number of static risk factors in addition to a lifelong pattern of antisocial personality disorder/psychopathy. In this regard, he will likely always be at high risk, and although some of the underlying personality traits could potentially be amenable to change, no such pattern has been observed in this case. Furthermore, he clearly continues to exhibit dynamic risk factors that include significant behavioral instability (including poor impulse and anger control) and proviolent ideation. His insight continues to be questionable, even if it has likely improved over the years. It is quite possible that Mr. C has learned to manipulate the system to his advantage and therefore avoids more serious ramifications of his behavior. Nevertheless, his dynamic risk appears to have attenuated to some degree, as objective evidence does indicate improved behavior overall. However, it was not the examiner's opinion that risk had sufficiently reduced to warrant conditional release into the community. Ultimately, the parole board concurred with this opinion, and Mr. C remains incarcerated.

CONCLUSIONS

The MMPI-2-RF can provide useful information about static and dynamic risk factors. Since research is only beginning to emerge with respect to future violence predictions, the scale scores should not be used for independent predictions of risk. Rather, the MMPI-2-RF can be useful in providing another source of information for a structured professional judgment, such the HCR-20-V3.

Chapter 7

Sexual Offender Risk Assessment

Few criminal acts engender as much societal concern and repulsion as sexual offenses, particularly when the victims are children. Psychologists and other mental health professionals are frequently requested to provide assistance in the assessment, treatment, and management of sexual offenders. The criminal justice system is tasked not only with punitive measures following a sexual offense, but also in determining which offenders pose the highest risk for future offending and violent behavior and which offenders are most amenable to treatment efforts designed to reduce the likelihood of future offending. As a whole, sexual offenses are a diverse group that vary with respect to the nature of the offense (e.g., contact or noncontact), age of the victim, and level of violence and coercion (among other factors). Moreover, some sexual offenses reflect distinct forms of psychopathology (e.g., pedophilia).

SEXUAL OFFENDER RISK ASSESSMENT

Sexual offender risk assessments can occur at various stages during a case that can range from the pretrial stage to postrelease from prison. Occasionally, defense attorneys will request to have their clients undergo a risk assessment before the case is adjudicated in court. In these instances, the attorney may wish to show the court that the defendant is low risk in order to work out a plea agreement with the prosecution. Consequently, the alleged offender is likely to be quite defensive during the evaluation and may be hesitant to acknowledge any sexually deviant behavior since he or she has not yet been adjudicated.

Many sexual offender risk assessments take place at the presentence phase of the trial. By this point, the offender has been convicted and the court may seek guidance with issues such as placement (incarceration vs. probation), risk for recidivism and sexual violence, treatment amenability, and community supervision/management. It is also common for offenders to be evaluated prior to release from prison, with respect to planning community supervision and treatment. In addition, approximately 20 states in the United States have civil commitment proceedings for sexual offenders deemed to be at a significantly high risk for sexual violence in the community. These commitments are typically reserved for high-risk offenders and include consideration of mental abnormality that results in volitional impairment and an increased risk for sexual offending (Conroy & Witt, 2013).

Similar to the prediction of violence (see Chapter 6), sexual offender risk assessment generally falls into three categories: unstructured clinical judgment, actuarial assessment, and structured professional judgment. The unstructured assessment approach in sexual offender evaluations is generally discouraged owing to limited reliability (Conroy & Witt, 2013).

The actuarial approach utilizes empirically identified variables, typically reflecting static factors (such as age of offender and history of sexual violence). The Static-99R (Helmus, Thornton, Hanson, & Babchishin, 2012) is a revised version of the original Static-99 (Hanson & Thornton, 1999), which is the most widely used actuarial risk assessment instrument in sexual offender evaluations across the world (Archer et al., 2006; Hanson, Thornton, Helmus, & Babchishin, 2016). Actuarial approaches for sex offender evaluations are generally considered to be more reliable than unstructured assessments, owing to the collection of readily available demographic and criminal history information (Hanson et al., 2016). However, recent research by Rice, Boccaccini, Harris, and Hawes (2014) found that the field reliability (interrater agreement) of the Static-99 was lowest for offenders scoring in the high range.

The final approach used in the assessment of sexual offenders is the SPJ guides. Sex offender SPJ guides include factors such as history of sexual violence as well as the presence of psychopathology (e.g., psychopathy, major mental illness). While SPJ provides more reliable guidance in an evaluation than an unstructured assessment, ensuring that factors empirically associated with recidivism are assessed (Conroy & Witt, 2013), the method is not without its faults. Indeed, little to no direction is provided with respect to how the evaluator weighs each risk factor in determining a global rating of risk for sexual violence.

The Risk for Sexual Violence Protocol (RSVP; Hart et al., 2003) is the most widely used SPJ guide in sexual offender risk assessment (Sutherland et al., 2012). The measure evolved from the earlier Sexual Violence Risk–20 (Boer, Hart, Kropp, & Webster, 1997), which was a direct descendant of HCR-20 (Webster, Douglas, Eaves, & Hart, 1997) that was developed for violence risk assessment. With the RSVP, the clinician rates the presence and relevance of 22 items that fall across five domains: sexual violence history, psychological adjustment, mental disorder, social adjustment, and manageability. In addition to guiding a summary judgment of risk, the RSVP helps the clinician identify and describe potential risk scenarios and provide recommendations for case management.

A recent meta-analysis of sexual offender recidivism found that actuarial measures were significantly more accurate for all outcomes (sexual offending, violent offending, or any recidivism) than unstructured approaches (Hanson & Morton-Bourgon, 2009). They also found that SPJ measures showed greater accuracy in predicting recidivism among sexual offenders, although the accuracy of SPJ measures was less than pure actuarial measures.

CONSIDERATIONS FOR USING THE MMPI-2-RF IN SEXUAL OFFENDER EVALUATIONS

Some have questioned the use of traditional assessment instruments (like the MMPI-2-RF) in sexual offender assessments, noting that they are limited in their ability to address specific psycho-legal issues (Conroy & Witt, 2013). Although broadband measures of personality and psychopathology may be limited in the direct prediction of sexual violence, they can nevertheless play an important role in assessing risk in a peripheral manner. It should also be noted that there is no "typical" sexual offender profile on the MMPI-2-RF, which is a point that was discussed by Graham (2012) more broadly with respect to MMPI and MMPI-2 profiles and certain types of criminal behaviors. The utility of the MMPI-2-RF in assessing sexual offenders is not in matching a distinct profile type, but rather in assessing dynamic characteristics that may be associated with the offender's risk for sexual violence and offending.

There is limited research investigating the predictive validity of the MMPI-2-RF scales with respect to sexual violence and deviancy. Tarescavage, Cappo, et al. (2016) discussed integrating the MMPI-2-RF in SPJ guides in assessing sexual offender risk. They emphasized the use of underreporting Validity Scales as a way of assessing overall defensiveness in this setting, noting that underreporting on the MMPI-2-RF generalizes to extratest measures (For-bey, Lee, Ben-Porath, Arbisi, & Gartland, 2013). They also noted that the MMPI-2-RF might reduce overall clinician bias by providing an objective measure that captures the severity of risk factors, such as degree of psycho-pathology and behavioral problems. Tarescavage, Cappo, et al. conceptually linked scales from the MMPI-2-RF with empirically supported dynamic risk factors identified by Mann, Hanson, and Thornton's (2010) meta-analysis. In addition to providing basic psychometric information on the MMPI-2-RF in a sample of 304 child sexual offenders in treatment, they correlated the scales with the Static-99 and static and dynamic risk factors on the Level of Service Inventory-Revised (Andrews & Bonta, 2000). Scores on the Static-99 were significantly associated with markers of externalizing on the MMPI-2-RF (BXD, RC9, JCP, DISC-r). Significant correlations with the Level of Service Inventory-Revised were found across the MMPI-2-RF, mainly in expected ways (e.g., JCP with criminal history).

As noted, denial and minimization are quite prevalent among sexual offenders, particularly during the course of a risk assessment. Tarescavage, Cappo, et al. (2016) noted that scores on (L-r tended to be higher than on K-r, suggesting that sexual offenders may be more likely to utilize an overt impression management approach rather than a covert self-deception approach (Sellbom & Bagby, 2008).

In many respects, the concepts pertaining to using the MMPI-2-RF in violence risk assessments that were discussed in Chapter 6 apply in sexual offender risk assessments as well. The strength of the MMPI-2-RF lies in its utility in general case formulation, which is important in the context of risk assessment. The test can also help inform the evaluator with specific targets of intervention by understanding the offender more fully. Psychopathology and personality dysfunction (particularly psychopathy) are often consid-ered risk factors for sexual violence. As discussed in Chapter 6, numerous studies have examined the ability of the MMPI-2-RF to capture psychopathic personality traits (e.g., Haneveld, Kamphuis, Smid, & Forbey, 2017; Kastner et al., 2012; Sellbom, Ben-Porath, et al, 2005; Sellbom, Ben-Porath, & Staf-ford, 2007; Wygant & Sellbom, 2012). In addition to sexual specific risk factors (e.g., deviant sexual interests, attitudes tolerant of sexual assault), Conroy and Murrie (2007) identified a number of dynamic risk factors that have been identified in the literature, such as intimacy deficits, impulsivity, severe emotional distress, poor self-management, hostility, and substance abuse (among others). All of these factors can be assessed by the internalizing and externalizing scales of the MMPI-2-RF to some degree. Additionally, Emmers-Sommer et al. (2004) discussed how sexual offenders, particularly child offenders, often exhibit ineptitude in their social interactions with others. The Interpersonal SP Scales, in particular IPP, SHY, and DSF can alert the clinician to such factors, which might prove useful in conceptualizing predisposing factors to offending, as well targets for intervention.

The MMPI-2-RF includes a comparison group of 304 male convicted child sexual offenders who were referred to a sex offender treatment program (Tarescavage, Cappo, et al., 2016). Although this comparison group may be helpful in characterizing convicted child sexual offenders with the MMPI-2-RF, it may be less useful in sexual offender risk assessments, many of which are conducted before the offender is fully adjudicated and sentenced. Evaluations conducted before the offender is sentenced provide a different context from testing completed postadjudication or while the offender is in treatment. At the preadjudication phase, evaluees may be more prone to minimizing aspects of their offense as well as indications of sexual deviancy.

CASE EXAMPLE 7-1

Case Background

Mr. D is a 25-year-old, single Caucasian male who was convicted of one count of sodomy first degree and one count of sexual abuse first degree. The victim in this case was the defendant's 13-year-old niece. Mr. D's sister and her daughter resided with him shortly after she separated from her husband. Over the course of 6 weeks, which occurred during the victim's summer break from school, he spent an increasing amount of time with his niece. The offenses took place on two separate occasions, 1 day apart. During the first offense, Mr. D asked his niece to stay up late with him watching a movie on the couch. He began to fondle her, eventually digitally penetrating her vagina. The next day, he once again asked her to stay up late to watch a movie, during which time he kissed her in a sexual manner and she briefly performed fellatio on him. The victim reported the two incidents to her mother 1 week later. The victim's mother contacted the police and Mr. D was arrested 2 days later. He admitted the offense to the police and pled guilty to both counts. He was referred for a psychological evaluation as part of his presentence investigation. The probation department requested a psychological evaluation to investigate his risk for sexual recidivism and treatment planning.

Mr. D was a high school graduate who worked on an assembly line at a factory. He had never been married and reported difficulty maintaining age-appropriate close relationships. He reported that his longest significant relationship, which occurred when he was 21 years of age, lasted only 3 months. He reported a history of depression, but had never received treatment. He acknowledged heavy use of alcohol several times per week and an almost daily use of marijuana since he was 19.

Mr. D received a score of 1 on the Static-99, which placed him in the low risk category. The evaluation utilized the RSVP to guide the assessment of his risk for sexual violence. Several RSVP items bear mentioning as background information. Within the sexual violence history domain, the defendant did not have a history of sexual acting out or escalation in behavior, although he did utilize psychological coercion and grooming in his victimization. With respect to the psychological adjustment and mental disorder domains, the defendant had poor emotional coping skills, limited insight and awareness, mental illness in the form of depression, and substance abuse. The Psychopathy Checklist-Revised was also used in this case to rate the presence of psychopathic characteristics. His Total Score on the Psychopathy Checklist-Revised was 10 and did not indicate significant psychopathic traits. Within the social adjustment domain, Mr. D had very limited interpersonal skills and he failed to establish normal intimate relationships.

MMPI-2-RF Results

As noted, the MMPI-2-RF includes a Sex Offender, Child Victim Evaluee comparison group. However, individuals in this group are postadjudication and are involved in treatment. As such, this group may be somewhat limited in a preadjudication setting such as a presentence evaluation. Therefore, we elected not to use a comparison group in this case.

PROTOCOL VALIDITY

Mr. D responded to each item (CNS = 0) and responded consistently to the items throughout the test (VRIN-r = 58, TRIN-r = 50). There was no

Minnesota Multiphasic
Personality Inventory-2
Restructured Form®

Score Report

MMPI-2-RF®

Minnesota Multiphasic Personality Inventory-2-Restructured Form®

Yossef S. Ben-Porath, PhD, & Auke Tellegen, PhD

Name:	Mr. D
ID Number:	7
Age:	25
Gender:	Male
Marital Status:	Never Married
Years of Education:	12
Date Assessed:	09/10/2012

ALWAYS LEARNING

PEARSON

FIGURE 7-1 Case Example 7-1: Mr. D's MMPI-2-RF Profile, continued.

137

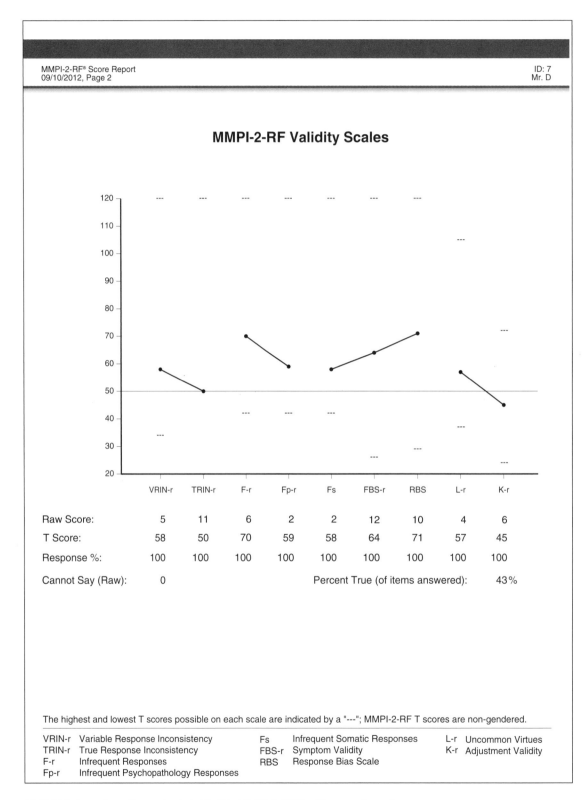

MMPI-2-RF Validity Scales

	VRIN-r	TRIN-r	F-r	Fp-r	Fs	FBS-r	RBS	L-r	K-r
Raw Score:	5	11	6	2	2	12	10	4	6
T Score:	58	50	70	59	58	64	71	57	45
Response %:	100	100	100	100	100	100	100	100	100

Cannot Say (Raw):   0   Percent True (of items answered):   43%

The highest and lowest T scores possible on each scale are indicated by a "---"; MMPI-2-RF T scores are non-gendered.

VRIN-r	Variable Response Inconsistency	Fs	Infrequent Somatic Responses	L-r	Uncommon Virtues
TRIN-r	True Response Inconsistency	FBS-r	Symptom Validity	K-r	Adjustment Validity
F-r	Infrequent Responses	RBS	Response Bias Scale		
Fp-r	Infrequent Psychopathology Responses				

FIGURE 7-1 Case Example 7-1: Mr. D's MMPI-2-RF Profile, continued.

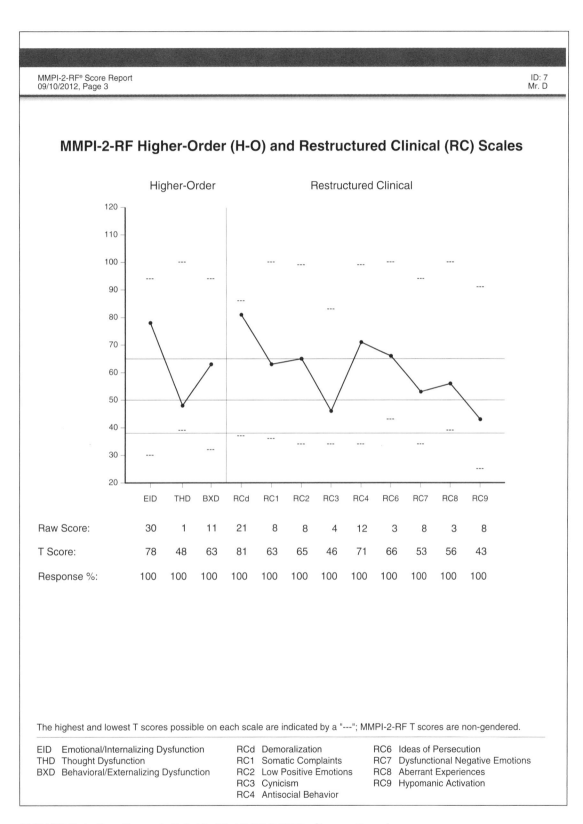

MMPI-2-RF Higher-Order (H-O) and Restructured Clinical (RC) Scales

	EID	THD	BXD	RCd	RC1	RC2	RC3	RC4	RC6	RC7	RC8	RC9
Raw Score:	30	1	11	21	8	8	4	12	3	8	3	8
T Score:	78	48	63	81	63	65	46	71	66	53	56	43
Response %:	100	100	100	100	100	100	100	100	100	100	100	100

The highest and lowest T scores possible on each scale are indicated by a "---"; MMPI-2-RF T scores are non-gendered.

EID Emotional/Internalizing Dysfunction
THD Thought Dysfunction
BXD Behavioral/Externalizing Dysfunction

RCd Demoralization
RC1 Somatic Complaints
RC2 Low Positive Emotions
RC3 Cynicism
RC4 Antisocial Behavior

RC6 Ideas of Persecution
RC7 Dysfunctional Negative Emotions
RC8 Aberrant Experiences
RC9 Hypomanic Activation

FIGURE 7-1 Case Example 7-1: Mr. D's MMPI-2-RF Profile, continued.

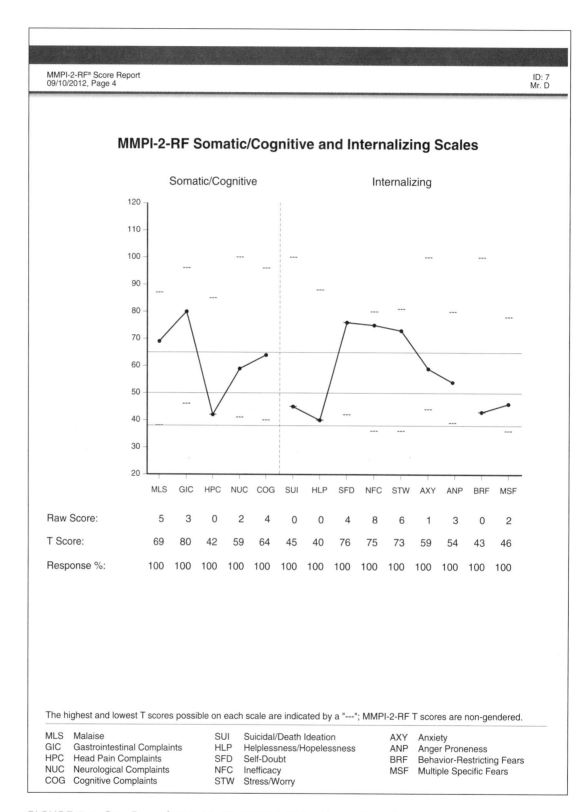

MMPI-2-RF Somatic/Cognitive and Internalizing Scales

Somatic/Cognitive   Internalizing

	MLS	GIC	HPC	NUC	COG	SUI	HLP	SFD	NFC	STW	AXY	ANP	BRF	MSF
Raw Score:	5	3	0	2	4	0	0	4	8	6	1	3	0	2
T Score:	69	80	42	59	64	45	40	76	75	73	59	54	43	46
Response %:	100	100	100	100	100	100	100	100	100	100	100	100	100	100

The highest and lowest T scores possible on each scale are indicated by a "---"; MMPI-2-RF T scores are non-gendered.

MLS	Malaise	SUI	Suicidal/Death Ideation	AXY	Anxiety
GIC	Gastrointestinal Complaints	HLP	Helplessness/Hopelessness	ANP	Anger Proneness
HPC	Head Pain Complaints	SFD	Self-Doubt	BRF	Behavior-Restricting Fears
NUC	Neurological Complaints	NFC	Inefficacy	MSF	Multiple Specific Fears
COG	Cognitive Complaints	STW	Stress/Worry		

FIGURE 7-1 Case Example 7-1: Mr. D's MMPI-2-RF Profile, continued.

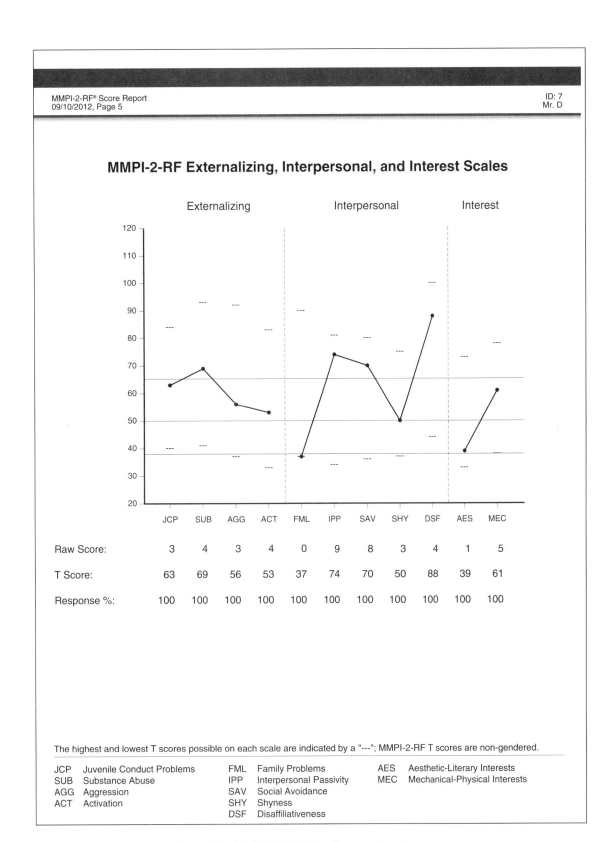

FIGURE 7-1 Case Example 7-1: Mr. D's MMPI-2-RF Profile, continued.

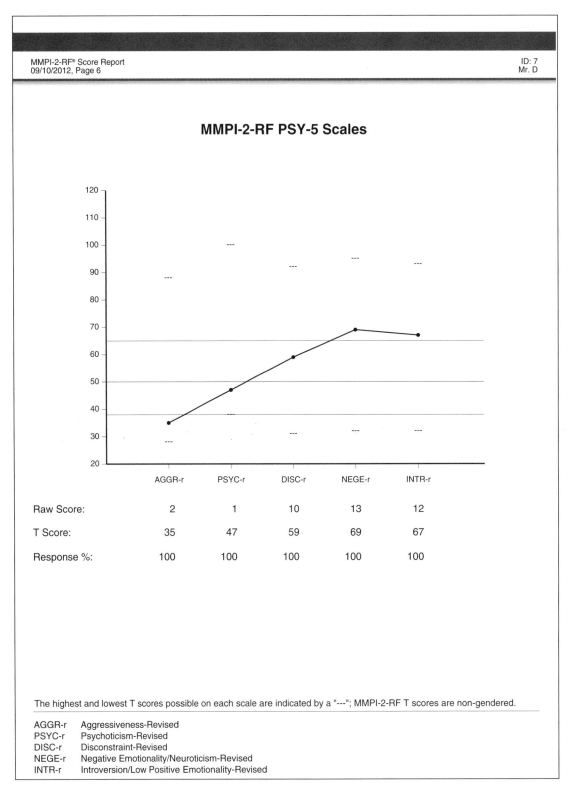

MMPI-2-RF PSY-5 Scales

	AGGR-r	PSYC-r	DISC-r	NEGE-r	INTR-r
Raw Score:	2	1	10	13	12
T Score:	35	47	59	69	67
Response %:	100	100	100	100	100

The highest and lowest T scores possible on each scale are indicated by a "---"; MMPI-2-RF T scores are non-gendered.

AGGR-r   Aggressiveness-Revised
PSYC-r   Psychoticism-Revised
DISC-r   Disconstraint-Revised
NEGE-r   Negative Emotionality/Neuroticism-Revised
INTR-r   Introversion/Low Positive Emotionality-Revised

FIGURE 7-1 Case Example 7-1: Mr. D's MMPI-2-RF Profile, continued.

MMPI-2-RF T SCORES (BY DOMAIN)

PROTOCOL VALIDITY

Content Non-Responsiveness

0	58	50
CNS	VRIN-r	TRIN-r

Over-Reporting

70	59		58	64	71
F-r	Fp-r		Fs	FBS-r	RBS

Under-Reporting

57	45
L-r	K-r

SUBSTANTIVE SCALES

Somatic/Cognitive Dysfunction

63	69	80	42	59	64
RC1	MLS	GIC	HPC	NUC	COG

Emotional Dysfunction

78		81	45	40	76	75
EID		RCd	SUI	HLP	SFD	NFC

65	67
RC2	INTR-r

53	73	59	54	43	46	69
RC7	STW	AXY	ANP	BRF	MSF	NEGE-r

Thought Dysfunction

48		66
THD		RC6

56
RC8

47
PSYC-r

Behavioral Dysfunction

63		71	63	69
BXD		RC4	JCP	SUB

43	56	53	35	59
RC9	AGG	ACT	AGGR-r	DISC-r

Interpersonal Functioning

37	46	74	70	50	88
FML	RC3	IPP	SAV	SHY	DSF

Interests

39	61
AES	MEC

Note. This information is provided to facilitate interpretation following the recommended structure for MMPI-2-RF interpretation in Chapter 5 of the *MMPI-2-RF Manual for Administration, Scoring, and Interpretation*, which provides details in the text and an outline in Table 5-1.

FIGURE 7-1 Case Example 7-1: Mr. D's MMPI-2-RF Profile, continued.

ITEM-LEVEL INFORMATION

Unscorable Responses

The test taker produced scorable responses to all the MMPI-2-RF items.

Critical Responses

Seven MMPI-2-RF scales--Suicidal/Death Ideation (SUI), Helplessness/Hopelessness (HLP), Anxiety (AXY), Ideas of Persecution (RC6), Aberrant Experiences (RC8), Substance Abuse (SUB), and Aggression (AGG)--have been designated by the test authors as having critical item content that may require immediate attention and follow-up. Items answered by the individual in the keyed direction (True or False) on a critical scale are listed below if his T score on that scale is 65 or higher. The percentage of the MMPI-2-RF normative sample that answered each item in the keyed direction is provided in parentheses following the item content.

Ideas of Persecution (RC6, T Score = 66)

194. Item Content Omitted. (True, 17.1%)
233. Item Content Omitted. (True, 5.5%)
310. Item Content Omitted. (True, 3.0%)

Substance Abuse (SUB, T Score = 69)

49. Item Content Omitted. (True, 29.6%)
141. Item Content Omitted. (True, 34.2%)
237. Item Content Omitted. (False, 27.4%)
266. Item Content Omitted. (True, 5.0%)

User-Designated Item-Level Information

The following item-level information is based on the report user's selection of additional scales, and/or of lower cutoffs for the critical scales from the previous section. Items answered by the test taker in the keyed direction (True or False) on a selected scale are listed below if his T score on that scale is at the user-designated cutoff score or higher. The percentage of the MMPI-2-RF normative sample that answered each item in the keyed direction is provided in parentheses following the item content.

Antisocial Behavior (RC4, T Score = 71)

49. Item Content Omitted. (True, 29.6%)
96. Item Content Omitted. (True, 18.8%)
126. Item Content Omitted. (False, 17.3%)
141. Item Content Omitted. (True, 34.2%)
156. Item Content Omitted. (True, 59.8%)
190. Item Content Omitted. (False, 28.6%)
205. Item Content Omitted. (True, 13.0%)
218. Item Content Omitted. (True, 4.9%)
223. Item Content Omitted. (True, 12.3%)

FIGURE 7-1 Case Example 7-1: Mr. D's MMPI-2-RF Profile, continued.

237. Item Content Omitted. (False, 27.4%)
266. Item Content Omitted. (True, 5.0%)
312. Item Content Omitted. (True, 5.5%)

Hypomanic Activation (RC9, T Score = 43)

72. Item Content Omitted. (True, 81.5%)
118. Item Content Omitted. (True, 57.4%)
166. Item Content Omitted.
    (True, 38.9%)
193. Item Content Omitted.
    (True, 32.8%)
207. Item Content Omitted. (True, 66.9%)
219. Item Content Omitted. (True, 51.5%)
256. Item Content Omitted. (True,
    65.7%)
337. Item Content Omitted. (True, 50.2%)

Behavior-Restricting Fears (BRF, T Score = 43)

No items that are scored on this scale were answered in the keyed direction.

Juvenile Conduct Problems (JCP, T Score = 63)

96. Item Content Omitted. (True, 18.8%)
205. Item Content Omitted. (True, 13.0%)
223. Item Content Omitted. (True, 12.3%)

Negative Emotionality/Neuroticism-Revised (NEGE-r, T Score = 69)

23. Item Content Omitted. (True, 39.0%)
29. Item Content Omitted. (True, 29.6%)
37. Item Content Omitted. (False, 56.3%)
73. Item Content Omitted. (False, 16.6%)
116. Item Content Omitted. (True, 40.0%)
123. Item Content Omitted. (True, 28.0%)
167. Item Content Omitted. (True, 43.7%)
209. Item Content Omitted. (True, 32.5%)
234. Item Content Omitted. (False, 53.9%)
263. Item Content Omitted.
    (True, 64.0%)
277. Item Content Omitted. (True, 8.0%)
293. Item Content Omitted. (False, 18.5%)
309. Item Content Omitted. (True, 34.0%)

End of Report

FIGURE 7-1 Case Example 7-1: Mr. D's MMPI-2-RF Profile, continued.

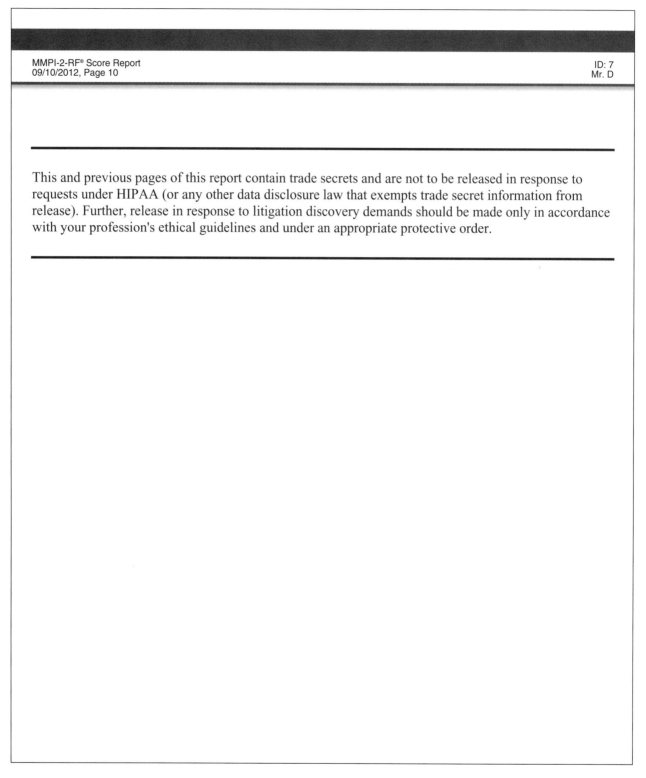

This and previous pages of this report contain trade secrets and are not to be released in response to requests under HIPAA (or any other data disclosure law that exempts trade secret information from release). Further, release in response to litigation discovery demands should be made only in accordance with your profession's ethical guidelines and under an appropriate protective order.

FIGURE 7-1 Case Example 7-1: Mr. D's MMPI-2-RF Profile.

evidence of overreporting with respect to psychopathology (F-r, Fp-r) or somatic/cognitive symptoms (Fs, FBS-r, RBS). Moreover, there was no evidence of underreporting on L-r or K-r. Consequently, his profile would be deemed valid for interpretation.

CLINICAL INTERPRETATION

Applying the interpretive strategy described in Chapter 1, we begin our interpretation with the highest elevation on the H-O Scales, which is EID (78T). Examining the RC Scales in this domain (RCd, RC2, RC7), we see that Mr. D had a very high score on RCd (81T). Taken together, his scores on EID and RCd indicate that he was likely experiencing a high degree of emotional turmoil. It would be important for the evaluator to determine the degree to which his score on RCd reflected dysphoria about his current legal situation and pending incarceration, or whether it was indicative of a more long-standing mood disorder. In addition to RCd, Mr. D produced elevated scores on RC2 (65T) and INTR-r (67T), indicating that he likely experiences significant anhedonia. The combination of RCd and RC2 is highly consistent with a depressive disorder (Sellbom, Ben-Porath, & Bagby, 2008), but the evaluation would also need to explore the degree to which depressive symptoms were a reaction to his current legal predicament. His scores on RC2 and INTR-r could also reflect social withdrawal and introversion. Although his score on RC7 was not elevated, his score on NEGE-r (69T) suggests that he does have the proclivity to experience various negative emotions. The SP Scales in this domain provide additional considerations about the particular nature of his internalized distress. He produced elevations on SFD (76T) and NFC (75T), which are both conceptually aligned with RCd (Ben-Porath, 2012b), that further indicate that the defendant experiences intense feelings of self-doubt, low self-esteem, and thoughts of inadequacy. Conceptually, his score on STW (73T) is more in line with NEGE-r and indicates that he likely feels burdened by many stressors. His interview suggested that his score on STW likely reflected concerns about his current legal situation rather than a more chronic proclivity to worry (e.g., generalized anxiety disorder). Taken together, his scores within the internalizing domain (particularly RCd, RC2, SFD, and NFC) are consistent with his history of depression that dates back to his adolescence. Within the context of the evaluation, the assessment would need to explore the ways in which his symptoms of depression impacted his sexual deviancy.

Turning to the somatic/cognitive domain, we see that Mr. D's score on RC1 is nearly elevated (63T). Consistent with this score, he has several elevations on the Somatic/Cognitive SP scales (Gastrointestinal Complaints [GIC], MLS) and almost on COG. Taken together, these scores suggest that he is preoccupied with his physical functioning and experiences gastrointestinal complaints. Given that he does not have any significant medical history, these scores (particularly MLS) suggest that he may experience physiological reactivity when stressed.

The next domain that we would review in this profile is externalizing. Although not above the traditional cutoff of 65T, Mr. D's score on BXD (63T) is nearly elevated and indicates the need to explore other indices of externalizing proclivities on the remainder of the test. His score on RC4 (71T) suggests potential problems with impulse control, antisocial tendencies, and substance abuse (Sellbom, Ben-Porath, & Stafford, 2007), which is supported by his scores on SUB (69T) and JCP (63T). RC9, AGG, and ACT, as well as AGGR-r and DISC-r, were not elevated. His score on SUB was consistent with the level of alcohol and drug misuse that he reported during the interview. He denied any previous adult legal history prior to his current case. His juvenile legal history only included one instance when the police brought him back home after he was out past curfew. However, Mr. D described several instances during which he was sanctioned with detention for "acting out" in school.

Since his score on the remaining H-O Scale (THD) was not elevated, we would turn to the RC Scales to examine any other elevations. Mr. D's only remaining RC scale that would need to be considered is RC6. His score on this scale (66T) could reflect suspiciousness and possible paranoid ideation. Review of the three items that he endorsed on this scale reveals that he believes others are likely making comments about him and treating him unkindly. It is quite possible that his endorsement of these three items reflects the negative effects of the stigma on sexual offenders, as well as his current legal situation, which has resulted in intense public scrutiny of his inappropriate sexual behavior. None of the remaining scales in the thought dysfunction domain are elevated, suggesting that it is unlikely that the defendant has a psychotic condition.

The interpersonal domain is the final one that we will examine in this profile. The RC Scale in this domain (RC3) was not elevated, but Mr. D had several elevations on the Interpersonal SP Scales, which suggested that he struggles with interpersonal relationships. His score on SAV (70T) indicated that he generally avoids social settings or endures them with discomfort. Moreover, IPP (74T) suggested that he is quite passive, unassertive, and submissive in relationships. Finally, his score on DSF reflected the intense social alienation that he experiences. Taken together, these scores are consistent with the social ineptitude displayed by many child offenders (Emmers-Sommer et al., 2004).

Overall, the defendant's scores on the MMPI-2-RF are consistent with a depressive condition. With regard to his risk assessment, the defendant's MMPI-2-RF results aligned with several of the RSVP domains, particularly major mental illness (EID, RCd, RC2), problems with substance use (RC4, SUB), problems with intimate and nonintimate relationships (RC6, DSF, IPP, SAV), and problems with planning (RCd, SFD, NFC).

Case Conclusion

The data gathered during this risk assessment indicated that the defendant's risk for sexual recidivism was in the moderate range. The defendant's limited interpersonal skills and passive-depressive personality played a significant role in him taking advantage of a vulnerable 13-year-old girl. Although the actuarial measure in this case (Static-99) placed the defendant's risk for sexual recidivism in the low category, various data gathered with the RSVP (including the MMPI-2-RF) revealed a number of concerning dynamic risk factors that pointed to a higher risk level. The defendant was sentenced to 15 years with the possibility of parole in 10 years pending completion of the sexual offender treatment program. In light of the assessments, particularly the factors identified with the MMPI-2-RF, the defendant was required to complete additional individual psychotherapy during the course of his incarceration.

CONCLUSIONS

Although the nature of sexual deviancy is not particularly well captured by the MMPI-2-RF, the instrument can nevertheless play an important role in sexual offender risk assessments. The MMPI-2-RF can provide an objective measure of response bias and capture various areas of psychopathology that have been important dynamic risk factors for sexual offenders (see Tarescavage, Cappo, et al., 2016).

Chapter 8

Mitigation in Sentencing

Psychologists are frequently called on by lawyers and courts to assist with different aspects of sentencing. These include, but are not necessarily limited to, providing information relevant to culpability (mitigation factors), identifying mental health needs relevant to sentencing and making treatment recommendations, and offering information about future risk of reoffending. Some jurisdictions (e.g., Australia and New Zealand) request information about whether a standard sentence would weigh more heavily on the defendant than on others because of his or her low intellectual functioning or mental health problems, or whether the otherwise appropriate sentence will exacerbate such problems (e.g., *R v. Verdins,* 2007, Victoria Court of Appeals). Furthermore, in some jurisdictions where the death penalty is available, mitigation assessments are frequently requested, which tend to be more extensive than standard presentence evaluations. Because the use of the MMPI-2-RF would not be meaningfully different in those evaluations compared to standard mitigation evaluations, this topic will not be discussed further (see e.g., Cunningham & Goldstein, 2013, for a review). Risk assessment has already been covered in Chapters 6 and 7. This chapter focuses explicitly on the evaluation of moral culpability (i.e., mitigation).

The issue of moral culpability is considered in virtually every jurisdiction's sentencing guidelines. It is assumed that an offender had full moral culpability for an offense of which he or she has been convicted unless proven otherwise. However, there are circumstances in which an offender's moral culpability for an offense is reduced in light of one or more mitigating factors. The most immediate mitigating factors are typically those that affect the offender's mental state at the time of the offense. These are not held to the same standard and threshold as the insanity defense (see Chapter 5) and would be inclusive of any factors that could have directly influenced the offender's mental state, as explanatory formulations do not have to be equally compelling as a formal defense (Melton et al., 2007). For instance, psychosocial factors, mental health problems, substance intoxication, and neurological impairment can all be woven into a formulation that explains the criminal conduct. Moreover, there are a number of general life circumstances that can be considered, and although they might not have a direct causal link with respect to explaining the offending behavior, they can nevertheless engender sympathy to a degree that results in a reduced sentence. For instance, neurodevelopmental factors (e.g., attention deficit hyperactivity disorder), growing up with violent, mentally ill, or substance-dependent parents; poor parental supervision; growing up in abject poverty; childhood abuse and neglect; community gang activity; recruitment into drug dealing as a child/teenager; or initiation into a gang at a young age would be potentially mitigating factors that could elicit sympathy for an offender and perhaps enhance the understanding for how the person could have eventually engaged in criminal activity. However, in some jurisdictions such information might have a lesser impact or be deemed outright inadmissible (Melton et al., 2007).

MITIGATION EVALUATIONS

The assessment of moral culpability for purposes of mitigation is similar to that of a criminal responsibility evaluation (Melton et al., 2007). The same type of information should be collected (see Chapter 5 for more detail), including clinical interview, third-party information, and psychological testing. However, the examiner should cast a much wider net with respect to life history, since there are no thresholds or constraints per se with respect to mitigation. The goal is to develop a good working formulation that provides an explanation (from a psychological perspective) of how the individual ended up committing the offense(s). Any information of what would have affected the defendant's mental state or ability to control his or her behavior could improve the judge's understanding in determining moral culpability. For instance, a young adult who grew up in an extremely violent home might have learned that violence is an acceptable manner of coping with stress and frustration. Such information would not qualify the person for a mental health defense, but could nevertheless serve to attenuate moral culpability. An individual with schizophrenia deemed to have the ability to appreciate the wrongfulness of his or her actions might nevertheless have an argument for reduced moral culpability in light of the mental state at the time of the offense. Furthermore, a more thorough life history examination would potentially reveal a number of potential factors that would elicit sympathy for the offender even if not directly or indirectly causal with respect to culpability.

CONSIDERATIONS FOR USING THE MMPI-2-RF IN MITIGATION ASSESSMENTS

The MMPI-2-RF is likely to be more useful in mitigation evaluations than for MSO evaluations. Although the issue of moral culpability is still retrospective in nature, and therefore, similar challenges apply to the use of the MMPI-2-RF, there is a greater emphasis on current functioning with respect to mitigation. The MMPI-2-RF can help elucidate potential psychopathology symptoms and maladaptive personality traits that can be considered mitigating factors. The MMPI-2-RF indeed measures a host of psychological symptoms and traits that can provide a full clinical picture that is helpful in case formulation in ways that have been covered in previous chapters. It is important to keep in mind that certain personality constellations (i.e., psychopathic personality traits) might be viewed as aggravating factors with respect to future risk and so should be considered as such, since they will also be considered at sentencing.

CASE EXAMPLE 8-1

Mr. E is a 36-year-old white New Zealand man who pleaded guilty to aggravated murder and violation of a domestic violence protection order (DVO). He had broken into his partner's home with an ax and killed her in front of her children. The victim's younger sister and two sons witnessed the attack. Mr. E was described to have been in a "rage" during the attack and multiple witnesses, including responding police officers, noted that he "seemed out of it" and was screaming uncontrollably and incoherently outside the victim's house after he had killed her. He confessed to the police on the scene and made no attempt to escape. He subsequently pleaded guilty to all charges and his lawyer requested a mitigation evaluation for sentencing purposes.

Mr. E had a life-long history of emotional difficulties, including depression, social anxiety, and poor frustration tolerance. He was emotionally and, at times, physically abused by his father who would frequently call him "stupid" and "an idiot," which was reflected in his school performance and self-perception. He was extremely shy as a child and always perceived himself as socially inept despite others suggesting he had good social skills and was generally likable. At age 18, he had become depressed to a degree where he attempted to end his life via overdose and was hospitalized for a brief time. Mr. E had a high school education and owned his construction business at the time of the offenses. He had no previous legal history.

Mr. E also had a history of emotionally volatile romantic relationships. His fiancée was unfaithful to him and he developed a general mistrust for women. About three years prior to the offense, he met a woman who was 10 years his junior. She was extremely emotionally manipulative, and when pregnant with their child, she would go back and forth about whether he was the father. Mr. E was emotionally scarred from the relationship, and, once it had ended, he sought treatment after having suicidal thoughts. Mr. E met the victim approximately 18 months prior to the offenses and he became suspicious of her when he found out she had been sending provocative pictures to her ex-partner. He claimed that there was an element of mistrust throughout the relationship, and he became more suspicious as time passed. After 9 months, she became pregnant with their child and the relationship improved somewhat. However, shortly thereafter, he found out that she had once again been communicating with an ex-boyfriend. Mr. E became so upset that he began abusing methamphetamine in an effort to self-destruct. He had previously begun using anabolic steroids about four months earlier to help with injuries to his back sustained during heavy construction work. Over time, he became more paranoid and more verbally abusive, and eventually the relationship broke down. About a month prior to the offenses, his previous partner came back into his life with their daughter and he resumed a relationship with her. The victim gave birth to their child a week prior to the offense. Because he proved difficult when trying to see his child and became verbally hostile with the victim's family members, she eventually filed for a temporary DVO.

On the day of the offenses, Mr. E found out that a DVO had been filed against him. His partner read the content of the DVO and accused him of having lied to her. She ended the relationship and said he would never see his daughter again. He felt that he had now lost both of his children; the chance for a family, which he desperately wanted; was struggling with drug abuse; and decided to end his life. First, he decided to stop by the victim's house and destroy his furniture that she refused to give back to him. As he was traveling to her house, he was becoming more and more enraged to a point where he tried to find Valium in his car. He called his sister, and, according to her report, was screaming incoherently. When he reached the victim's house, he described being in a state of rage, he grabbed an ax from his vehicle, cut down the door, and once he saw the victim, he chased after her and struck her down with the ax. She died instantly. Mr. E stated that "I knew what I was doing, but could not control myself. I was in a fucking rage." He added that "it felt like an out of body experience. I was looking down at myself doing this horrible act." Once he had realized what he had done, he walked outside and started screaming continuously.

Issues Pertaining to Moral Culpability

In developing a conceptual model for explaining the offending behavior, these are several factors to examine. Mr. E suffered from life-long emotional instability, social anxiety, and depression. He had either attempted or tried to attempt suicide several times in his life. He was prone to strong self-deprecating reactions when romantic relationships broke down. He was further interpersonally suspicious, which intensified once he started abusing methamphetamine in an effort to self-destruct. His anger and hostility also became gradually worse, likely owing to his steroid abuse. At the time of the offense he experienced the breakdown in his relationship and the loss of his children as intense emotional trauma, and he wanted to end his life. However, he was also very angry (because of the DVO, but also because she had been keeping his furniture from him for months) and decided to go over to the victim's house to destroy his property. Upon arrival, he entered a rage state, likely influenced by steroids, and was quite possibly in a stress-induced dissociative state.

Furthermore, mitigation factors that might elicit sympathy but not be directly affecting his mental state at the time of the offenses would be childhood abuse, life-long depression, and social anxiety. In addition, he had never previously engaged in illegal activity and was generally a prosocial member of society.

MMPI-2-RF Results

PROTOCOL VALIDITY

Mr. E did not produce a response to five of the items on the test (CNS = 5). Most of the items dealt directly with anger control and aggression, which was particularly relevant in his current case, with ANP and AGG having less than 90 percent scorable responses. It is possible he elected to not respond to items with content that could have been viewed as incriminating. He responded consistently to the items throughout the test (VRIN-r = 53, TRIN-r = 50). In terms of overreporting, his F-r score was 101T, which raises concerns about protocol validity. However, in light of his long history of emotional problems and the fact that Fp-r was 68T, overreporting of psychopathology was deemed less likely than genuine psychopathology, which can also produce high F-r scores. There was no evidence of overreporting with respect to somatic/cognitive symptoms (Fs, FBS-r, RBS). Moreover, there was no evidence of underreporting on L-r or K-r. Consequently, the profile would be deemed valid for interpretation.

CLINICAL INTERPRETATION

As noted, with regard to substantive scale interpretive framework, the H-O Scales are to be consulted first to organize the interpretation. In this case, EID, with a T score of 82, means that the emotional dysfunction domain should be considered first. The combination of these scales indicates that Mr. E is likely experiencing significant emotional turmoil (EID, RCd). He is likely distressed, unhappy, and dissatisfied with his life. He is further likely experiencing considerable symptoms of depression and anxiety (EID, RCd, RC2, RC7), and with NEGE-r at 66T he is dispositionally prone to experience a wide array of negative emotions, including sadness, anxiety, anger, and guilt. He is likely to be stress reactive, worry to an obsessive degree, and experience intense levels of anxiety (STW), including potential posttraumatic stress reactions as a result of trauma (AXY; see Sellbom, Lee, et al., 2012). Mr. E is very likely experiencing considerable thoughts about death and suicide (SUI = 100T), and thus, is at risk for such behaviors. Indeed, he explained in the interview that he exhibited considerable self-hatred, which was further exacerbated by what he had done to his ex-partner, and it was consistent with his general responses to feeling emotionally overwhelmed. Moreover, he tends to feel helpless about his circumstances and hopeless regarding

Minnesota Multiphasic
Personality Inventory-2
Restructured Form®

Score Report

MMPI-2-RF®

Minnesota Multiphasic Personality Inventory-2-Restructured Form®

Yossef S. Ben-Porath, PhD, & Auke Tellegen, PhD

Name:	Mr. E
ID Number:	8
Age:	36
Gender:	Male
Marital Status:	Not reported
Years of Education:	Not reported
Date Assessed:	10/09/2015

ALWAYS LEARNING

PEARSON

FIGURE 8-1 Case Example 8-1: Mr. E's MMPI-2-RF Profile, continued.

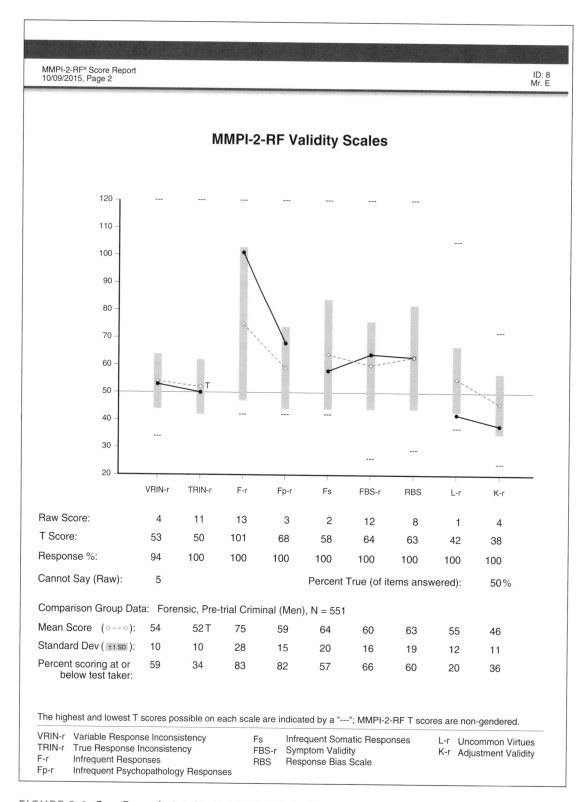

MMPI-2-RF Validity Scales

	VRIN-r	TRIN-r	F-r	Fp-r	Fs	FBS-r	RBS	L-r	K-r
Raw Score:	4	11	13	3	2	12	8	1	4
T Score:	53	50	101	68	58	64	63	42	38
Response %:	94	100	100	100	100	100	100	100	100

Cannot Say (Raw): 5   Percent True (of items answered): 50%

Comparison Group Data: Forensic, Pre-trial Criminal (Men), N = 551

Mean Score (◇‑‑‑◇):	54	52 T	75	59	64	60	63	55	46
Standard Dev (±1 SD):	10	10	28	15	20	16	19	12	11
Percent scoring at or below test taker:	59	34	83	82	57	66	60	20	36

The highest and lowest T scores possible on each scale are indicated by a "---"; MMPI-2-RF T scores are non-gendered.

VRIN-r	Variable Response Inconsistency	Fs	Infrequent Somatic Responses	L-r Uncommon Virtues
TRIN-r	True Response Inconsistency	FBS-r	Symptom Validity	K-r Adjustment Validity
F-r	Infrequent Responses	RBS	Response Bias Scale	
Fp-r	Infrequent Psychopathology Responses			

FIGURE 8-1 Case Example 8-1: Mr. E's MMPI-2-RF Profile, continued.

MMPI-2-RF Higher-Order (H-O) and Restructured Clinical (RC) Scales

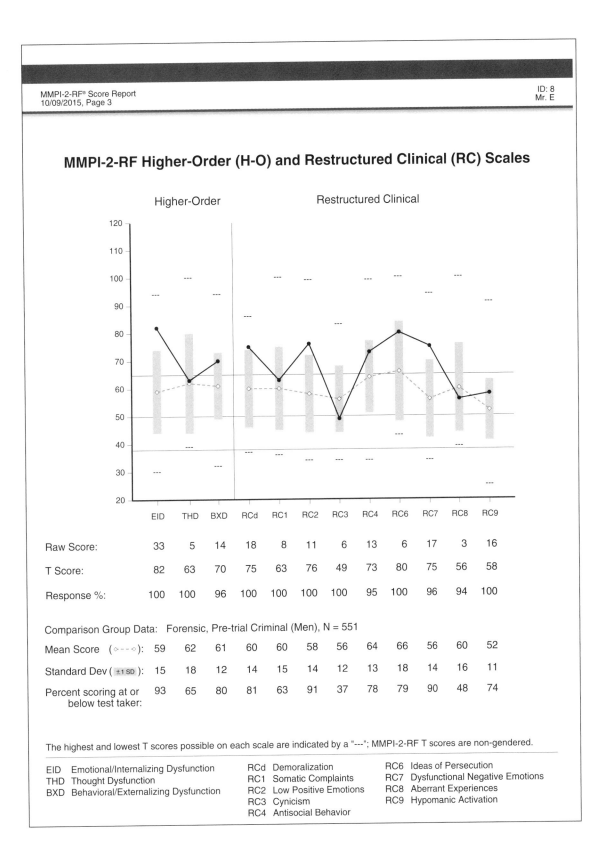

	EID	THD	BXD	RCd	RC1	RC2	RC3	RC4	RC6	RC7	RC8	RC9
Raw Score:	33	5	14	18	8	11	6	13	6	17	3	16
T Score:	82	63	70	75	63	76	49	73	80	75	56	58
Response %:	100	100	96	100	100	100	100	95	100	96	94	100

Comparison Group Data: Forensic, Pre-trial Criminal (Men), N = 551

	EID	THD	BXD	RCd	RC1	RC2	RC3	RC4	RC6	RC7	RC8	RC9
Mean Score (◇---◇):	59	62	61	60	60	58	56	64	66	56	60	52
Standard Dev (±1 SD):	15	18	12	14	15	14	12	13	18	14	16	11
Percent scoring at or below test taker:	93	65	80	81	63	91	37	78	79	90	48	74

The highest and lowest T scores possible on each scale are indicated by a "---"; MMPI-2-RF T scores are non-gendered.

EID Emotional/Internalizing Dysfunction	RCd Demoralization	RC6 Ideas of Persecution
THD Thought Dysfunction	RC1 Somatic Complaints	RC7 Dysfunctional Negative Emotions
BXD Behavioral/Externalizing Dysfunction	RC2 Low Positive Emotions	RC8 Aberrant Experiences
	RC3 Cynicism	RC9 Hypomanic Activation
	RC4 Antisocial Behavior	

FIGURE 8-1 Case Example 8-1: Mr. E's MMPI-2-RF Profile, continued.

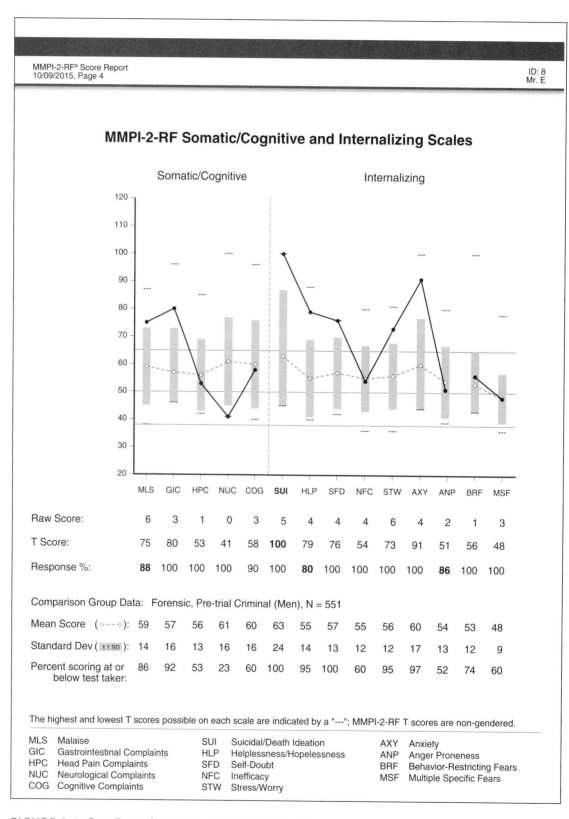

MMPI-2-RF Somatic/Cognitive and Internalizing Scales

Somatic/Cognitive   Internalizing

	MLS	GIC	HPC	NUC	COG	SUI	HLP	SFD	NFC	STW	AXY	ANP	BRF	MSF
Raw Score:	6	3	1	0	3	5	4	4	4	6	4	2	1	3
T Score:	75	80	53	41	58	**100**	79	76	54	73	91	51	56	48
Response %:	**88**	100	100	100	90	100	**80**	100	100	100	100	**86**	100	100

Comparison Group Data: Forensic, Pre-trial Criminal (Men), N = 551

	MLS	GIC	HPC	NUC	COG	SUI	HLP	SFD	NFC	STW	AXY	ANP	BRF	MSF
Mean Score (◇--◇):	59	57	56	61	60	63	55	57	55	56	60	54	53	48
Standard Dev (±1 SD):	14	16	13	16	16	24	14	13	12	12	17	13	12	9
Percent scoring at or below test taker:	86	92	53	23	60	100	95	100	60	95	97	52	74	60

The highest and lowest T scores possible on each scale are indicated by a "---"; MMPI-2-RF T scores are non-gendered.

MLS	Malaise	SUI	Suicidal/Death Ideation	AXY	Anxiety
GIC	Gastrointestinal Complaints	HLP	Helplessness/Hopelessness	ANP	Anger Proneness
HPC	Head Pain Complaints	SFD	Self-Doubt	BRF	Behavior-Restricting Fears
NUC	Neurological Complaints	NFC	Inefficacy	MSF	Multiple Specific Fears
COG	Cognitive Complaints	STW	Stress/Worry		

FIGURE 8-1   Case Example 8-1: Mr. E's MMPI-2-RF Profile, continued.

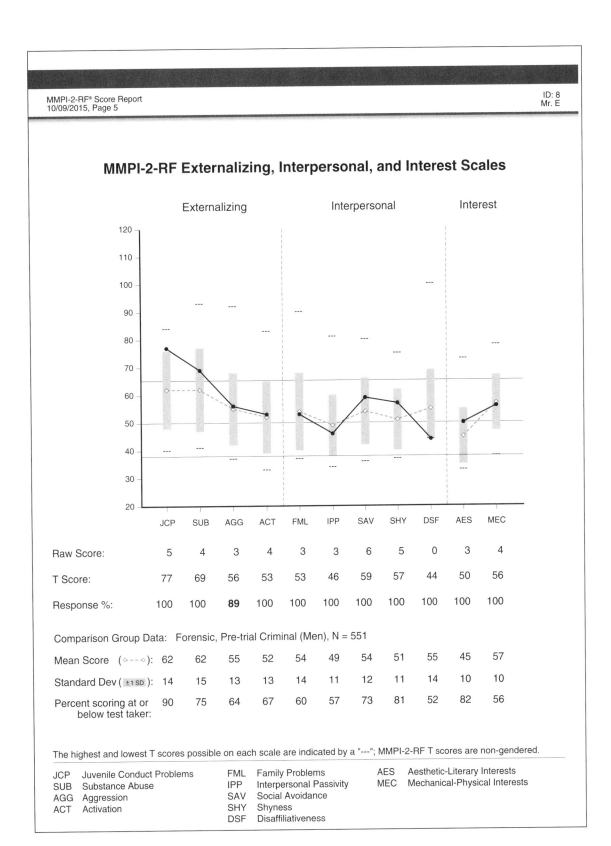

MMPI-2-RF Externalizing, Interpersonal, and Interest Scales

	JCP	SUB	AGG	ACT	FML	IPP	SAV	SHY	DSF	AES	MEC
Raw Score:	5	4	3	4	3	3	6	5	0	3	4
T Score:	77	69	56	53	53	46	59	57	44	50	56
Response %:	100	100	**89**	100	100	100	100	100	100	100	100

Comparison Group Data: Forensic, Pre-trial Criminal (Men), N = 551

Mean Score (◇--◇):	62	62	55	52	54	49	54	51	55	45	57
Standard Dev (±1 SD):	14	15	13	13	14	11	12	11	14	10	10
Percent scoring at or below test taker:	90	75	64	67	60	57	73	81	52	82	56

The highest and lowest T scores possible on each scale are indicated by a "---"; MMPI-2-RF T scores are non-gendered.

JCP	Juvenile Conduct Problems	FML	Family Problems	AES	Aesthetic-Literary Interests
SUB	Substance Abuse	IPP	Interpersonal Passivity	MEC	Mechanical-Physical Interests
AGG	Aggression	SAV	Social Avoidance		
ACT	Activation	SHY	Shyness		
		DSF	Disaffiliativeness		

FIGURE 8-1 Case Example 8-1: Mr. E's MMPI-2-RF Profile, continued.

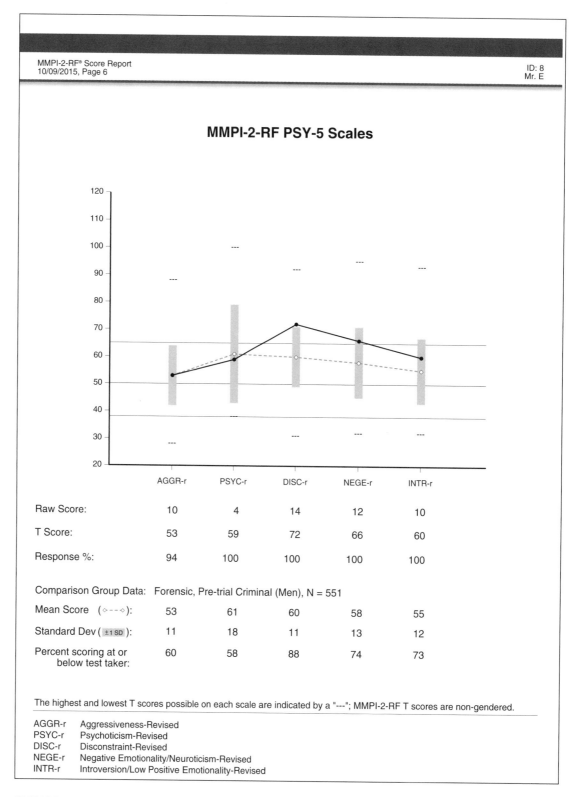

MMPI-2-RF PSY-5 Scales

	AGGR-r	PSYC-r	DISC-r	NEGE-r	INTR-r
Raw Score:	10	4	14	12	10
T Score:	53	59	72	66	60
Response %:	94	100	100	100	100

Comparison Group Data: Forensic, Pre-trial Criminal (Men), N = 551

Mean Score (◇- - -◇):	53	61	60	58	55
Standard Dev (±1 SD):	11	18	11	13	12
Percent scoring at or below test taker:	60	58	88	74	73

The highest and lowest T scores possible on each scale are indicated by a "---"; MMPI-2-RF T scores are non-gendered.

AGGR-r	Aggressiveness-Revised
PSYC-r	Psychoticism-Revised
DISC-r	Disconstraint-Revised
NEGE-r	Negative Emotionality/Neuroticism-Revised
INTR-r	Introversion/Low Positive Emotionality-Revised

FIGURE 8-1 Case Example 8-1: Mr. E's MMPI-2-RF Profile, continued.

MMPI-2-RF T SCORES (BY DOMAIN)

PROTOCOL VALIDITY

Content Non-Responsiveness	5	53	50
	CNS	VRIN-r	TRIN-r

Over-Reporting	101	68		58	64	63
	F-r	Fp-r		Fs	FBS-r	RBS

Under-Reporting	42	38
	L-r	K-r

SUBSTANTIVE SCALES

Somatic/Cognitive Dysfunction	63	75*	80	53	41	58
	RC1	MLS	GIC	HPC	NUC	COG

Emotional Dysfunction	82	75	100	79*	76	54	
	EID	RCd	SUI	HLP	SFD	NFC	
		76	60				
		RC2	INTR-r				
		75	73	91	51*	56	48	66
		RC7	STW	AXY	ANP	BRF	MSF	NEGE-r

Thought Dysfunction	63	80	
	THD	RC6	
		56	
		RC8	
		59	
		PSYC-r	

Behavioral Dysfunction	70	73	77	69		
	BXD	RC4	JCP	SUB		
		58	56*	53	53	72
		RC9	AGG	ACT	AGGR-r	DISC-r

Interpersonal Functioning	53	49	46	59	57	44
	FML	RC3	IPP	SAV	SHY	DSF

Interests	50	56
	AES	MEC

*The test taker provided scorable responses to less than 90% of the items scored on this scale. See the relevant profile page for the specific percentage.

Note. This information is provided to facilitate interpretation following the recommended structure for MMPI-2-RF interpretation in Chapter 5 of the *MMPI-2-RF Manual for Administration, Scoring, and Interpretation*, which provides details in the text and an outline in Table 5-1.

FIGURE 8-1 Case Example 8-1: Mr. E's MMPI-2-RF Profile, continued.

ITEM-LEVEL INFORMATION

Unscorable Responses

Following is a list of items to which the test taker did not provide scorable responses. Unanswered or double answered (both True and False) items are unscorable. The scales on which the items appear are in parentheses following the item content.

257. Item Content Omitted. (VRIN-r, RC8, COG)
318. Item Content Omitted. (VRIN-r, RC7, ANP)
329. Item Content Omitted. (VRIN-r, BXD, RC4, AGG, AGGR-r)
333. Item Content Omitted. (MLS)
336. Item Content Omitted. (HLP)

Critical Responses

Seven MMPI-2-RF scales--Suicidal/Death Ideation (SUI), Helplessness/Hopelessness (HLP), Anxiety (AXY), Ideas of Persecution (RC6), Aberrant Experiences (RC8), Substance Abuse (SUB), and Aggression (AGG)--have been designated by the test authors as having critical item content that may require immediate attention and follow-up. Items answered by the individual in the keyed direction (True or False) on a critical scale are listed below if his T score on that scale is 65 or higher. The percentage of the MMPI-2-RF normative sample (NS) and of the Forensic, Pre-trial Criminal (Men) comparison group (CG) that answered each item in the keyed direction are provided in parentheses following the item content.

Suicidal/Death Ideation (SUI, T Score = 100)
  93. Item Content Omitted. (True; NS 3.7%, CG 27.6%)
  120. Item Content Omitted. (True; NS 2.4%, CG 20.1%)
  164. Item Content Omitted. (True; NS 1.7%, CG 19.4%)
  251. Item Content Omitted. (True; NS 3.0%, CG 17.1%)
  334. Item Content Omitted. (True; NS 13.5%, CG 26.1%)

Helplessness/Hopelessness (HLP, T Score = 79)
  135. Item Content Omitted. (True; NS 24.2%, CG 35.4%)
  169. Item Content Omitted. (True; NS 4.3%, CG 26.0%)
  214. Item Content Omitted. (True; NS 10.4%, CG 24.3%)
  282. Item Content Omitted. (False; NS 17.3%, CG 37.4%)

Anxiety (AXY, T Score = 91)
  79. Item Content Omitted. (True; NS 6.2%, CG 30.5%)
  146. Item Content Omitted. (True; NS 1.8%, CG 9.3%)
  228. Item Content Omitted. (True; NS 17.3%, CG 31.8%)
  275. Item Content Omitted. (True; NS 5.0%, CG 28.1%)

FIGURE 8-1 Case Example 8-1: Mr. E's MMPI-2-RF Profile, continued.

Ideas of Persecution (RC6, T Score = 80)

    110. Item Content Omitted. (True; NS 9.9%, CG 36.3%)
    150. Item Content Omitted. (True; NS 2.0%, CG 7.8%)
    194. Item Content Omitted. (True; NS 17.1%, CG 42.5%)
    212. Item Content Omitted. (False; NS 9.1%, CG 38.1%)
    233. Item Content Omitted. (True; NS 5.5%, CG 32.3%)
    264. Item Content Omitted. (True; NS 5.3%, CG 28.5%)

Substance Abuse (SUB, T Score = 69)

    141. Item Content Omitted. (True; NS 34.2%, CG 60.1%)
    192. Item Content Omitted. (True; NS 11.2%, CG 26.7%)
    237. Item Content Omitted. (False; NS 27.4%, CG 55.4%)
    266. Item Content Omitted. (True; NS 5.0%, CG 51.9%)

User-Designated Item-Level Information

The following item-level information is based on the report user's selection of additional scales, and/or of lower cutoffs for the critical scales from the previous section. Items answered by the test taker in the keyed direction (True or False) on a selected scale are listed below if his T score on that scale is at the user-designated cutoff score or higher. The percentage of the MMPI-2-RF normative sample (NS) and of the Forensic, Pre-trial Criminal (Men) comparison group (CG) that answered each item in the keyed direction are provided in parentheses following the item content.

Behavioral/Externalizing Dysfunction (BXD, T Score = 70)

    21. Item Content Omitted. (True; NS 47.1%, CG 64.2%)
    61. Item Content Omitted. (False; NS 61.6%, CG 67.9%)
    66. Item Content Omitted. (True; NS 20.3%, CG 60.3%)
    96. Item Content Omitted. (True; NS 18.8%, CG 49.4%)
    107. Item Content Omitted. (True; NS 47.3%, CG 40.1%)
    131. Item Content Omitted. (True; NS 43.3%, CG 43.0%)
    156. Item Content Omitted. (True; NS 59.8%, CG 61.2%)
    190. Item Content Omitted. (False; NS 28.6%, CG 85.8%)
    193. Item Content Omitted.
        (True; NS 32.8%, CG 30.7%)
    223. Item Content Omitted. (True; NS 12.3%, CG 50.1%)
    237. Item Content Omitted. (False; NS 27.4%, CG 55.4%)
    253. IItem Content Omitted. (True; NS 5.8%, CG 25.8%)
    266. Item Content Omitted. (True; NS 5.0%, CG 51.9%)
    316. Item Content Omitted. (True; NS 45.1%, CG 59.7%)

FIGURE 8-1 Case Example 8-1: Mr. E's MMPI-2-RF Profile, continued.

Antisocial Behavior (RC4, T Score = 73)

    5. Item Content Omitted. (True; NS 36.7%, CG 54.3%)
   21. Item Content Omitted. (True; NS 47.1%, CG 64.2%)
   38. Item Content Omitted. (False; NS 18.8%, CG 20.3%)
   66. Item Content Omitted. (True; NS 20.3%, CG 60.3%)
   96. Item Content Omitted. (True; NS 18.8%, CG
      49.4%)
 126. Item Content Omitted. (False; NS 17.3%, CG 36.7%)
 141. Item Content Omitted. (True; NS 34.2%, CG 60.1%)
 156. Item Content Omitted. (True; NS 59.8%, CG 61.2%)
 190. Item Content Omitted. (False; NS 28.6%, CG 85.8%)
 223. Item Content Omitted. (True; NS 12.3%, CG 50.1%)
 237. Item Content Omitted. (False; NS 27.4%, CG 55.4%)
 253. Item Content Omitted. (True; NS 5.8%, CG
      25.8%)
 266. Item Content Omitted. (True; NS 5.0%, CG 51.9%)

Dysfunctional Negative Emotions (RC7, T Score = 75)

   23. Item Content Omitted. (True; NS 39.0%, CG 43.6%)
   35. Item Content Omitted. (True; NS 36.6%, CG 37.7%)
   51. Item Content Omitted. (True; NS 15.4%, CG
      24.3%)
   63. Item Content Omitted. (True; NS 24.3%, CG 43.9%)
   91. Item Content Omitted. (True; NS 37.7%, CG 41.0%)
 119. Item Content Omitted. (True; NS 39.5%, CG 40.7%)
 132. Item Content Omitted. (True; NS 10.5%, CG 21.2%)
 146. Item Content Omitted. (True; NS 1.8%, CG 9.3%)
 161. Item Content Omitted. (True; NS
      8.8%, CG 24.0%)
 206. Item Content Omitted.
      (True; NS 41.6%, CG 53.5%)
 228. Item Content Omitted. (True; NS 17.3%, CG 31.8%)
 235. Item Content Omitted. (True; NS 12.1%,
      CG 26.1%)
 263. Item Content Omitted.
      (True; NS 64.0%, CG 60.1%)
 275. Item Content Omitted. (True; NS 5.0%, CG
      28.1%)
 303. Item Content Omitted. (True; NS 28.6%, CG 38.8%)
 322. Item Content Omitted. (True; NS 46.8%, CG 44.3%)
 335. Item Content Omitted. (True; NS 30.1%, CG 48.5%)

FIGURE 8-1 Case Example 8-1: Mr. E's MMPI-2-RF Profile, continued.

Hypomanic Activation (RC9, T Score = 58)

    39. Item Content Omitted. (True; NS
        51.0%, CG 62.4%)

    61. Item Content Omitted. (False; NS 61.6%, CG 67.9%)

    72. Item Content Omitted. (True; NS 81.5%, CG
        75.7%)

    107. Item Content Omitted. (True; NS 47.3%, CG 40.1%)

    131. Item Content Omitted. (True; NS 43.3%, CG 43.0%)

    143. Item Content Omitted. (True; NS 27.5%, CG 29.6%)

    166. Item Content Omitted.
        (True; NS 38.9%, CG 39.2%)

    181. Item Content Omitted. (True; NS 35.3%, CG 39.2%)

    193. Item Content Omitted.
        (True; NS 32.8%, CG 30.7%)

    207. Item Content Omitted. (True; NS 66.9%,
        CG 54.4%)

    244. Item Content Omitted. (True; NS
        56.9%, CG 71.1%)

    256. Item Content Omitted. (True; NS
        65.7%, CG 63.5%)

    305. Item Content Omitted. (True; NS 37.6%, CG 39.9%)

    316. Item Content Omitted. (True; NS 45.1%, CG
        59.7%)

    327. Item Content Omitted.
        (True; NS 41.7%, CG 47.2%)

    337. Item Content Omitted. (True; NS 50.2%,
        CG 55.2%)

Behavior-Restricting Fears (BRF, T Score = 56)

    90. Item Content Omitted. (True; NS 15.7%, CG 25.4%)

Juvenile Conduct Problems (JCP, T Score = 77)

    21. Item Content Omitted. (True; NS 47.1%, CG 64.2%)

    66. Item Content Omitted. (True; NS 20.3%, CG 60.3%)

    96. Item Content Omitted. (True; NS 18.8%, CG
        49.4%)

    223. Item Content Omitted. (True; NS 12.3%, CG 50.1%)

    253. Item Content Omitted. (True; NS 5.8%, CG
        25.8%)

Disconstraint-Revised (DISC-r, T Score = 72)

    21. Item Content Omitted. (True; NS 47.1%, CG 64.2%)

    61. Item Content Omitted. (False; NS 61.6%, CG 67.9%)

    66. Item Content Omitted. (True; NS 20.3%, CG 60.3%)

FIGURE 8-1 Case Example 8-1: Mr. E's MMPI-2-RF Profile, continued.

75. Item Content Omitted. (True; NS 50.3%, CG 60.3%)
107. Item Content Omitted. (True; NS 47.3%, CG 40.1%)
115. Item Content Omitted. (True; NS 55.0%, CG 56.1%)
131. Item Content Omitted. (True; NS 43.3%, CG 43.0%)
156. Item Content Omitted. (True; NS 59.8%, CG 61.2%)
190. Item Content Omitted. (False; NS 28.6%, CG 85.8%)
193. Item Content Omitted.
    (True; NS 32.8%, CG 30.7%)
223. Item Content Omitted. (True; NS 12.3%, CG 50.1%)
237. Item Content Omitted. (False; NS 27.4%, CG 55.4%)
253. Item Content Omitted. (True; NS 5.8%, CG
    25.8%)
300. Item Content Omitted. (True; NS 26.5%, CG 54.4%)

Negative Emotionality/Neuroticism-Revised (NEGE-r, T Score = 66)
23. Item Content Omitted. (True; NS 39.0%, CG 43.6%)
37. Item Content Omitted. (False; NS 56.3%, CG 57.7%)
73. Item Content Omitted. (False; NS 16.6%, CG 35.6%)
116. Item Content Omitted. (True; NS 40.0%, CG 55.7%)
123. Item Content Omitted. (True; NS 28.0%, CG 52.3%)
146. Item Content Omitted. (True; NS 1.8%, CG 9.3%)
167. Item Content Omitted. (True; NS 43.7%, CG 48.3%)
206. Item Content Omitted.
    (True; NS 41.6%, CG 53.5%)
209. Item Content Omitted. (True; NS 32.5%, CG 80.6%)
234. Item Content Omitted. (False; NS 53.9%, CG 75.3%)
263. Item Content Omitted.
    (True; NS 64.0%, CG 60.1%)
309. Item Content Omitted. (True; NS 34.0%, CG 56.4%)

End of Report

FIGURE 8-1 Case Example 8-1: Mr. E's MMPI-2-RF Profile.

the future (HLP), which is not unexpected in light of the uncertain (and likely very lengthy) prison sentence. He is also likely to feel worthless and exhibit thoughts of inadequacy (SFD, NFC). Moreover, Mr. E is unlikely to experience positive emotions such as happiness, or to be socially engaged (RC2, INTR-r). Overall, these findings are quite corroborating of his depression, life-long anxiety, and emotional instability. It is noteworthy that the ANP scale could not be interpreted, since only 86 percent of items could be scored.

It is recommended that the somatic/cognitive domain be interpreted immediately after the emotional dysfunction domain, if applicable. Here, the only elevated scales were MLS (75T) and GIC (80T). These scales might be suggestive of significant somatic preoccupation, especially if medical problems can be ruled out. In Mr. E's case, however, he exhibited a long history of debilitating back problems and gastroesophageal reflux disease, which would be potential reasons for why he endorsed these items, especially as he was quite concerned about his back injuries to a degree where he began abusing anabolic steroids.

The next domain that warrants interpretation is the behavioral dysfunction domain given that BXD is the second most elevated H-O scale at 70T. Indeed, Mr. E endorsed a wide range of externalizing proclivities (BXD). The externalizing scales (RC4, JCP, SUB, DISC-r) collectively indicate that he is likely prone to acting out, had difficulties in school as a child, and may have acted in socially deviant ways. Moreover, he likely has a proclivity toward impulsive and thrill-seeking behavior (DISC-r). It is important to consider corroborating information. Mr. E does not have a substantial antisocial history nor has he displayed considerable evidence of lifestyle impulsivity. However, he did act out in school, is emotionally impulsive, and had recently engaged in self-destructive substance abuse, which could be the sources of elevation for these scales.

Since no additional H-O Scales were elevated, the RC Scales should be considered next. The only RC Scale not yet interpreted is RC6 (80T). This elevation indicates that Mr. E tends to be mistrustful and fears being victimized and hurt by others. He is likely to be guarded in interactions with others and exhibit paranoid ideation, which was consistent with his interpersonal sensitivity, especially in romantic relationships. Although RC6 scores this high might be indicative of persecutory delusions, it is important to consider that he has never before shown evidence of such symptoms and did not impress as such during the interview. Indeed, a review of the critical items (see also Chapter 4) did not indicate endorsement of the more pathological items.

Case Conclusion

The MMPI-2-RF results provided a clear picture of emotional dysregulation, generalized anxiety, social deviance, substance abuse, and a paranoid interpersonal style that corroborated both the clinical interview and third-party information. This information allowed the forensic examiner to argue more strongly for emotional instability and interpersonal sensitivity that, when coupled with substance abuse (anabolic steroids and methamphetamine), provided an explanatory formulation of his mental state at the time of the offenses. Moreover, it provided further evidence for his proneness to depression and suicidal ideation, which were key issues in his mitigation defense. Upon considering the report and evidence heard in court, the judge decided there was a sufficient reduction in moral culpability and other mitigating factors to set a time-limited sentence of 20 years, rather than imposing life-imprisonment.

CONCLUSIONS

The MMPI-2-RF can be very helpful in mitigation evaluations. Although similar challenges to MSO evaluations exist with respect to the retrospective aspects of the evaluation, a mitigation evaluation casts a much wider net and can include current functioning. In the case just presented, the MMPI-2-RF results provided significant corroborating information about the persistence of emotional instability, depression, suicidality, and paranoid ideation. It also captured more recent externalizing proclivities, including substance abuse.

PART III

Civil Forensic Applications of the MMPI-2-RF

Chapter 9

Child Custody

Child custody evaluations are undertaken to provide assistance to family courts in making decisions regarding custody and visitation in accordance with criteria provided in state statutes. These evaluations are among the most difficult of forensic psychological evaluations to complete because of their multifaceted nature and the high stakes for all involved. Unlike most forensic evaluations that involve assessing one evaluee for a particular circumscribed legal issue (e.g., criminal responsibility), child custody evaluations typically involve the assessment of numerous individuals (e.g., parents, children) as well potential stepparents and grandparents. Moreover, child custody evaluations involve not only an assessment of the psychological functioning of those involved, but also consideration of additional factors, such as parenting ability, medical/health status, family finances/insurance, housing situations, schools, and legal issues. Parents involved in child custody disputes are often highly emotional, antagonistic toward each other, and greatly invested in obtaining their particular desired outcome.

Since the 1970s, child custodial decisions in family court have been based on the "best interests of the child" standard (Cooke & Norris, 2011; Gould & Martindale, 2013). This standard has been adopted by most states and family courts as the guiding principle and legal standard for determining custody arrangements. In 2010, the American Psychological Association published "Guidelines for Child Custody Evaluations in Family Law Proceedings" to assist evaluators by providing objectives for child custody evaluations (e.g., striving for the child's welfare, striving for impartiality). These guidelines incorporate the American Psychological Association Ethics Codes that apply to child custody evaluations (e.g., avoiding conflicts of interest and multiple relationships). They define the purpose of a child custody evaluation as:

Psychologists strive to identify the psychological best interests of the child. To this end, they are encouraged to weigh and incorporate such overlapping factors as family dynamics and interactions; cultural and environmental variables; relevant challenges and aptitudes for all examined parties; and the child's educational, physical, and psychological needs.

In contrast to other forensic psychological evaluations (particularly in the criminal arena), where statutory language often requires the presence of a mental disease, condition, or defect, in child custody evaluations, psychiatric diagnoses are only part of the overall scope of the assessment. Moreover, psychiatric diagnoses are important only to the extent that they have an impact on the parents' ability to provide an environment that is in the best interests of the child. For example, an anxiety or depressive condition would not by itself indicate that a parent was not fit to maintain custody of their child. However, if these or any other psychiatric conditions interfere with the parent providing a safe, stable, and supportive home environment in the best interest of the child, then the evaluator might opine that the condition is relevant to custody arrangements.

CHILD CUSTODY ASSESSMENT

Consistent with the American Psychological Association guidelines, child custody evaluations should incorporate multiple sources of information. Various sources, including surveys of clinicians conducting child custody evaluations, suggest that most evaluations include clinical interviews of the parents and children, collateral interviews with other relevant individuals (e.g., teachers, health care providers), extensive record reviews, observations of parent-child interactions, home visits, and psychological testing (Ackerman & Ackerman, 1997; Ackerman & Pritzl, 2011; Bow & Quinnell, 2001; Gould & Martindale, 2013; Martindale & Gould, 2007; Otto, Buffington-Vollum, & Edens, 2003). Although the American Psychological Association guidelines provide some assistance in planning an evaluation, they do not identify specific evaluation methods, test instruments, or interview questions.

Martindale and Gould (2004) established a basis for a forensic model of child custody evaluations, so that courts would be provided with scientifically informed and evidence-based opinions. In their various works, Martindale and Gould noted that any custody evaluation should, among other things, begin with a clear indication of the evaluator's role, and that the purpose and focus of the evaluation should be defined by the court. They also note that the evaluation should be completed under the auspices of specific psycho-legal issues or questions requested by the court. In their list of components for a forensic model of child custody evaluation, Martindale and Gould noted that the selection of psychological tests for these evaluations should be guided by the 1985 and 1999 (updated again in 2014) *Standards for Educational and Psychological Testing* (American Educational Research Association, American Psychological Association, & National Council on Measurement in Education, 1985/1999/2014), with particular attention to issues of reliability and validity. Numerous studies have examined the psychometric properties of the MMPI-2-RF, and several have specifically examined them in child custody settings (Archer et al., 2012; Kauffman et al., 2015; Pinsoneault & Ezzo, 2012; Sellbom & Bagby, 2008).

Psychological testing is a common component of child custody evaluations. Self-report measures are among the most commonly used tests in these evaluations (Ackerman & Ackerman, 1997; Ackerman & Pritzl, 2011; Bow & Quinnell, 2001). Psychological test results provide additional data that can be integrated with information gathered through other means (e.g., clinical interviews and collateral records).

CONSIDERATIONS FOR USING THE MMPI-2-RF IN CHILD CUSTODY EVALUATIONS

Gould and Martindale (2013) provided specific considerations for child custody evaluators in selecting psychological tests for child custody evaluations. Their considerations are quite sound in preparing the forensic evaluator to select measures in a manner consistent with an evidence-based and scientific model for the gathering of data and formulating of an opinion. Although a review of the 13 points Gould and Martindale raise is beyond the scope of this chapter, several issues will be specifically discussed as they pertain to the MMPI-2-RF. These considerations (which are paraphrased from the original in Gould and Martindale [2013]) include the following:

What theoretical or rational basis was used for selecting the measure for the present evaluation? Is the test relevant to the psycho-legal issues of the evaluation?

Given the complexity of child custody evaluations and the various components that go into a custodial decision, the MMPI-2-RF (like any psychological measure) will play only a limited role. Some have noted that psychological test results have limited ability to capture relevant characteristics of parents and children in child custody evaluations, such as parenting abilities and child attachment (Erikson, Lilienfeld, & Vitacco, 2007). Moreover, research examining the link between scores on the MMPI-2-RF (or any version of the MMPI) and parental effectiveness is quite limited. Kauffman et al. (2015) noted that although the MMPI-2, and MMPI-2-RF, for that matter, are limited in their ability to directly measure parental effectiveness, psychological and psychopathological characteristics captured by the tests can inform indirect impressions about parenting skills.

Child custody evaluators should be clear that use of the MMPI-2-RF is limited to assessing the psychological functioning of the parents. When administered to both parties, the test can provide an objective source of data regarding various psychopathological constructs (e.g., depression, anxiety, substance misuse), behavioral proclivities (e.g., aggression and poor impulse control), and personality characteristics (e.g., interpersonal passivity). If the link between the test results and the psycho-legal issues is indirect, Gould and Martindale (2013) suggested that the link must be explained by the evaluator. Therefore, if the presence of psychopathology or maladaptive personality characteristics is identified in the MMPI-2-RF results, the evaluator must clearly explain how those issues are related to the psycho-legal issues at hand. For example, in Kentucky, where one of the authors (D.B.W.) practices, the statute that guides custodial decisions states that the court shall consider the mental and physical health of all individuals involved when determining a custodial decision. Thus, an evaluator can reasonably utilize the MMPI-2-RF as a means of screening parents for psychopathology. Regardless of the jurisdiction, the evaluator must be prepared to explain the rational for using the MMPI-2-RF and how the test results inform the evaluator's overall opinions. It should also be noted that within the broader context of a child custody evaluation, clinicians can also utilize the downward extension of the MMPI-2-RF, the Restructured Form of the MMPI-A (MMPI-A-RF; Archer, Handel, Ben-Porath, & Tellegen, 2016), to evaluate the psychological functioning of adolescents impacted by the custodial decision.

Did the evaluator review and reference the peer-reviewed literature pertaining to the tests' use in child custody assessment?

Three studies have directly examined the MMPI-2-RF in custody settings. Archer et al. (2012) examined the test in a sample of 344 child custody litigants. Their sample had completed the MMPI-2, from which the MMPI-2-RF was rescored. Therefore, they had the ability to compare results from both tests in their sample. Basic psychometric properties of the MMPI-2-RF in this setting were similar to those from other settings. The authors provided means and standard deviations for all 50 of the 51 scales (this article was published before the RBS was added to the test), which can be consulted by child custody examiners for comparison purposes. Most evaluees produced normal limits profiles with both instruments. RC6 was the most frequently elevated RC Scale, with 15 percent of males and 18 percent of females scoring above 65T. Twenty-four percent of males and 27 percent of females in the sample elevated at least one RC Scale above 65T.

Pinsoneault and Ezzo (2012) compared MMPI-2-RF profiles of 61 parents referred for parental fitness evaluations in child maltreatment cases with 168 child custody litigants. Fifty-five percent of the child custody litigants had at least one clinical elevation on the test, and 8 percent had at least six clinical elevations. Similar to Archer et al. (2012), Pinsoneault and Ezzo found that RC6 was the most commonly elevated scale in the child custody group.

Most recently, Kauffman et al. (2015) examined the MMPI-2-RF in a sample of 49 child custody litigants. The mean profile was similar to the Archer et al. (2012) sample. Once again, RC6 had the highest mean elevation among the RC Scales.

Did the evaluator explain how test response style/bias was interpreted?

As a routine practice, forensic clinicians should provide statements in their reports regarding the protocol validity of psychological test results. The same practice should be applied in a child custody evaluation. The clinician may consider adding a statement that interpretation of the MMPI-2-RF Validity Scales should be made within the context of this particular forensic setting, in which individuals tend to be more defensive than are other groups (Archer et al., 2012).

Chapter 3 of this book reviews matters of response bias in detail. It is important to consider that although there have been only three published studies that provide mean scores on the underreporting Validity Scales in child custody settings, along with a child custody comparison group that is available to use in the scoring of the test, the data from Tellegen and Ben-Porath (2008/2011), Archer et al. (2012), and Kauffman et al. (2015) suggest that L-r and K-r function very similarly to their MMPI-2 counterparts. L-r and L (similar to K-r and K) are highly correlated, have similar reliability estimates, and show similar mean elevations in child custody settings. It is not surprising that parents undergoing child custody evaluations are motivated to put their best foot forward, which may be perceived as defensiveness, guardedness, or "faking good." The Validity Scales of the MMPI-2-RF allow the clinician to form an opinion about the degree to which the results on L-r and K-r align with others who completed the test under a similar situation. The MMPI-2-RF Forensic, Child Custody Litigant comparison group (238 females and 243 males) and several publications (Archer et al., 2012; Kauffman et al., 2015; Pinsoneault & Ezzo, 2012; Sellbom & Bagby, 2008) provide descriptive data for L-r and K-r in child custody samples (see Table 9-1).

TABLE 9-1

Descriptive Data for Underreporting Validity Scales in Child Custody Setting

Sample		L-r		K-r	
	Size	Mean	SD	Mean	SD
Tellegen and Ben-Porath (2008/2011) child custody group (male)	243	56	12	60	9
Tellegen and Ben-Porath (2008/2011) child custody group (female)	238	55	12	58	9
Archer et al., 2012 (male)	172	52	10	58	9
Archer et al., 2012 (female)	172	53	11	57	10
Sellbom and Bagby (2008) (mixed gender)	109	60	12	56	11
Kauffman et al. (2015) (mixed gender)	51	60	12	59	9
Pinsoneault and Ezzo (2012) (mixed gender)	171	59	14	59	9

Note. K-r = Adjustment Validity; L-r = Uncommon Virtues.

Sellbom and Bagby (2008) used a simulation design to examine L-r and K-r. Both scales exhibited large effects in differentiating undergraduates instructed to fake good from child custody litigants who completed the test under standard instructions.

How do objective test results line up with other sources of information, such as third-party collateral sources?

A primary utility of the MMPI-2-RF is to formulate hypotheses about psychological functioning that can be corroborated by extratest data. The results can also be used to confirm hypotheses generated by collateral sources of data. The point made by Martindale and Gould (2004) is that evidence-based and scientifically oriented child custody evaluations should illustrate how psychological test results corroborate extratest data. This practice is good regardless of the forensic context. In Case Example 9-1, we will illustrate how the MMPI-2-RF results align with collateral data.

Erikson et al. (2007) noted that contextual factors must be considered when interpreting psychological tests in child custody evaluations. Those litigating contested custody often harbor intense hostility toward one another and are highly suspicious of the motives and agenda of the other parent. Several items on RC6, which was designed to capture self-referential persecutory ideation, may reflect the resentment and hostility that is more common in contested custody cases. Moreover, an endorsement of only three items on this scale will elevate the T score above 65. Therefore, the evaluator must be careful not to ascribe paranoid or delusional symptoms to the evaluee with an elevated RC6 score unless it is corroborated by other data.

CASE EXAMPLE 9-1

Case Background

The parents involved in this case were a 43-year-old Caucasian male (Mr. F) and a 47-year-old Caucasian female (Ms. F). They had two daughters, aged 16 and 14 years. The couple had been married for 18 years at the time of their separation in 2008. Prior to the separation, both parents were employed.

The father owned a small but successful business, and the mother worked as a realtor.

Both parents presented a significantly negative view of the other parent, externalizing much of the blame on their partner for the decline in the marriage. The father described the mother as "crazy" and indicated that she had poor anger management, often "screaming at me and blaming me." He also indicated that she was physically abusive and "punched me in the face a couple of times." He claimed that she had two extramarital affairs. The mother characterized her husband as a "pathological liar" and claimed that he had extramarital affairs. She said that he told her to "go have affairs" because he "was gone more than he was home." However, she also stated that he "threatened suicide if I left him."

Father's MMPI-2-RF Results

PROTOCOL VALIDITY

As you can see in Mr. F's MMPI-2-RF results, he responded to each item (CNS = 0) and responded consistently to the items throughout the test (VRIN-r = 58, TRIN-r = 57F). Although his score on VRIN-r placed him at the 97th percentile in relation to other males in the child custody comparison group, we would not be concerned with respect to this aspect of protocol validity in his profile. The mean T score in the comparison group of male child custody litigants is 43, which equates to a raw score of 2, suggesting that most males in this setting are likely to be very consistent in their responding. Although he scored significantly higher than this group, we would not be concerned that his results on VRIN-r reflect any problems with random or inconsistent responding, just that he was less careful than others in this setting. There was no evidence of overreporting with respect to psychopathology (F-r, Fp-r) or somatic/cognitive symptoms (Fs, FBS-r, RBS), which is consistent with most evaluees in this setting. Moreover, there was no significant evidence of underreporting on L-r or K-r. His T scores of 62 and 55 on L-r and K-r, respectively, are consistent with most male evaluees in this setting and do not represent significant levels of underreporting. Several scales in the clinically substantive portion of his profile are elevated, which suggests he was willing to acknowledge symptoms and problems on the test. Consequently, his profile was considered valid for interpretation.

Minnesota Multiphasic
Personality Inventory-2
Restructured Form®

Score Report

MMPI-2-RF®

Minnesota Multiphasic Personality Inventory-2-Restructured Form®

Yossef S. Ben-Porath, PhD, & Auke Tellegen, PhD

Name:	Mr. F
ID Number:	9
Age:	43
Gender:	Male
Marital Status:	Separated
Years of Education:	17
Date Assessed:	02/09/2009

ALWAYS LEARNING

PEARSON

FIGURE 9-1 Case Example 9-1: Mr. F's MMPI-2-RF Profile, continued.

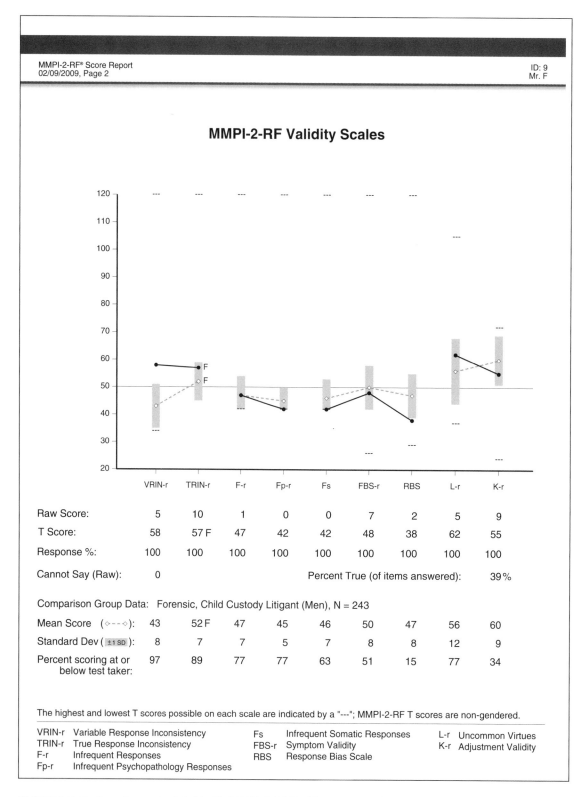

MMPI-2-RF Validity Scales

	VRIN-r	TRIN-r	F-r	Fp-r	Fs	FBS-r	RBS	L-r	K-r
Raw Score:	5	10	1	0	0	7	2	5	9
T Score:	58	57 F	47	42	42	48	38	62	55
Response %:	100	100	100	100	100	100	100	100	100

Cannot Say (Raw):   0   Percent True (of items answered):   39 %

Comparison Group Data: Forensic, Child Custody Litigant (Men), N = 243

	VRIN-r	TRIN-r	F-r	Fp-r	Fs	FBS-r	RBS	L-r	K-r
Mean Score (◇- - -◇):	43	52 F	47	45	46	50	47	56	60
Standard Dev (±1 SD):	8	7	7	5	7	8	8	12	9
Percent scoring at or below test taker:	97	89	77	77	63	51	15	77	34

The highest and lowest T scores possible on each scale are indicated by a "---"; MMPI-2-RF T scores are non-gendered.

VRIN-r	Variable Response Inconsistency	Fs	Infrequent Somatic Responses	L-r Uncommon Virtues
TRIN-r	True Response Inconsistency	FBS-r	Symptom Validity	K-r Adjustment Validity
F-r	Infrequent Responses	RBS	Response Bias Scale	
Fp-r	Infrequent Psychopathology Responses			

FIGURE 9-1   Case Example 9-1: Mr. F's MMPI-2-RF Profile, continued.

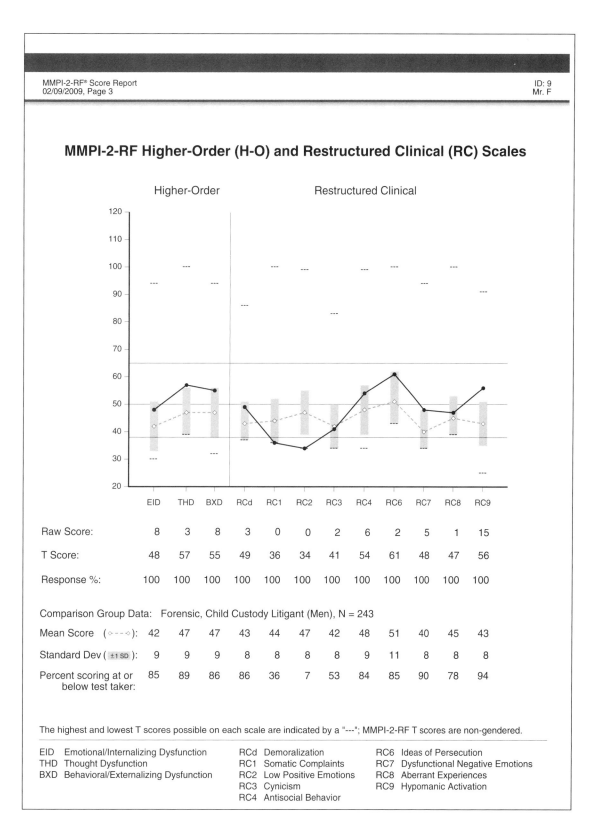

MMPI-2-RF Higher-Order (H-O) and Restructured Clinical (RC) Scales

Higher-Order   Restructured Clinical

	EID	THD	BXD	RCd	RC1	RC2	RC3	RC4	RC6	RC7	RC8	RC9
Raw Score:	8	3	8	3	0	0	2	6	2	5	1	15
T Score:	48	57	55	49	36	34	41	54	61	48	47	56
Response %:	100	100	100	100	100	100	100	100	100	100	100	100

Comparison Group Data: Forensic, Child Custody Litigant (Men), N = 243

Mean Score (◇- - -◇):	42	47	47	43	44	47	42	48	51	40	45	43
Standard Dev (±1 SD):	9	9	9	8	8	8	8	9	11	8	8	8
Percent scoring at or below test taker:	85	89	86	86	36	7	53	84	85	90	78	94

The highest and lowest T scores possible on each scale are indicated by a "---"; MMPI-2-RF T scores are non-gendered.

EID	Emotional/Internalizing Dysfunction	RCd	Demoralization
THD	Thought Dysfunction	RC1	Somatic Complaints
BXD	Behavioral/Externalizing Dysfunction	RC2	Low Positive Emotions
		RC3	Cynicism
		RC4	Antisocial Behavior

RC6	Ideas of Persecution
RC7	Dysfunctional Negative Emotions
RC8	Aberrant Experiences
RC9	Hypomanic Activation

FIGURE 9-1   Case Example 9-1: Mr. F's MMPI-2-RF Profile, continued.

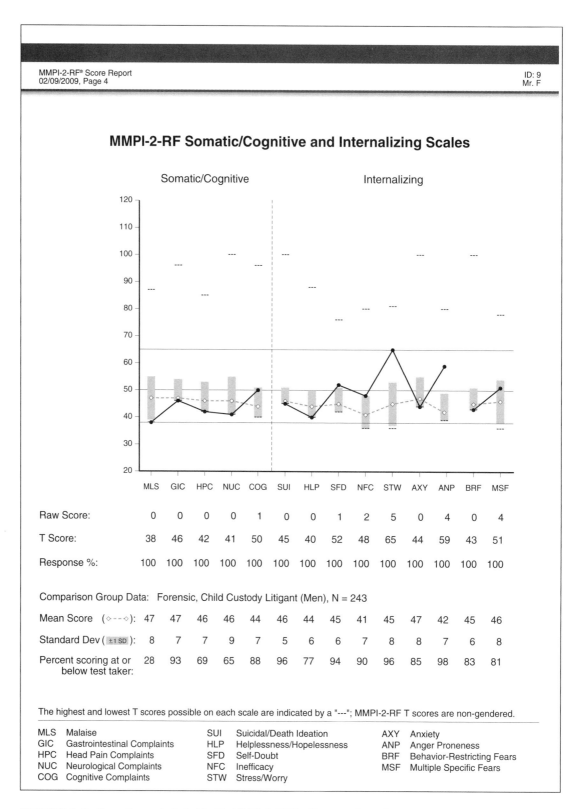

MMPI-2-RF Somatic/Cognitive and Internalizing Scales

Somatic/Cognitive   Internalizing

	MLS	GIC	HPC	NUC	COG	SUI	HLP	SFD	NFC	STW	AXY	ANP	BRF	MSF
Raw Score:	0	0	0	0	1	0	0	1	2	5	0	4	0	4
T Score:	38	46	42	41	50	45	40	52	48	65	44	59	43	51
Response %:	100	100	100	100	100	100	100	100	100	100	100	100	100	100

Comparison Group Data: Forensic, Child Custody Litigant (Men), N = 243

	MLS	GIC	HPC	NUC	COG	SUI	HLP	SFD	NFC	STW	AXY	ANP	BRF	MSF
Mean Score (◇- - -◇):	47	47	46	46	44	46	44	45	41	45	47	42	45	46
Standard Dev (±1 SD):	8	7	7	9	7	5	6	6	7	8	8	7	6	8
Percent scoring at or below test taker:	28	93	69	65	88	96	77	94	90	96	85	98	83	81

The highest and lowest T scores possible on each scale are indicated by a "---"; MMPI-2-RF T scores are non-gendered.

MLS	Malaise	SUI	Suicidal/Death Ideation	AXY	Anxiety
GIC	Gastrointestinal Complaints	HLP	Helplessness/Hopelessness	ANP	Anger Proneness
HPC	Head Pain Complaints	SFD	Self-Doubt	BRF	Behavior-Restricting Fears
NUC	Neurological Complaints	NFC	Inefficacy	MSF	Multiple Specific Fears
COG	Cognitive Complaints	STW	Stress/Worry		

FIGURE 9-1 Case Example 9-1: Mr. F's MMPI-2-RF Profile, continued.

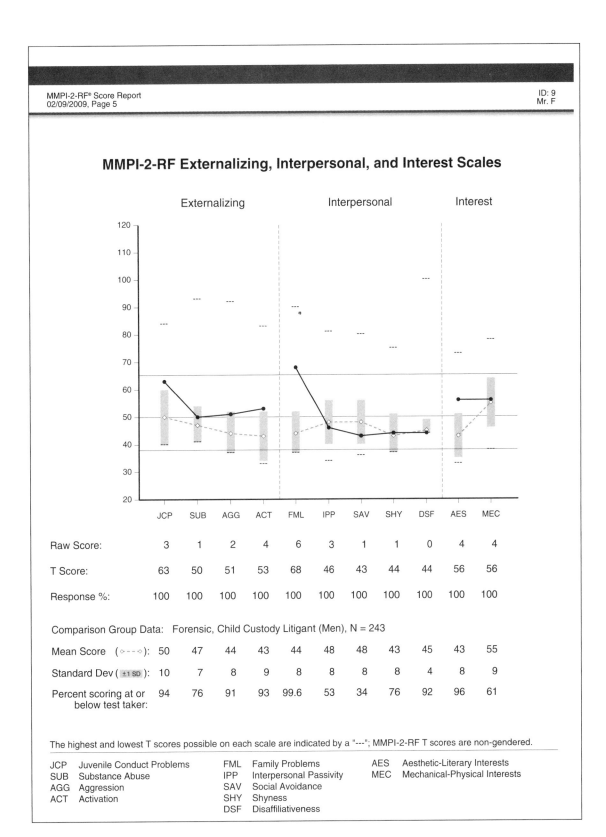

MMPI-2-RF Externalizing, Interpersonal, and Interest Scales

Externalizing   Interpersonal   Interest

	JCP	SUB	AGG	ACT	FML	IPP	SAV	SHY	DSF	AES	MEC
Raw Score:	3	1	2	4	6	3	1	1	0	4	4
T Score:	63	50	51	53	68	46	43	44	44	56	56
Response %:	100	100	100	100	100	100	100	100	100	100	100

Comparison Group Data: Forensic, Child Custody Litigant (Men), N = 243

	JCP	SUB	AGG	ACT	FML	IPP	SAV	SHY	DSF	AES	MEC
Mean Score (◇---◇):	50	47	44	43	44	48	48	43	45	43	55
Standard Dev (±1 SD):	10	7	8	9	8	8	8	8	4	8	9
Percent scoring at or below test taker:	94	76	91	93	99.6	53	34	76	92	96	61

The highest and lowest T scores possible on each scale are indicated by a "---"; MMPI-2-RF T scores are non-gendered.

JCP	Juvenile Conduct Problems	FML	Family Problems	AES	Aesthetic-Literary Interests
SUB	Substance Abuse	IPP	Interpersonal Passivity	MEC	Mechanical-Physical Interests
AGG	Aggression	SAV	Social Avoidance		
ACT	Activation	SHY	Shyness		
		DSF	Disaffiliativeness		

FIGURE 9-1 Case Example 9-1: Mr. F's MMPI-2-RF Profile, continued.

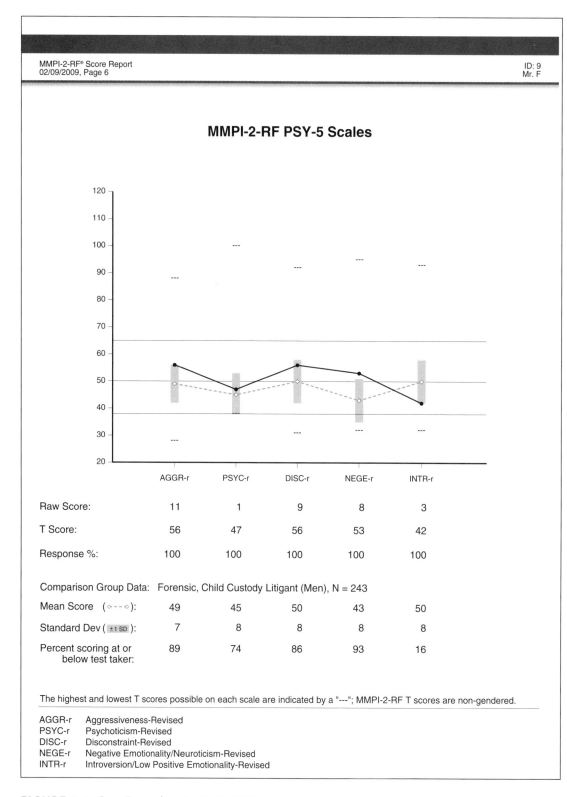

MMPI-2-RF PSY-5 Scales

	AGGR-r	PSYC-r	DISC-r	NEGE-r	INTR-r
Raw Score:	11	1	9	8	3
T Score:	56	47	56	53	42
Response %:	100	100	100	100	100

Comparison Group Data: Forensic, Child Custody Litigant (Men), N = 243

Mean Score (◇- - -◇):	49	45	50	43	50
Standard Dev (±1 SD):	7	8	8	8	8
Percent scoring at or below test taker:	89	74	86	93	16

The highest and lowest T scores possible on each scale are indicated by a "---"; MMPI-2-RF T scores are non-gendered.

AGGR-r   Aggressiveness-Revised
PSYC-r   Psychoticism-Revised
DISC-r   Disconstraint-Revised
NEGE-r   Negative Emotionality/Neuroticism-Revised
INTR-r   Introversion/Low Positive Emotionality-Revised

FIGURE 9-1 Case Example 9-1: Mr. F's MMPI-2-RF Profile, continued.

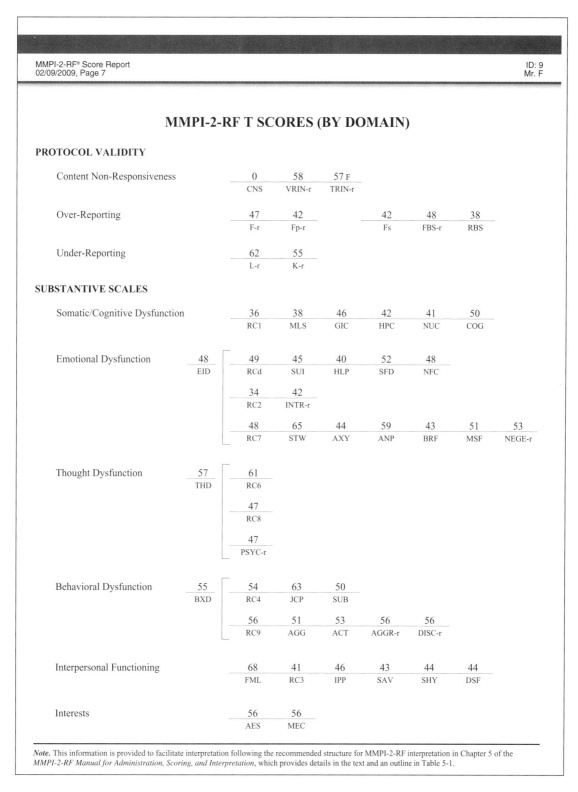

MMPI-2-RF T SCORES (BY DOMAIN)

PROTOCOL VALIDITY

| Content Non-Responsiveness | 0 | 58 | 57 F |
| | CNS | VRIN-r | TRIN-r |

| Over-Reporting | 47 | 42 | | 42 | 48 | 38 |
| | F-r | Fp-r | | Fs | FBS-r | RBS |

| Under-Reporting | 62 | 55 |
| | L-r | K-r |

SUBSTANTIVE SCALES

| Somatic/Cognitive Dysfunction | 36 | 38 | 46 | 42 | 41 | 50 |
| | RC1 | MLS | GIC | HPC | NUC | COG |

Emotional Dysfunction	48	49	45	40	52	48
	EID	RCd	SUI	HLP	SFD	NFC
		34	42
		RC2	INTR-r
		48	65	44	59	43	51	53
		RC7	STW	AXY	ANP	BRF	MSF	NEGE-r

Thought Dysfunction	57	61
	THD	RC6
		47
		RC8
		47
		PSYC-r

Behavioral Dysfunction	55	54	63	50
	BXD	RC4	JCP	SUB
		56	51	53	56	56
		RC9	AGG	ACT	AGGR-r	DISC-r

| Interpersonal Functioning | 68 | 41 | 46 | 43 | 44 | 44 |
| | FML | RC3 | IPP | SAV | SHY | DSF |

| Interests | 56 | 56 |
| | AES | MEC |

Note. This information is provided to facilitate interpretation following the recommended structure for MMPI-2-RF interpretation in Chapter 5 of the *MMPI-2-RF Manual for Administration, Scoring, and Interpretation*, which provides details in the text and an outline in Table 5-1.

FIGURE 9-1 Case Example 9-1: Mr. F's MMPI-2-RF Profile, continued.

ITEM-LEVEL INFORMATION

Unscorable Responses

The test taker produced scorable responses to all the MMPI-2-RF items.

Critical Responses

Seven MMPI-2-RF scales--Suicidal/Death Ideation (SUI), Helplessness/Hopelessness (HLP), Anxiety (AXY), Ideas of Persecution (RC6), Aberrant Experiences (RC8), Substance Abuse (SUB), and Aggression (AGG)--have been designated by the test authors as having critical item content that may require immediate attention and follow-up. Items answered by the individual in the keyed direction (True or False) on a critical scale are listed below if his T score on that scale is 65 or higher.

The test taker has not produced an elevated T score ($\geq$ 65) on any of these scales.

User-Designated Item-Level Information

The following item-level information is based on the report user's selection of additional scales, and/or of lower cutoffs for the critical scales from the previous section. Items answered by the test taker in the keyed direction (True or False) on a selected scale are listed below if his T score on that scale is at the user-designated cutoff score or higher. The percentage of the MMPI-2-RF normative sample (NS) and of the Forensic, Child Custody Litigant (Men) comparison group (CG) that answered each item in the keyed direction are provided in parentheses following the item content.

Ideas of Persecution (RC6, T Score = 61)

    110. Item Content Omitted. (True; NS 9.9%, CG 6.2%)
    212. Item Content Omitted. (False; NS 9.1%, CG 25.9%)

Hypomanic Activation (RC9, T Score = 56)

    13. Item Content Omitted. (True; NS 40.9%, CG 21.8%)
    39. Item Content Omitted. (True; NS 51.0%, CG 33.3%)
    47. Item Content Omitted. (True; NS 42.7%, CG 43.2%)
    61. Item Content Omitted. (False; NS 61.6%, CG 67.9%)
    72. Item Content Omitted. (True; NS 81.5%, CG 55.1%)
    97. Item Content Omitted. (True; NS 50.5%, CG 23.5%)
    107. Item Content Omitted. (True; NS 47.3%, CG 37.4%)
    118. Item Content Omitted. (True; NS 57.4%, CG 50.6%)
    155. Item Content Omitted. (True; NS 41.6%, CG 15.6%)
    193. Item Content Omitted. (True; NS 32.8%, CG 9.9%)

FIGURE 9-1 Case Example 9-1: Mr. F's MMPI-2-RF Profile, continued.

MMPI-2-RF® Score Report
02/09/2009, Page 9

ID: 9
Mr. F

207. Item Content Omitted. (True; NS 66.9%, CG 39.9%)
219. Item Content Omitted. (True; NS 51.5%, CG 30.0%)
244. Item Content Omitted. (True; NS 56.9%, CG 60.5%)
256. Item Content Omitted. (True; NS 65.7%, CG 37.4%)
337. Item Content Omitted. (True; NS 50.2%, CG 30.0%)

Behavior-Restricting Fears (BRF, T Score = 43)

No items that are scored on this scale were answered in the keyed direction.

Juvenile Conduct Problems (JCP, T Score = 63)

21. Item Content Omitted. (True; NS 47.1%, CG 42.8%)
66. Item Content Omitted. (True; NS 20.3%, CG 31.7%)
223. Item Content Omitted. (True; NS 12.3%, CG 14.0%)

End of Report

This and previous pages of this report contain trade secrets and are not to be released in response to requests under HIPAA (or any other data disclosure law that exempts trade secret information from release). Further, release in response to litigation discovery demands should be made only in accordance with your profession's ethical guidelines and under an appropriate protective order.

FIGURE 9-1 Case Example 9-1: Mr. F's MMPI-2-RF Profile.

CLINICAL INTERPRETATION

As noted in Chapter 1, interpretation begins with a review of the H-O Scales to determine which domain to start interpreting. Mr. F did not elevate any of the three H-O Scales, although his scores on these scales were relatively high in relation to the male child custody group (85th to 89th percentiles). The highest score among the three H-O Scales was THD (57T). This is consistent with his score on RC6, which was 61T. As discussed earlier, it is not uncommon for individuals involved in child custody cases to exhibit normative beliefs that others are the cause of their problems (i.e., their spouse/former spouse and the attorneys involved in the case) as well as a belief that their behaviors and attitudes are highly scrutinized. Consequently, although his score on RC6 is over one standard deviation above the mean with respect to the normative sample, this is not alarming in a child custody setting and not likely to reflect paranoia or delusional thinking.

Since none of the RC Scales were in the clinically elevated range, we next examine the SP Scales. Mr. F did not endorse many of the somatic/cognitive items (which is consistent with his raw score of 0 on RC1). This was also consistent with his positive description of his physical health, and his denial of any significant medical issues. Turning to the Internalizing Scales, we see that he had an elevation on STW (65T), suggesting that he experiences a high level of worry and has numerous stressors. These symptoms were consistent with his presentation during the evaluation, when he stated "my stress level is through the roof" and "I'm constantly worrying about how this will turn out in court." Since none of the RC Scales (including those that pertain to internalizing distress, RCd, RC2, RC7) were in the elevated range, his score on STW was considered to reflect his current circumstances rather than a pervasive anxiety condition. None of the remaining Internalizing SP Scales were elevated, although his score on ANP (59T) was almost a standard deviation above the normative group. Although this score was not clinically elevated, it was consistent with his presentation during the evaluation when he made statements regarding his deeply held resentment of his former spouse. He also stated during the interview "I sometimes let my anger get the best of me."

Consistent with his generally normal range profile, none of Mr. F's Externalizing SP Scales were elevated, although his score on JCP (63T), while not above a clinical cutoff of 65T, nevertheless suggests that he may have had difficulty with authority in the past. It is also worth noting that his score on the scale would place him at the 94th percentile compared to others in the male child custody comparison group. During his clinical interview, Mr. F acknowledged a history of in-school detentions for unruly behavior during middle school. He also reported that he had been returned home by the police after he had been caught "out with some friends too late" when he was 15 years old. On the two PSY-5 Scales in the externalizing domain, we see that neither were in the clinical range. His scores on AGGR-r (56T) and DISC-r (56T) were at the 89th and 86th percentiles, respectively, in relation to the male child custody litigant group. Although not in the clinical range, the traits captured by these two scales were exhibited to some degree during the clinical interview. As an example, he characterized his interpersonal style as "I know how to get what I want out of people." He also made several statements during the interview characteristic of a grandiose sense of self-worth and egocentricity. He also stated "I don't always think things through" when making decisions.

The Interpersonal SP Scales were significant for a clinical elevation on Family Problems (FML) (68), which was consistent with Mr. F's history of marital problems and his report of familial discord growing up. He reported that his father was emotionally and physically abusive toward his mother, and he witnessed domestic violence between his parents on several occasions.

Mr. F produced a valid MMPI-2-RF profile that was consistent with his emotional adjustment. It accurately reflected his level of stress and familial discord (both historically and currently), and some of the moderate (albeit not clinically elevated) scores were consistent with his personality characteristics. There was nothing in his MMPI-2-RF profile that would indicate any inherent difficulties in providing a stable environment for his children. Ultimately, Mr. F did not meet criteria for any clinical disorder, but he did exhibit enough characteristics of narcissistic personality (independent of the test results) to be diagnosed with narcissistic personality traits.

Mother's MMPI-2-RF Results

PROTOCOL VALIDITY

As you can see in Ms. F's MMPI-2-RF results, she also gave a scorable response to each item (CNS = 0) and did so consistently to the items throughout the test (VRIN-r = 48, TRIN-r = 50). There was no evidence of overreporting with respect to psychopathology (F-r, Fp-r) or somatic/cognitive

Minnesota Multiphasic
Personality Inventory-2
Restructured Form®

Score Report

MMPI-2-RF®

Minnesota Multiphasic Personality Inventory-2-Restructured Form®

Yossef S. Ben-Porath, PhD, & Auke Tellegen, PhD

Name:	Ms. F
ID Number:	9
Age:	47
Gender:	Female
Marital Status:	Separated
Years of Education:	13
Date Assessed:	02/11/2009

ALWAYS LEARNING　　　　　　　　　　　　　　　　　**PEARSON**

FIGURE 9-2 Case Example 9-1: Ms. F's MMPI-2-RF Profile, continued.

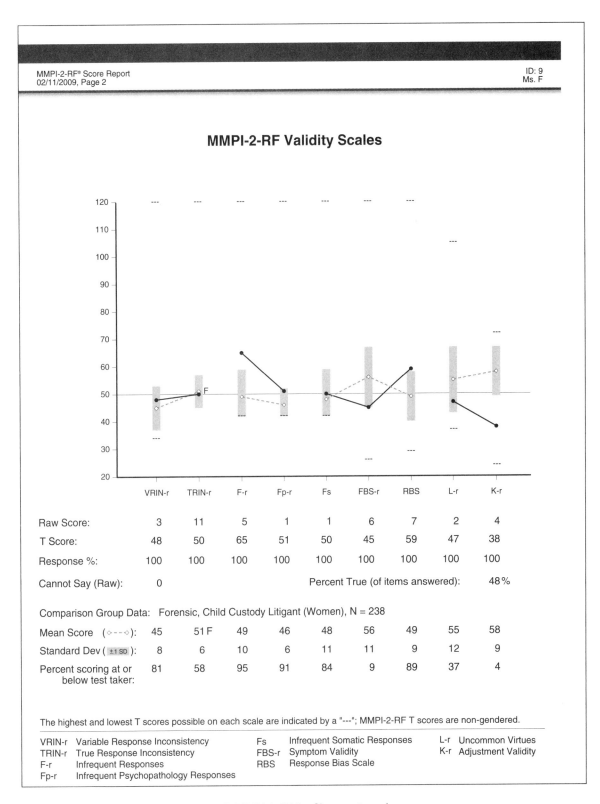

MMPI-2-RF Validity Scales

	VRIN-r	TRIN-r	F-r	Fp-r	Fs	FBS-r	RBS	L-r	K-r
Raw Score:	3	11	5	1	1	6	7	2	4
T Score:	48	50	65	51	50	45	59	47	38
Response %:	100	100	100	100	100	100	100	100	100

Cannot Say (Raw):   0   Percent True (of items answered):   48%

Comparison Group Data: Forensic, Child Custody Litigant (Women), N = 238

	VRIN-r	TRIN-r	F-r	Fp-r	Fs	FBS-r	RBS	L-r	K-r
Mean Score (◇- - -◇):	45	51 F	49	46	48	56	49	55	58
Standard Dev (±1 SD):	8	6	10	6	11	11	9	12	9
Percent scoring at or below test taker:	81	58	95	91	84	9	89	37	4

The highest and lowest T scores possible on each scale are indicated by a "---"; MMPI-2-RF T scores are non-gendered.

VRIN-r	Variable Response Inconsistency	Fs	Infrequent Somatic Responses	L-r Uncommon Virtues
TRIN-r	True Response Inconsistency	FBS-r	Symptom Validity	K-r Adjustment Validity
F-r	Infrequent Responses	RBS	Response Bias Scale	
Fp-r	Infrequent Psychopathology Responses			

FIGURE 9-2 Case Example 9-1: Ms. F's MMPI-2-RF Profile, continued.

193

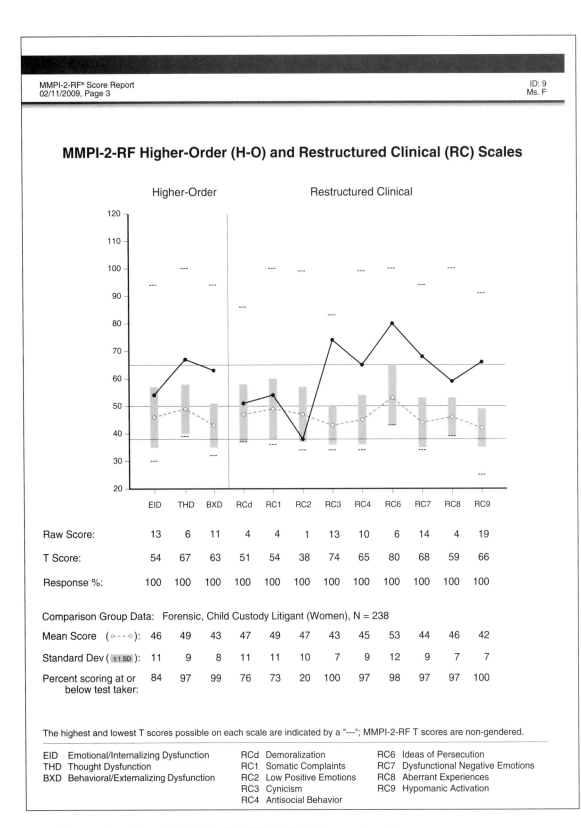

MMPI-2-RF Higher-Order (H-O) and Restructured Clinical (RC) Scales

Higher-Order   Restructured Clinical

	EID	THD	BXD	RCd	RC1	RC2	RC3	RC4	RC6	RC7	RC8	RC9
Raw Score:	13	6	11	4	4	1	13	10	6	14	4	19
T Score:	54	67	63	51	54	38	74	65	80	68	59	66
Response %:	100	100	100	100	100	100	100	100	100	100	100	100

Comparison Group Data: Forensic, Child Custody Litigant (Women), N = 238

Mean Score (◇--◇):	46	49	43	47	49	47	43	45	53	44	46	42
Standard Dev (±1 SD):	11	9	8	11	11	10	7	9	12	9	7	7
Percent scoring at or below test taker:	84	97	99	76	73	20	100	97	98	97	97	100

The highest and lowest T scores possible on each scale are indicated by a "---"; MMPI-2-RF T scores are non-gendered.

EID	Emotional/Internalizing Dysfunction	RCd	Demoralization	RC6	Ideas of Persecution
THD	Thought Dysfunction	RC1	Somatic Complaints	RC7	Dysfunctional Negative Emotions
BXD	Behavioral/Externalizing Dysfunction	RC2	Low Positive Emotions	RC8	Aberrant Experiences
		RC3	Cynicism	RC9	Hypomanic Activation
		RC4	Antisocial Behavior		

FIGURE 9-2 Case Example 9-1: Ms. F's MMPI-2-RF Profile, continued.

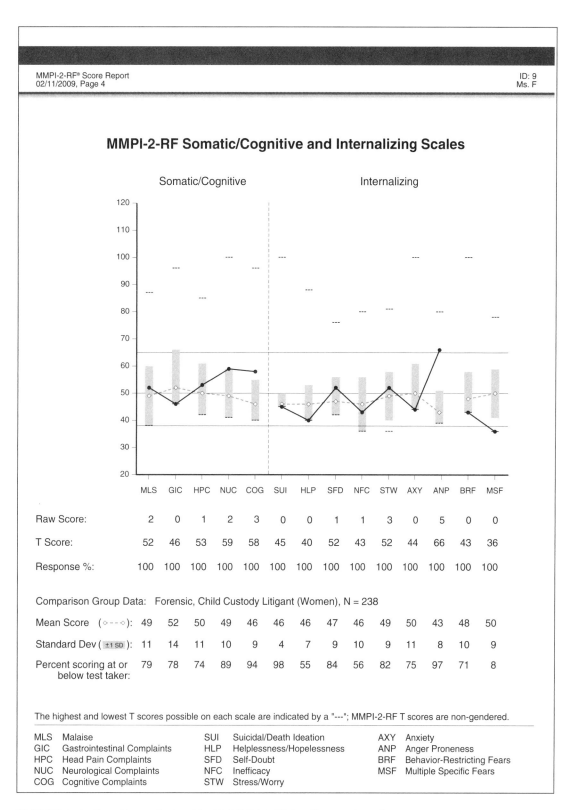

MMPI-2-RF Somatic/Cognitive and Internalizing Scales

Somatic/Cognitive   Internalizing

	MLS	GIC	HPC	NUC	COG	SUI	HLP	SFD	NFC	STW	AXY	ANP	BRF	MSF
Raw Score:	2	0	1	2	3	0	0	1	1	3	0	5	0	0
T Score:	52	46	53	59	58	45	40	52	43	52	44	66	43	36
Response %:	100	100	100	100	100	100	100	100	100	100	100	100	100	100

Comparison Group Data: Forensic, Child Custody Litigant (Women), N = 238

	MLS	GIC	HPC	NUC	COG	SUI	HLP	SFD	NFC	STW	AXY	ANP	BRF	MSF
Mean Score (◇--◇):	49	52	50	49	46	46	46	47	46	49	50	43	48	50
Standard Dev (±1 SD):	11	14	11	10	9	4	7	9	10	9	11	8	10	9
Percent scoring at or below test taker:	79	78	74	89	94	98	55	84	56	82	75	97	71	8

The highest and lowest T scores possible on each scale are indicated by a "---"; MMPI-2-RF T scores are non-gendered.

MLS	Malaise	SUI	Suicidal/Death Ideation	AXY	Anxiety
GIC	Gastrointestinal Complaints	HLP	Helplessness/Hopelessness	ANP	Anger Proneness
HPC	Head Pain Complaints	SFD	Self-Doubt	BRF	Behavior-Restricting Fears
NUC	Neurological Complaints	NFC	Inefficacy	MSF	Multiple Specific Fears
COG	Cognitive Complaints	STW	Stress/Worry		

FIGURE 9-2 Case Example 9-1: Ms. F's MMPI-2-RF Profile, continued.

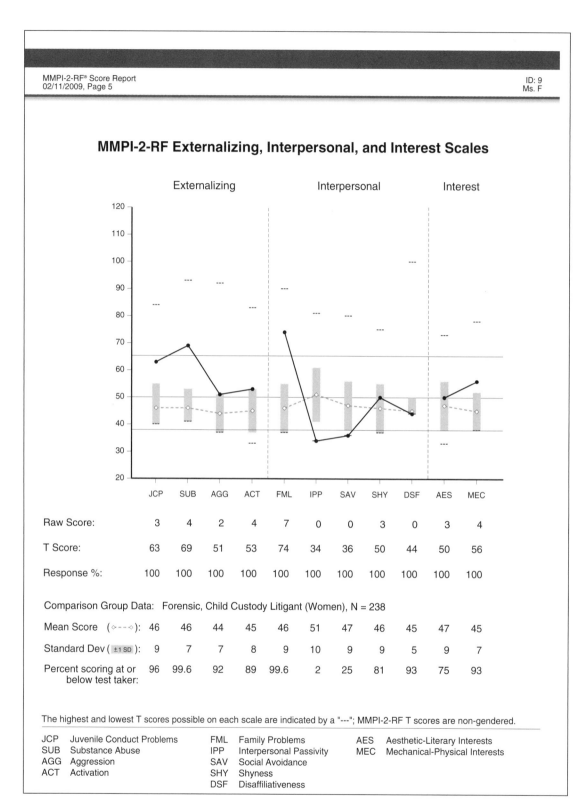

MMPI-2-RF Externalizing, Interpersonal, and Interest Scales

Externalizing   Interpersonal   Interest

	JCP	SUB	AGG	ACT	FML	IPP	SAV	SHY	DSF	AES	MEC
Raw Score:	3	4	2	4	7	0	0	3	0	3	4
T Score:	63	69	51	53	74	34	36	50	44	50	56
Response %:	100	100	100	100	100	100	100	100	100	100	100

Comparison Group Data: Forensic, Child Custody Litigant (Women), N = 238

	JCP	SUB	AGG	ACT	FML	IPP	SAV	SHY	DSF	AES	MEC
Mean Score (◇- - -◇):	46	46	44	45	46	51	47	46	45	47	45
Standard Dev (±1 SD):	9	7	7	8	9	10	9	9	5	9	7
Percent scoring at or below test taker:	96	99.6	92	89	99.6	2	25	81	93	75	93

The highest and lowest T scores possible on each scale are indicated by a "---"; MMPI-2-RF T scores are non-gendered.

JCP	Juvenile Conduct Problems	FML	Family Problems	AES	Aesthetic-Literary Interests
SUB	Substance Abuse	IPP	Interpersonal Passivity	MEC	Mechanical-Physical Interests
AGG	Aggression	SAV	Social Avoidance		
ACT	Activation	SHY	Shyness		
		DSF	Disaffiliativeness		

FIGURE 9-2 Case Example 9-1: Ms. F's MMPI-2-RF Profile, continued.

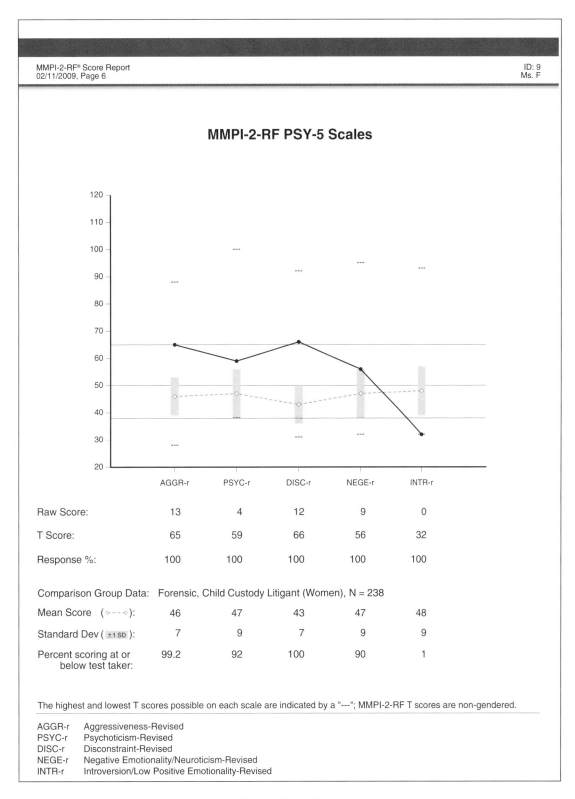

MMPI-2-RF PSY-5 Scales

	AGGR-r	PSYC-r	DISC-r	NEGE-r	INTR-r
Raw Score:	13	4	12	9	0
T Score:	65	59	66	56	32
Response %:	100	100	100	100	100

Comparison Group Data: Forensic, Child Custody Litigant (Women), N = 238

Mean Score (◇---◇):	46	47	43	47	48
Standard Dev (±1 SD):	7	9	7	9	9
Percent scoring at or below test taker:	99.2	92	100	90	1

The highest and lowest T scores possible on each scale are indicated by a "---"; MMPI-2-RF T scores are non-gendered.

AGGR-r	Aggressiveness-Revised
PSYC-r	Psychoticism-Revised
DISC-r	Disconstraint-Revised
NEGE-r	Negative Emotionality/Neuroticism-Revised
INTR-r	Introversion/Low Positive Emotionality-Revised

FIGURE 9-2 Case Example 9-1: Ms. F's MMPI-2-RF Profile, continued.

MMPI-2-RF T SCORES (BY DOMAIN)

PROTOCOL VALIDITY

Content Non-Responsiveness

0	48	50
CNS	VRIN-r	TRIN-r

Over-Reporting

65	51		50	45	59
F-r	Fp-r		Fs	FBS-r	RBS

Under-Reporting

47	38
L-r	K-r

SUBSTANTIVE SCALES

Somatic/Cognitive Dysfunction

54	52	46	53	59	58
RC1	MLS	GIC	HPC	NUC	COG

Emotional Dysfunction

54		51	45	40	52	43	
EID		RCd	SUI	HLP	SFD	NFC	

		38	32
		RC2	INTR-r

		68	52	44	66	43	36	56
		RC7	STW	AXY	ANP	BRF	MSF	NEGE-r

Thought Dysfunction

67		80
THD		RC6

		59
		RC8

		59
		PSYC-r

Behavioral Dysfunction

63		65	63	69
BXD		RC4	JCP	SUB

		66	51	53	65	66
		RC9	AGG	ACT	AGGR-r	DISC-r

Interpersonal Functioning

74	74	34	36	50	44
FML	RC3	IPP	SAV	SHY	DSF

Interests

50	56
AES	MEC

Note. This information is provided to facilitate interpretation following the recommended structure for MMPI-2-RF interpretation in Chapter 5 of the *MMPI-2-RF Manual for Administration, Scoring, and Interpretation*, which provides details in the text and an outline in Table 5-1.

FIGURE 9-2 Case Example 9-1: Ms. F's MMPI-2-RF Profile, continued.

ITEM-LEVEL INFORMATION

Unscorable Responses

The test taker produced scorable responses to all the MMPI-2-RF items.

Critical Responses

Seven MMPI-2-RF scales--Suicidal/Death Ideation (SUI), Helplessness/Hopelessness (HLP), Anxiety (AXY), Ideas of Persecution (RC6), Aberrant Experiences (RC8), Substance Abuse (SUB), and Aggression (AGG)--have been designated by the test authors as having critical item content that may require immediate attention and follow-up. Items answered by the individual in the keyed direction (True or False) on a critical scale are listed below if her T score on that scale is 65 or higher. The percentage of the MMPI-2-RF normative sample (NS) and of the Forensic, Child Custody Litigant (Women) comparison group (CG) that answered each item in the keyed direction are provided in parentheses following the item content.

Ideas of Persecution (RC6, T Score = 80)

    71. Item Content Omitted. (True; NS 2.0%, CG 12.6%)
  110. Item Content Omitted. (True; NS 9.9%, CG 11.3%)
  194. Item Content Omitted. (True; NS 17.1%, CG 21.8%)
  212. Item Content Omitted. (False; NS 9.1%, CG 27.3%)
  233. Item Content Omitted. (True; NS 5.5%, CG 9.7%)
  264. Item Content Omitted. (True; NS 5.3%, CG 18.1%)

Substance Abuse (SUB, T Score = 69)

    49. Item Content Omitted. (True; NS 29.6%, CG 17.2%)
    86. Item Content Omitted. (True; NS 3.8%, CG 1.7%)
  141. Item Content Omitted. (True; NS 34.2%, CG 18.5%)
  237. Item Content Omitted. (False; NS 27.4%, CG 22.7%)

User-Designated Item-Level Information

The following item-level information is based on the report user's selection of additional scales, and/or of lower cutoffs for the critical scales from the previous section. Items answered by the test taker in the keyed direction (True or False) on a selected scale are listed below if her T score on that scale is at the user-designated cutoff score or higher. The percentage of the MMPI-2-RF normative sample (NS) and of the Forensic, Child Custody Litigant (Women) comparison group (CG) that answered each item in the keyed direction are provided in parentheses following the item content.

Thought Dysfunction (THD, T Score = 67)

    71. Item Content Omitted. (True; NS 2.0%, CG 12.6%)
  110. Item Content Omitted. (True; NS 9.9%, CG 11.3%)
  179. Item Content Omitted. (True; NS 12.6%, CG
    7.1%)
  212. Item Content Omitted. (False; NS 9.1%, CG 27.3%)

FIGURE 9-2 Case Example 9-1: Ms. F's MMPI-2-RF Profile, continued.

264. Item Content Omitted. (True; NS 5.3%, CG 18.1%)
311. Item Content Omitted. (True; NS 32.4%, CG
     26.1%)

Cynicism (RC3, T Score = 74)

10. Item Content Omitted. (True; NS 35.9%, CG 13.4%)
36. Item Content Omitted.
     (True; NS 58.3%, CG 26.5%)
55. Item Content Omitted. (True; NS 47.7%, CG 25.2%)
87. Item Content Omitted. (True; NS 39.7%, CG
     18.9%)
99. Item Content Omitted.
     (True; NS 53.6%, CG 27.7%)
121. Item Content Omitted. (True; NS 16.8%, CG 10.1%)
142. Item Content Omitted. (True; NS 22.0%, CG
     11.3%)
171. Item Content Omitted. (True; NS 51.5%, CG 33.2%)
185. Item Content Omitted. (True; NS 29.3%, CG
     13.4%)
213. Item Content Omitted.
     (True; NS 71.4%, CG 67.6%)
238. Item Content Omitted. (True; NS
     32.6%, CG 16.8%)
260. Item Content Omitted.
     (True; NS 36.2%, CG
     16.8%)
279. Item Content Omitted. (True; NS 39.1%, CG 24.4%)

Antisocial Behavior (RC4, T Score = 65)

19. Item Content Omitted. (False; NS 17.0%, CG
     18.1%)
21. Item Content Omitted. (True; NS 47.1%, CG 29.4%)
38. Item Content Omitted. (False; NS 18.8%, CG 16.8%)
49. Item Content Omitted. (True; NS 29.6%, CG 17.2%)
66. Item Content Omitted. (True; NS 20.3%, CG 10.1%)
141. Item Content Omitted. (True; NS 34.2%, CG 18.5%)
173. Item Content Omitted. (True; NS 13.4%, CG 11.8%)
190. Item Content Omitted. (False; NS 28.6%, CG 24.4%)
205. Item Content Omitted. (True; NS 13.0%,
     CG 14.7%)
237. Item Content Omitted. (False; NS 27.4%, CG 22.7%)

Dysfunctional Negative Emotions (RC7, T Score = 68)

23. Item Content Omitted. (True; NS 39.0%, CG 13.0%)
35. Item Content Omitted. (True; NS 36.6%, CG 18.1%)

FIGURE 9-2 Case Example 9-1: Ms. F's MMPI-2-RF Profile, continued.

51. Item Content Omitted. (True; NS 15.4%, CG
    7.6%)
63. Item Content Omitted. (True; NS 24.3%, CG 9.7%)
91. Item Content Omitted. (True; NS 37.7%, CG 32.8%)
112. Item Content Omitted.
    (True; NS 23.1%, CG 17.6%)
119. Item Content Omitted. (True; NS 39.5%, CG 13.0%)
206. Item Content Omitted.
    (True; NS 41.6%, CG 24.8%)
250. Item Content Omitted. (True; NS 42.4%, CG 20.6%)
263. Item Content Omitted.
    (True; NS 64.0%, CG 44.1%)
303. Item Content Omitted. (True; NS 28.6%, CG 10.1%)
318. Item Content Omitted. (True; NS 19.9%, CG
    9.2%)
322. Item Content Omitted. (True; NS 46.8%, CG 34.9%)
335. Item Content Omitted. (True; NS 30.1%, CG 26.5%)

Hypomanic Activation (RC9, T Score = 66)
13. Item Content Omitted. (True; NS 40.9%, CG
    25.6%)
39. Item Content Omitted. (True; NS
    51.0%, CG 28.2%)
47. Item Content Omitted. (True; NS 42.7%, CG
    45.8%)
61. Item Content Omitted. (False; NS 61.6%, CG 43.3%)
72. Item Content Omitted. (True; NS 81.5%, CG
    63.4%)
97. Item Content Omitted. (True; NS 50.5%, CG
    21.8%)
107. Item Content Omitted. (True; NS 47.3%, CG 21.8%)
118. Item Content Omitted. (True; NS 57.4%, CG 52.1%)
143. Item Content Omitted. (True; NS 27.5%, CG 21.8%)

166. Item Content Omitted.
    (True; NS 38.9%, CG 21.8%)
181. Item Content Omitted. (True; NS 35.3%, CG 27.7%)
193. Item Content Omitted.
    (True; NS 32.8%, CG 2.5%)
207. Item Content Omitted. (True; NS 66.9%,
    CG 48.7%)
244. Item Content Omitted. (True; NS
    56.9%, CG 73.5%)
248. Item Content Omitted. (True; NS 16.1%, CG 5.9%)
256. Item Content Omitted. (True; NS
    65.7%, CG 37.8%)

FIGURE 9-2 Case Example 9-1: Ms. F's MMPI-2-RF Profile, continued.

305. Item Content Omitted. (True; NS 37.6%, CG 20.2%)
327. Item Content Omitted.
(True; NS 41.7%, CG 23.9%)
337. Item Content Omitted. (True; NS 50.2%,
CG 40.8%)

Anger Proneness (ANP, T Score = 66)
119. Item Content Omitted. (True; NS 39.5%, CG 13.0%)
248. Item Content Omitted. (True; NS 16.1%, CG 5.9%)
293. Item Content Omitted. (False; NS 18.5%, CG 10.9%)
303. Item Content Omitted. (True; NS 28.6%, CG 10.1%)
318. Item Content Omitted. (True; NS 19.9%, CG
9.2%)

Behavior-Restricting Fears (BRF, T Score = 43)
No items that are scored on this scale were answered in the keyed direction.

Juvenile Conduct Problems (JCP, T Score = 63)
21. Item Content Omitted. (True; NS 47.1%, CG 29.4%)
66. Item Content Omitted. (True; NS 20.3%, CG 10.1%)
205. Item Content Omitted. (True; NS 13.0%,
CG 14.7%)

Aggressiveness-Revised (AGGR-r, T Score = 65)
24. Item Content Omitted. (False; NS 74.6%, CG 72.7%)
39. Item Content Omitted. (True; NS
51.0%, CG 28.2%)
104. Item Content Omitted. (True; NS 67.1%, CG 55.0%)
147. Item Content Omitted. (True; NS 75.2%, CG 83.6%)
182. Item Content Omitted. (True; NS 33.6%, CG 30.3%)
197. Item Content Omitted. (True; NS 62.5%, CG
58.4%)
239. Item Content Omitted. (True; NS 60.7%, CG 63.9%)
256. Item Content Omitted. (True; NS
65.7%, CG 37.8%)
276. Item Content Omitted. (True; NS
50.0%, CG 62.6%)
302. Item Content Omitted. (True; NS 67.9%, CG 60.1%)
319. Item Content Omitted. (False; NS 64.7%,
CG 76.9%)
321. Item Content Omitted. (True; NS 31.3%, CG 20.2%)
327. Item Content Omitted.
(True; NS 41.7%, CG 23.9%)

FIGURE 9-2 Case Example 9-1: Ms. F's MMPI-2-RF Profile, continued.

Disconstraint-Revised (DISC-r, T Score = 66)
  21. Item Content Omitted. (True; NS 47.1%, CG 29.4%)
  49. Item Content Omitted. (True; NS 29.6%, CG 17.2%)
  61. Item Content Omitted. (False; NS 61.6%, CG 43.3%)
  66. Item Content Omitted. (True; NS 20.3%, CG 10.1%)
  75. Item Content Omitted. (True; NS 50.3%, CG 33.6%)
107. Item Content Omitted. (True; NS 47.3%, CG 21.8%)
115. Item Content Omitted. (True; NS 55.0%, CG 47.5%)
190. Item Content Omitted. (False; NS 28.6%, CG 24.4%)
193. Item Content Omitted.
    (True; NS 32.8%, CG 2.5%)
205. Item Content Omitted. (True; NS 13.0%,
    CG 14.7%)
226. Item Content Omitted. (True; NS 21.5%, CG 10.9%)
237. Item Content Omitted. (False; NS 27.4%, CG 22.7%)

End of Report

This and previous pages of this report contain trade secrets and are not to be released in response to requests under HIPAA (or any other data disclosure law that exempts trade secret information from release). Further, release in response to litigation discovery demands should be made only in accordance with your profession's ethical guidelines and under an appropriate protective order.

FIGURE 9-2 Case Example 9-1: Ms. F's MMPI-2-RF Profile.

symptoms (Fs, FBS-r, RBS), although her score on F-r (65T) was significantly higher than most in the female child custody comparison group. Although this score is not in the elevated range and does not reflect overreporting, it does indicate to the clinician that there are likely to be some elevations in clinically substantive portions of the profile (which is the case here). It is important to note that in this setting Ms. F did not exhibit any evidence of underreporting. Moreover, her scores on L-r (47T) and K-r (38T) were lower than most women in the female child custody comparison group, suggesting a greater level of openness into her psychological functioning than is typical in this context. Overall, her profile was valid for interpretation.

CLINICAL INTERPRETATION

Using the same interpretive strategy, we would start by examining the H-O scales, where we see that Ms. F's highest score was on THD (67T). Turning to other scales in this domain (RC6, RC8, PSYC-r), we see that she has a significantly elevated score on RC6 (80T). This is quite elevated, even in a child custody setting (98th percentile in the child custody comparison group), where those involved may already be prone to displaying a heightened level of suspiciousness of their partner, the attorneys involved, and the court. However, the six RC6 items she endorsed include those with the theme of others plotting against her, punishing her, and insulting her. Although a T score of 80 on RC6 could lead one to formulate a hypothesis about paranoia or delusional thinking, it is also quite possible that endorsement of these six items reflects feelings of resentment and hostility that have been exacerbated by the contextual experience of child custody litigation. It is also possible that her score on RC6 reflects situational/contextual stress as well as a more deeply engrained paranoia. This was explored during the clinical interview as well as with other collateral sources, and there was no historical evidence or indication that she experienced symptoms of psychosis or thought disorder. She presented as quite hostile toward her husband and two daughters, believing that he had "turned them against me." None of the remaining scales in this domain were elevated.

BXD was the next highest H-O Scale and was nearly elevated at a T score of 63. Similar to her score on THD, a T score of 63 on BXD is at the 97th percentile in relation to the female child custody comparison group and suggested the possibility of some behavioral problems, although we need to look at other scales on the test to form more specific impressions. Her scores on RC4 (65T), SUB (69T), JCP (63T), and DISC-r (66T) were all at or above the 96th percentile in relation to the child custody comparison group and suggested that she has problems with drugs and alcohol, poor impulse control, difficulty with authority, and general antisocial proclivities. Elevations on RC9 (66T) and AGGR-r (65T) have been found to be related to grandiose and narcissistic personality traits (Haneveld et al., 2017; Sellbom et al., 2013; Wygant & Sellbom, 2012).

With respect to the internalizing domain, neither EID nor two of the internalizing RC Scales (RCd and RC2) were elevated. On the contrary, her scores on both RC2 (38T) and INTR-r (32T) were both significantly low, suggesting that she is quite extroverted and experiences an abundance of positive emotions. Low scores on RC2 and INTR-r are also associated with social potency (Sellbom & Ben-Porath, 2005). Ms. F's score on RC7 (68T) was in the clinically significant range and suggested that she is prone to various negative emotional states. She did not present as particularly anxious or one who experiences internalizing dysfunction. The Internalizing SP Scales were helpful in characterizing her elevation on RC7. We see that she had only one elevation on this set of scales, ANP (66T). Thus, it is likely that her score on RC7 can be attributed to anger and hostility, which she harbors a great deal of in her interpersonal relationships. Indeed, during the clinical interview she acknowledged that she "snaps" at people "especially when I don't get what I want."

None of the scales in the somatic/cognitive domain were elevated, which is consistent with her description of her physical health as good. In the interpersonal domain, Ms. F had a score of 74T on RC3. Individuals scoring in that range on RC3 are particularly cynical in their general outlook and believe others will look out only for their own interests. She provided numerous statements during the clinical interview that were consistent with a misanthropic view of others, particularly those involved in the court. She believed the judge in her case was "against me" and she had been represented by three separate attorneys during the course of the divorce proceedings. She terminated her first two attorneys because "they weren't looking out for my best interests" and "I didn't trust that they would fight for me." It was apparent from her clinical interview that she had become increasingly alienated from others in the three years leading up to the separation, exhibiting a general contempt for those around her and weak interpersonal bonds. Her scores on RC3 and RC6 seem quite consistent with her level of mistrust of others and blame externalization. Other scores in the interpersonal domain include an elevation on FML (74T), which is congruent with her reported history of familial discord. She also obtained a low score on IPP (34T) which, consistent with her elevated scores on AGGR-r and RC9, would characterize her as domineering, assertive, and direct in her dealings with others. Her low score on SAV (36T) is consistent with her extroverted personality.

Overall, Ms. F produced a valid MMPI-2-RF profile that revealed significant maladaptive psychological functioning. Her test scores characterized the narcissistic qualities of her personality, suggesting that she likely thrives from attention, is interpersonally demanding, manipulative, and emotionally reactive. Her scores were also consistent with substance misuse. Unlike the father in this case, the mother's profile raised concern about several factors that could impact her ability to provide a stable environment for her children, namely her potential for substance abuse and angry, aggressive outbursts. As a result of the clinical interview, MMPI-2-RF results, and collateral sources, she was diagnosed with alcohol abuse and narcissistic personality disorder.

CASE OUTCOME

Although both parents expressed genuine concern about the welfare of their children, the evaluation revealed that that the negative aspects of their personalities and hostility toward each other had interfered with their parenting abilities, causing undue stress on their children. The mother had reportedly been physically assaultive toward the children on multiple occasions (which was unsubstantiated by police investigation) and her alcohol consumption had had a negative impact on her relationship with them. During the evaluation, the older daughter described numerous incidents during which her mother was intoxicated and exhibited violent and erratic behaviors. Although the children expressed a desire to maintain contact with their mother, they were strongly concerned about her emotional instability, poor anger management, and problematic use of alcohol in their presence. The daughters were in agreement that they preferred to reside with their father, whom they viewed as more emotionally stable.

Based on all of the information gathered during the evaluation, the judge's ruling designated the father as the sole residential and custodial parent for both children. In the judge's opinion, she noted that although Mr. F had several maladaptive personality characteristics and exhibited poor boundaries during the divorce proceedings, there was no evidence that he was abusive to the children. Moreover, the evidence from the custody evaluation suggested that he was more emotionally stable than Ms. F and the children were more emotionally attached to him. The judge noted concern in her ruling about Ms. F's misuse of alcohol and poorly managed angry outbursts. Nevertheless, she granted Ms. F a standard order of visitation with her two daughters.

CONCLUSIONS

Child custody evaluations are quite challenging and require the evaluator to make serious decisions that have the potential to profoundly impact those involved. Advances in child custody assessment (see Gould & Martindale, 2013; Martindale & Gould, 2004, 2007; Otto et al., 2003) have established a best-practices model that emphasizes scientific and ethical principles (see American Psychological Association, 2010). The MMPI-2-RF has the potential to contribute to the systematic and scientifically informed process of gathering information in a child custody evaluation. The MMPI-2-RF can provide objective data on response bias (including underreporting and defensiveness, which is of primary concern in this setting) as well as inform clinical and diagnostic impressions relevant to determining what is in the best interest of the children involved.

Chapter 10

Parental Fitness

The relationship and bond between parents and their children is by default unquestioned and sacred. Unfortunately, there are times when society must intervene in an effort to protect children's welfare owing to parental maltreatment (e.g., abuse and/or neglect). This process is complicated and involves legal proceedings to determine whether parents are sufficiently competent or invested in caring for their children. Psychologists and other mental health professionals are often sought out to assist legal decision makers by evaluating parents' psychological functioning as it pertains to their competence and caregiving abilities in light of children's safety and welfare. Ultimately, the decision makers need to determine custodial arrangements, which include visitation and permanency planning as well as the possibility for termination of parental rights (Budd, Connell, & Clark, 2013). A full account of the legal process is beyond the scope of this chapter, but Budd et al. (2013) provided a comprehensive review of the process and psychologists' role in it.

Typically, as in child custody evaluations (see Chapter 9), the "best interest of the child" is at the heart of child welfare laws, but is typically operationalized differently in parental fitness (sometimes referred to as parental capacity) as opposed to child custody evaluations (Budd et al., 2013). Often the definition is indeterminate and depends on the jurisdiction at hand, but it usually takes into account the child's age and developmental needs, safety, emotional and physical needs, parental and sibling bonds, and need for continuity (Budd et al., 2013). Psychologists are often asked to provide a functional assessment of the parents' capacity to meet the child's needs (developmental and psychological) as well as the quality of their relationship (Budd, 2001, 2005). A major feature of such determinations is that it typically applies to a minimal parental standard. Psychologists are not asked to consider the threshold for acceptable parenting as the optimal parent, or even the average parent. Rather, the threshold is typically the floor: the minimally acceptable level of parenting (Budd, 2001).

PARENTAL FITNESS EVALUATIONS

There are a number of challenges in assessing parental fitness. The most important is the lack of widely accepted standards for what constitutes minimally accepted parenting (Budd, 2001). In the absence of clear criteria, which is often a function of the jurisdiction, forensic examiners must use their best judgment in light of the evidence available to them. It is therefore very important that opinions are clearly elaborated and the evidence for the opinions clearly documented. For areas where the evidence is unclear or outright missing, it is important that examiners acknowledge the weaknesses in their opinions. This approach will allow legal decision makers to use the examiner's report and testimony in an optimal manner. Another challenge is the fact that parents are typically coerced into undergoing evaluations and will therefore often be defensive and may minimize significant faults (Budd, 2001; Budd et al., 2013). Such response bias is important to consider and evaluate directly when conducting these evaluations. Moreover, there are no straightforward measures of parenting fitness (Melton et al., 2007). The Child Abuse Potential Inventory (CAPI; Milner, 1986) has received some support (Milner, 1994), but Melton et al. (2007) recommended against it because it is primarily a research measure, not a clinical instrument. Budd (2001) therefore recommended that examiners consider and acknowledge the limitations of any psychological tests used for assessing parental fitness. Finally, it is also worth noting that parental fitness assessment involves a formulation about how a parent will treat his or her child in the future. This endeavor is quite difficult, as the base rates for child maltreatment are extremely difficult to estimate, and the tools available for other risk assessment purposes (e.g., general violence, sexual offending) are simply not applicable in this context (Budd, 2001; Budd et al., 2013; Melton et al., 2007).

The process of a parental fitness evaluation is not unlike other forensic psychological evaluations that we have already reviewed. The first step is to carefully review all records available from the child protection agency in the forensic examiner's jurisdiction. Although this is important in every case, in abuse and neglect cases, parents have a tendency to underreport, and inconsistencies in records are important to investigate during the interview. The clinical interview should, whenever possible, come after record reviews and serves as the vehicle for getting an impression of the parents' account of the situation that led to the removal of children from the home, history of any maltreatment, any parenting services received, current living situation, and personal background history. It is imperative to explore and develop an understanding of the parents' perception of the parent–child relationship, including the children's needs, developmental progress and associated expectations, attachment, empathy, etc. An understanding of the parents' expectations of how to handle the current situation, how to best move forward, and the ultimate outcome is very useful (Budd, 2001).

Third-party information, such as collateral sources, in addition to available records can be quite useful. Although family members and friends of the parents might be biased in their information, others such as long-time case workers and lawyers (particularly those serving as guardian ad litem for the child) can be helpful. Observing parent and child interactions is helpful when feasible. Often, however, parents will have supervised visitation of children while in foster care, and social workers reports documenting parent–child interactions are important to consider. Furthermore, the administration of psychological testing is important, considering the limitations described earlier. In some cases, intelligence tests of parents are needed to rule out any intellectual challenges in caring for children as well as successfully completing necessary interventions. Personality and symptom inventories can be helpful in elucidating any mental health problems or maladaptive personality traits that could interfere with parenting and child welfare, as well as potential personal strengths that would be adaptive for parenting. Finally, although interview or evaluation of the children is not a typical practice, it might occasionally be necessary when certain aspects of child functioning and needs are important in a particular case (Budd et al., 2013).

CONSIDERATIONS FOR USING THE MMPI-2-RF IN PARENTAL FITNESS EVALUATIONS

Budd et al. (2013) recommended that psychological tests in parental fitness evaluations be considered according to four broad factors: (a) adds information to other sources; (b) provides valuable data on relevant constructs; (c) has good psychometric properties for their intended use; and (d) provides evidence for use with the parents' cultural group.

The MMPI-2-RF is not a measure of parenting skills nor will it have substantial utility in directly predicting future child maltreatment. Nonetheless, we believe that the MMPI-2-RF is useful in assessing the psychological functioning of the parents. More specifically, the test can provide an objective source of data regarding various psychopathological constructs (e.g., depression, anxiety, substance misuse), behavioral proclivities (e.g., aggression and poor impulse control), and both adaptive (e.g., resilience, interpersonal affiliation) and maladaptive personality characteristics (e.g., interpersonal passivity). Moreover, the MMPI-2-RF, unlike many other assessment sources, includes an assessment of response bias. Validity Scales L-r and K-r are well-validated measures of underreporting (e.g., Sellbom & Bagby, 2008), which is critical in these evaluations. Furthermore, the MMPI-2-RF has good psychometric properties, as described in previous chapters, including in samples with a wide range of diversity.

Research has been published on the MMPI-2-RF in parental fitness evaluations. A few studies have shown descriptive data for MMPI-2-RF scale scores in such evaluations, which is important because they allow the forensic examiner to get an indication of typical and atypical scores in this population. Stredny et al. (2006) and Resendes and Lecci (2012) showed average profiles for the RC Scales only. These studies were remarkably similar, with RC6 being the highest average score (60T), with RC3 and RC4 being the next two highest scales (~55T). Pinsoneault and Ezzo (2012) observed similar scores in parents evaluated for parental fitness owing to child maltreatment. Moreover, they found that scores on scales L-r, THD, RC3, RC6, and FML were higher for these parents than for a group of parents undergoing child custody evaluations without a history of child maltreatment. Furthermore, L-r (67T) was associated with the largest mean scale score, which should signal to the forensic examiner that underreporting is indeed prevalent in this setting. The MMPI-2-RF scoring software (Q-global and Q Local) now includes a parental fitness comparison group to frame the results of an evaluee in relation to others in this context.

Most recently, Solomon, Morgan, Asberg, and McCord (2014) examined the concurrent associations between MMPI-2-RF H-O Scale scores and CAPI scores in a sample of 178 parents who were court-ordered to undergo parental fitness evaluations. They found that the EID Scale, but not BXD or THD, predicted CAPI scores. Although these results were somewhat surprising, the authors speculated that the content similarity of EID and CAPI could have explained these associations.

CASE EXAMPLE 10-1

Case Background

Ms. G is a 27-year-old Caucasian woman whose four children had been removed from her custody.[1] She and her partner of 12 years had shown a long history of abuse and neglect toward the children, with numerous interventions by the local child and family services. The current case was primarily neglect. The home was found to be in extremely poor condition, very dirty, moldy, and generally disordered. There were used diapers laying on the floor and the home was heavily insect-infested. The children all evidenced extremely poor hygiene and exhibited psychiatric and/or severe behavioral problems. For instance, her 11-year-old son was diagnosed with attention deficit/hyperactivity disorder and was suspended numerous times in school, on the verge of expulsion. Her 9-year-old daughter was aggressive and broke her younger brother's arm. She also acted in a hypersexual manner toward her older brother, such as walking into his room naked. Her youngest son was 3 years old, highly uncoordinated, and unable to form full sentences. The state of neglect was in part attributed to the parents' severe substance (narcotic) abuse. The children were removed from the home and placed in foster care with their maternal grandmother.

Ms. G had been with her partner "off and on" for the past 12 years. They had their first child when Ms. G was 16 years old. The relationship was described as extremely toxic. There were numerous instances of domestic violence and emotional abuse perpetrated by the father, though the physical violence was often mutual. After the children were removed from the home, they ended their relationship and blamed each other for the circumstances. Ms. G described growing up in a similar environment as her own children. Her mother (current custodian of Ms. G's children) was reportedly emotionally and physically abusive as well as dismissive and invalidating of her feelings. Ms. G explained that she was raped twice as a teenager and her mother did not express any care in the matter. Furthermore, Ms. G had major behavioral problems as an adolescent. She started drinking alcohol and smoking marijuana in her early teens, and described herself as promiscuous prior to meeting her children's father at age 15. She also acknowledged chronic opiate abuse since the age of 21 and had at times been dependent on heroin. Ms. G also had a history of mental health treatment; she stated that she had been diagnosed with "bipolar" and other conditions which all share symptoms of emotional and behavioral dysregulation. During the interview, Ms. G voiced significant interpersonal suspiciousness (including of the examiner), significant anger, and blame externalizing.

Issues Pertaining to Parental Fitness

Ms. G appeared to have a fair amount of parental knowledge; she could adequately describe developmental milestones and had a basic perception of her children's developmental states. She expressed some realization that her youngest son was delayed in language and her other children were hyperactive. However, Ms. G displayed very poor parental judgment. She showed severe neglect of her children's needs including hygiene and proper medical attention. She acknowledged that she would medicate her children with sedatives at times when they were disobeying. Ms. G and her partner would also occasionally sell their children's medication. She acknowledged verbal abuse of the children but denied physical abuse (despite recorded history of such). She would frequently drink alcohol, smoke marijuana, and abuse opiates in the home in front of the children. Ms. G and her partner would also engage in verbal and physical violence in front of the children. Moreover, Ms. G displayed questionable empathy. Despite her own reported experiences, she was quite dismissive of allegations that her brother had sexually abused her daughter and did not view them as worthy of investigation, despite a formal ongoing police inquiry into the matter. Ms. G would also inform her children that she had a brain tumor and would soon die without considering the impact such statements might have on them. At other times, she made fleeting statements in front of her children about committing suicide. She displayed an incredibly poor understanding of her children's emotional difficulties and psychiatric problems and expressed mostly indifference toward them, saying "that's just how kids are." Finally, Ms. G displayed extremely poor insight into her own functioning. She did not believe that her substance abuse was creating substantial problems in her life. She blamed her mother (or her partner) for most of her problems.

MMPI-2-RF Results

PROTOCOL VALIDITY

Ms. G provided scorable responses to all of the MMPI-2-RF items (CNS = 0). Her VRIN-r score was somewhat elevated (73T), suggesting some possibility for careless/inconsistent responding. Therefore, some caution should be exercised when interpreting this profile. There was no evidence of indiscriminant fixed responding (TRIN-r) or overreporting (F-r, Fp-r, Fs, FBS-r, RBS). The underreporting scales show an opposing pattern. Ms. G's L-r score was high (71T), which indicates significant concerns about underreporting, particularly presenting herself in an overly virtuous manner. On the other hand, her K-r score was quite low (38T), indicating that she might have been quite open about psychological maladjustment. In other words, she was open about having psychological problems, but wanted to ensure that she presented as a "good person." The comparison group (Parental Fitness Evaluee [Woman]) is very useful here. Her level of underreporting from the perspective of L-r is well within the range of what is typical in these evaluations, but her score on K-r is substantially lower than typical.

CLINICAL INTERPRETATION

The H-O Scales allow us to organize the interpretation of Ms. G's substantive scales. The only elevated H-O Scale was BXD (65T), which indicated pervasive behavioral dysfunction in several areas. RC4, SUB, AGG, and DISC-r were elevated within this domain (JCP at 63T was close to being elevated). This pattern of scale elevations pointed to a nonadherence to social norms and standards, authority problems, impulsivity, substance abuse problems, a proneness to engage in verbal and physical aggression, and thrill-seeking tendencies. Moreover, her DISC-r score suggested a personality proclivity toward externalizing behavior.

Because no additional H-O Scales were elevated, the RC Scales were consulted next. Both RC1 and RC7 were elevated at 65T. We will cover the emotional dysfunction domain first. Both RC7 and NEGE-r (66T) indicated a dispositional proclivity toward experiencing negative emotions, including poor stress-reactivity and anxious apprehension (STW = 65T), as well as anger, irritability, and poor frustration tolerance (ANP = 73T). It is interesting that her RCd scale score was 49T, so she is unlikely to be significantly distressed about her current circumstances. Her SFD and NFC scores were at the floor,

Minnesota Multiphasic
Personality Inventory-2
Restructured Form®

Score Report

MMPI-2-RF®

Minnesota Multiphasic Personality Inventory-2-Restructured Form®

Yossef S. Ben-Porath, PhD, & Auke Tellegen, PhD

Name:	Ms. G
ID Number:	10
Age:	27
Gender:	Female
Marital Status:	Not reported
Years of Education:	12
Date Assessed:	06/19/2013

ALWAYS LEARNING

PEARSON

FIGURE 10-1 Case Example 10-1: Ms. G's MMPI-2-RF Profile, continued.

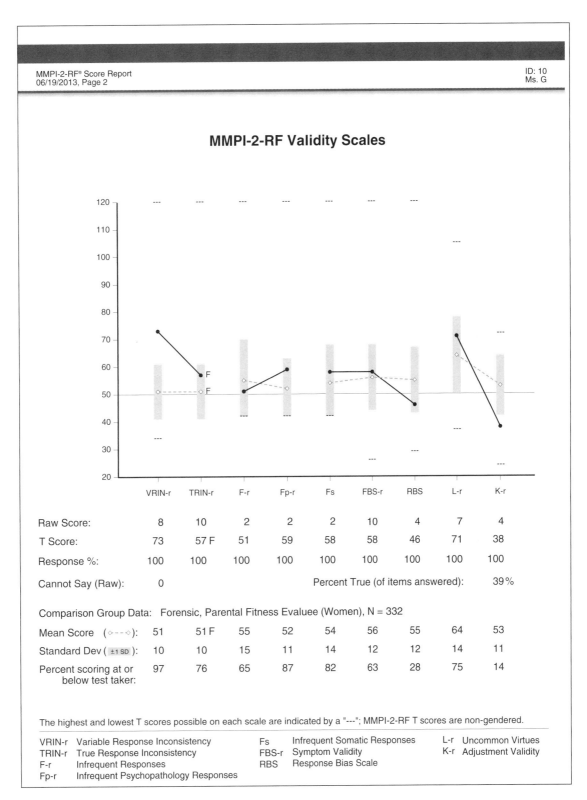

MMPI-2-RF Validity Scales

	VRIN-r	TRIN-r	F-r	Fp-r	Fs	FBS-r	RBS	L-r	K-r
Raw Score:	8	10	2	2	2	10	4	7	4
T Score:	73	57 F	51	59	58	58	46	71	38
Response %:	100	100	100	100	100	100	100	100	100

Cannot Say (Raw):   0   Percent True (of items answered):   39%

Comparison Group Data: Forensic, Parental Fitness Evaluee (Women), N = 332

	VRIN-r	TRIN-r	F-r	Fp-r	Fs	FBS-r	RBS	L-r	K-r
Mean Score (◇---◇):	51	51 F	55	52	54	56	55	64	53
Standard Dev (±1 SD):	10	10	15	11	14	12	12	14	11
Percent scoring at or below test taker:	97	76	65	87	82	63	28	75	14

The highest and lowest T scores possible on each scale are indicated by a "---"; MMPI-2-RF T scores are non-gendered.

VRIN-r	Variable Response Inconsistency	Fs	Infrequent Somatic Responses	L-r	Uncommon Virtues
TRIN-r	True Response Inconsistency	FBS-r	Symptom Validity	K-r	Adjustment Validity
F-r	Infrequent Responses	RBS	Response Bias Scale		
Fp-r	Infrequent Psychopathology Responses				

FIGURE 10-1 Case Example 10-1: Ms. G's MMPI-2-RF Profile, continued.

217

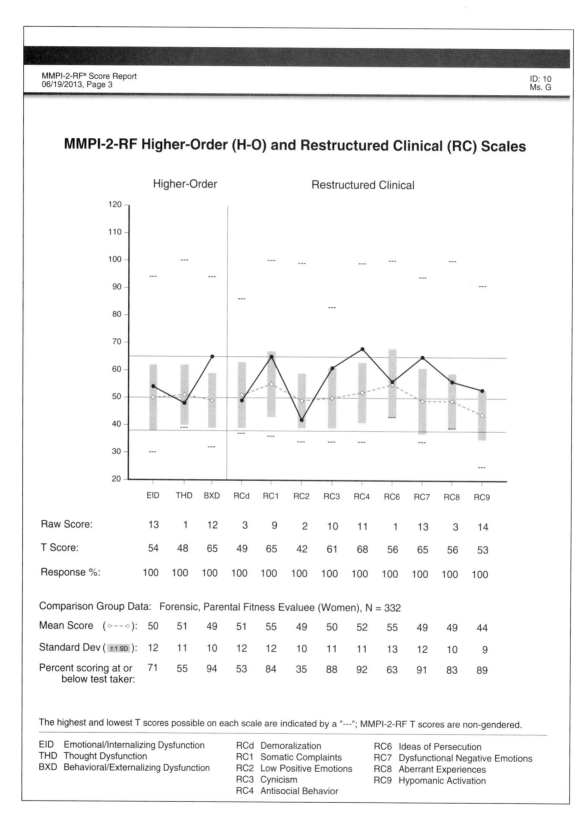

MMPI-2-RF Higher-Order (H-O) and Restructured Clinical (RC) Scales

	EID	THD	BXD	RCd	RC1	RC2	RC3	RC4	RC6	RC7	RC8	RC9
Raw Score:	13	1	12	3	9	2	10	11	1	13	3	14
T Score:	54	48	65	49	65	42	61	68	56	65	56	53
Response %:	100	100	100	100	100	100	100	100	100	100	100	100

Comparison Group Data: Forensic, Parental Fitness Evaluee (Women), N = 332

	EID	THD	BXD	RCd	RC1	RC2	RC3	RC4	RC6	RC7	RC8	RC9
Mean Score (◇---◇):	50	51	49	51	55	49	50	52	55	49	49	44
Standard Dev (±1 SD):	12	11	10	12	12	10	11	11	13	12	10	9
Percent scoring at or below test taker:	71	55	94	53	84	35	88	92	63	91	83	89

The highest and lowest T scores possible on each scale are indicated by a "---"; MMPI-2-RF T scores are non-gendered.

EID Emotional/Internalizing Dysfunction	RCd Demoralization	RC6 Ideas of Persecution
THD Thought Dysfunction	RC1 Somatic Complaints	RC7 Dysfunctional Negative Emotions
BXD Behavioral/Externalizing Dysfunction	RC2 Low Positive Emotions	RC8 Aberrant Experiences
	RC3 Cynicism	RC9 Hypomanic Activation
	RC4 Antisocial Behavior	

FIGURE 10-1 Case Example 10-1: Ms. G's MMPI-2-RF Profile, continued.

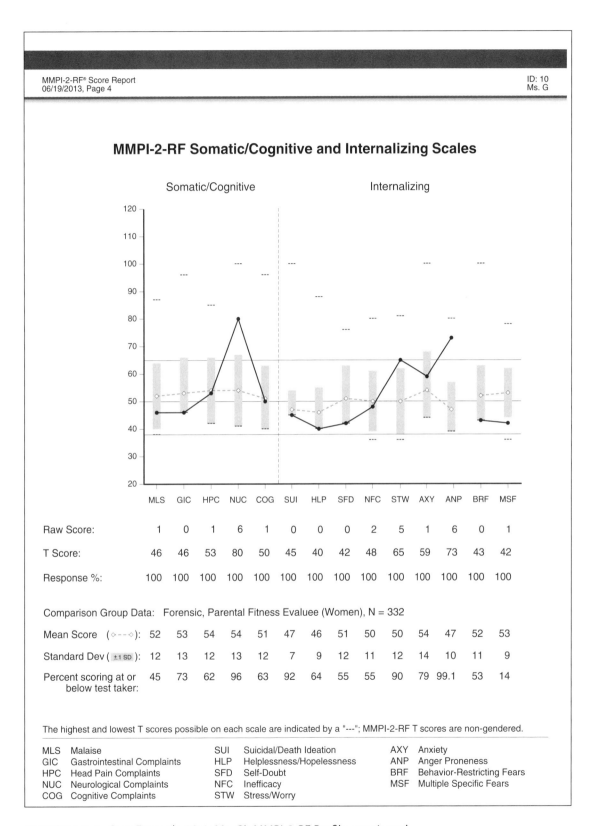

MMPI-2-RF Somatic/Cognitive and Internalizing Scales

Somatic/Cognitive   Internalizing

	MLS	GIC	HPC	NUC	COG	SUI	HLP	SFD	NFC	STW	AXY	ANP	BRF	MSF
Raw Score:	1	0	1	6	1	0	0	0	2	5	1	6	0	1
T Score:	46	46	53	80	50	45	40	42	48	65	59	73	43	42
Response %:	100	100	100	100	100	100	100	100	100	100	100	100	100	100

Comparison Group Data: Forensic, Parental Fitness Evaluee (Women), N = 332

	MLS	GIC	HPC	NUC	COG	SUI	HLP	SFD	NFC	STW	AXY	ANP	BRF	MSF
Mean Score (◇- -◇):	52	53	54	54	51	47	46	51	50	50	54	47	52	53
Standard Dev (±1 SD):	12	13	12	13	12	7	9	12	11	12	14	10	11	9
Percent scoring at or below test taker:	45	73	62	96	63	92	64	55	55	90	79	99.1	53	14

The highest and lowest T scores possible on each scale are indicated by a "---"; MMPI-2-RF T scores are non-gendered.

MLS	Malaise	SUI	Suicidal/Death Ideation	AXY	Anxiety
GIC	Gastrointestinal Complaints	HLP	Helplessness/Hopelessness	ANP	Anger Proneness
HPC	Head Pain Complaints	SFD	Self-Doubt	BRF	Behavior-Restricting Fears
NUC	Neurological Complaints	NFC	Inefficacy	MSF	Multiple Specific Fears
COG	Cognitive Complaints	STW	Stress/Worry		

FIGURE 10-1 Case Example 10-1: Ms. G's MMPI-2-RF Profile, continued.

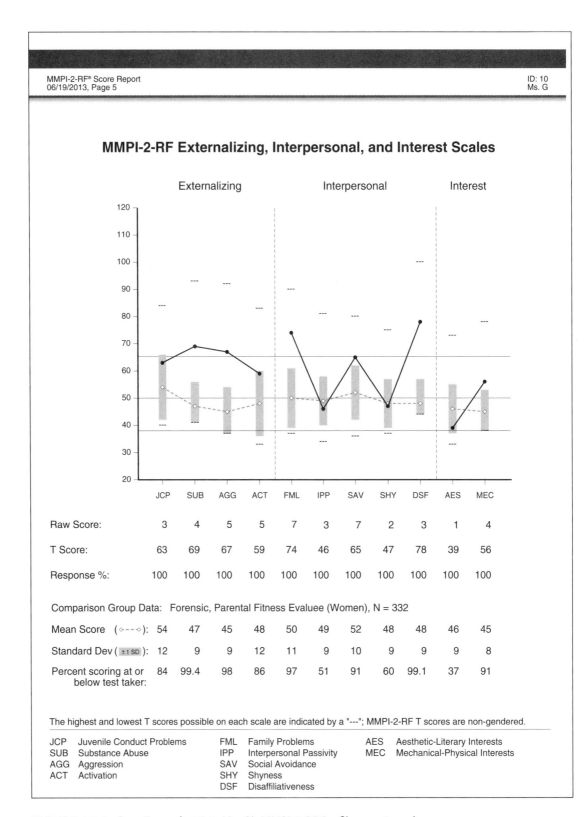

MMPI-2-RF Externalizing, Interpersonal, and Interest Scales

	Externalizing				Interpersonal					Interest	
	JCP	SUB	AGG	ACT	FML	IPP	SAV	SHY	DSF	AES	MEC
Raw Score:	3	4	5	5	7	3	7	2	3	1	4
T Score:	63	69	67	59	74	46	65	47	78	39	56
Response %:	100	100	100	100	100	100	100	100	100	100	100

Comparison Group Data: Forensic, Parental Fitness Evaluee (Women), N = 332

	JCP	SUB	AGG	ACT	FML	IPP	SAV	SHY	DSF	AES	MEC
Mean Score (◇--◇):	54	47	45	48	50	49	52	48	48	46	45
Standard Dev (±1 SD):	12	9	9	12	11	9	10	9	9	9	8
Percent scoring at or below test taker:	84	99.4	98	86	97	51	91	60	99.1	37	91

The highest and lowest T scores possible on each scale are indicated by a "---"; MMPI-2-RF T scores are non-gendered.

JCP	Juvenile Conduct Problems	FML	Family Problems	AES	Aesthetic-Literary Interests
SUB	Substance Abuse	IPP	Interpersonal Passivity	MEC	Mechanical-Physical Interests
AGG	Aggression	SAV	Social Avoidance		
ACT	Activation	SHY	Shyness		
		DSF	Disaffiliativeness		

FIGURE 10-1 Case Example 10-1: Ms. G's MMPI-2-RF Profile, continued.

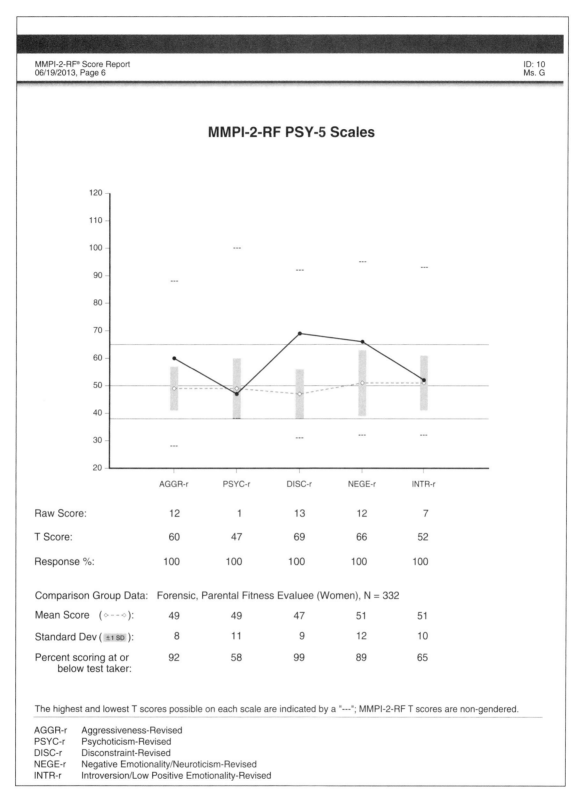

MMPI-2-RF PSY-5 Scales

	AGGR-r	PSYC-r	DISC-r	NEGE-r	INTR-r
Raw Score:	12	1	13	12	7
T Score:	60	47	69	66	52
Response %:	100	100	100	100	100

Comparison Group Data: Forensic, Parental Fitness Evaluee (Women), N = 332

Mean Score (◇---◇):	49	49	47	51	51
Standard Dev (±1 SD):	8	11	9	12	10
Percent scoring at or below test taker:	92	58	99	89	65

The highest and lowest T scores possible on each scale are indicated by a "---"; MMPI-2-RF T scores are non-gendered.

AGGR-r Aggressiveness-Revised
PSYC-r Psychoticism-Revised
DISC-r Disconstraint-Revised
NEGE-r Negative Emotionality/Neuroticism-Revised
INTR-r Introversion/Low Positive Emotionality-Revised

FIGURE 10-1 Case Example 10-1: Ms. G's MMPI-2-RF Profile, continued.

MMPI-2-RF T SCORES (BY DOMAIN)

PROTOCOL VALIDITY

Content Non-Responsiveness

0	73	57 F
CNS	VRIN-r	TRIN-r

Over-Reporting

51	59		58	58	46
F-r	Fp-r		Fs	FBS-r	RBS

Under-Reporting

71	38
L-r	K-r

SUBSTANTIVE SCALES

Somatic/Cognitive Dysfunction

65	46	46	53	80	50
RC1	MLS	GIC	HPC	NUC	COG

Emotional Dysfunction

54					
EID					

49	45	40	42	48
RCd	SUI	HLP	SFD	NFC

42	52
RC2	INTR-r

65	65	59	73	43	42	66
RC7	STW	AXY	ANP	BRF	MSF	NEGE-r

Thought Dysfunction

48
THD

56
RC6

56
RC8

47
PSYC-r

Behavioral Dysfunction

65
BXD

68	63	69
RC4	JCP	SUB

53	67	59	60	69
RC9	AGG	ACT	AGGR-r	DISC-r

Interpersonal Functioning

74	61	46	65	47	78
FML	RC3	IPP	SAV	SHY	DSF

Interests

39	56
AES	MEC

Note. This information is provided to facilitate interpretation following the recommended structure for MMPI-2-RF interpretation in Chapter 5 of the *MMPI-2-RF Manual for Administration, Scoring, and Interpretation*, which provides details in the text and an outline in Table 5-1.

FIGURE 10-1 Case Example 10-1: Ms. G's MMPI-2-RF Profile, continued.

ITEM-LEVEL INFORMATION

Unscorable Responses

The test taker produced scorable responses to all the MMPI-2-RF items.

Critical Responses

Seven MMPI-2-RF scales--Suicidal/Death Ideation (SUI), Helplessness/Hopelessness (HLP), Anxiety (AXY), Ideas of Persecution (RC6), Aberrant Experiences (RC8), Substance Abuse (SUB), and Aggression (AGG)--have been designated by the test authors as having critical item content that may require immediate attention and follow-up. Items answered by the individual in the keyed direction (True or False) on a critical scale are listed below if her T score on that scale is 65 or higher. The percentage of the MMPI-2-RF normative sample (NS) and of the Forensic, Parental Fitness Evaluee (Women) comparison group (CG) that answered each item in the keyed direction are provided in parentheses following the item content.

Substance Abuse (SUB, T Score = 69)

    49. Item Content Omitted. (True; NS 29.6%, CG 18.7%)
  237. Item Content Omitted. (False; NS 27.4%, CG 24.4%)
  266. Item Content Omitted. (True; NS 5.0%, CG 17.5%)
  297. Item Content Omitted. (True; NS 14.4%, CG 1.8%)

Aggression (AGG, T Score = 67)

    23. Item Content Omitted. (True; NS 39.0%, CG 17.5%)
    84. Item Content Omitted. (True; NS 12.1%, CG 3.9%)
  316. Item Content Omitted. (True; NS 45.1%, CG 31.3%)
  329. Item Content Omitted. (True; NS 12.7%, CG 9.6%)
  337. Item Content Omitted. (True; NS 50.2%, CG 35.8%)

User-Designated Item-Level Information

The following item-level information is based on the report user's selection of additional scales, and/or of lower cutoffs for the critical scales from the previous section. Items answered by the test taker in the keyed direction (True or False) on a selected scale are listed below if her T score on that scale is at the user-designated cutoff score or higher. The percentage of the MMPI-2-RF normative sample (NS) and of the Forensic, Parental Fitness Evaluee (Women) comparison group (CG) that answered each item in the keyed direction are provided in parentheses following the item content.

Behavioral/Externalizing Dysfunction (BXD, T Score = 65)

  21. Item Content Omitted. (True; NS 47.1%, CG 37.0%)
  49. Item Content Omitted. (True; NS 29.6%, CG 18.7%)
  61. Item Content Omitted. (False; NS 61.6%, CG 41.3%)

FIGURE 10-1 Case Example 10-1: Ms. G's MMPI-2-RF Profile, continued.

66. Item Content Omitted. (True; NS 20.3%, CG 29.8%)
84. Item Content Omitted. (True; NS 12.1%, CG 3.9%)
190. Item Content Omitted. (False; NS 28.6%, CG 62.3%)
223. Item Content Omitted. (True; NS 12.3%, CG 26.2%)
237. Item Content Omitted. (False; NS 27.4%, CG 24.4%)
266. Item Content Omitted. (True; NS 5.0%, CG 17.5%)
292. Item Content Omitted. (True; NS 26.1%, CG 18.7%)
316. Item Content Omitted. (True; NS 45.1%, CG
    31.3%)
329. Item Content Omitted. (True; NS 12.7%, CG
    9.6%)

Antisocial Behavior (RC4, T Score = 68)

19. Item Content Omitted. (False; NS 17.0%, CG
    25.6%)
21. Item Content Omitted. (True; NS 47.1%, CG 37.0%)
49. Item Content Omitted. (True; NS 29.6%, CG 18.7%)
66. Item Content Omitted. (True; NS 20.3%, CG 29.8%)
80. Item Content Omitted. (False; NS 21.2%, CG 29.8%)
190. Item Content Omitted. (False; NS 28.6%, CG 62.3%)
223. Item Content Omitted. (True; NS 12.3%, CG 26.2%)
237. Item Content Omitted. (False; NS 27.4%, CG 24.4%)
266. Item Content Omitted. (True; NS 5.0%, CG 17.5%)
297. Item Content Omitted. (True; NS 14.4%, CG 1.8%)
329. Item Content Omitted. (True; NS 12.7%, CG
    9.6%)

Ideas of Persecution (RC6, T Score = 56)

233. Item Content Omitted. (True; NS 5.5%, CG 22.3%)

Dysfunctional Negative Emotions (RC7, T Score = 65)

23. Item Content Omitted. (True; NS 39.0%, CG 17.5%)
51. Item Content Omitted. (True; NS 15.4%, CG
    16.0%)
63. Item Content Omitted. (True; NS 24.3%, CG 28.9%)
77. Item Content Omitted. (True; NS 24.8%, CG 37.7%)
112. Item Content Omitted.
    (True; NS 23.1%, CG 23.5%)
119. Item Content Omitted. (True; NS 39.5%, CG 20.2%)
228. Item Content Omitted. (True; NS 17.3%, CG 22.0%)
235. Item Content Omitted. (True; NS 12.1%,
    CG 13.0%)
263. Item Content Omitted.
    (True; NS 64.0%, CG 49.7%)
303. Item Content Omitted. (True; NS 28.6%, CG 18.7%)

FIGURE 10-1 Case Example 10-1: Ms. G's MMPI-2-RF Profile, continued.

224

318. Item Content Omitted. (True; NS 19.9%, CG
    17.5%)
322. Item Content Omitted. (True; NS 46.8%, CG 41.6%)
335. Item Content Omitted. (True; NS 30.1%, CG 39.5%)

Hypomanic Activation (RC9, T Score = 53)

  61. Item Content Omitted. (False; NS 61.6%, CG 41.3%)
  72. Item Content Omitted. (True; NS 81.5%, CG
    55.1%)
  84. Item Content Omitted. (True; NS 12.1%, CG 3.9%)
118. Item Content Omitted. (True; NS 57.4%, CG 44.9%)
155. Item Content Omitted. (True; NS 41.6%, CG 30.7%)
166. Item Content Omitted.
    (True; NS 38.9%, CG 30.1%)
181. Item Content Omitted. (True; NS 35.3%, CG 42.2%)
219. Item Content Omitted. (True; NS 51.5%, CG 41.9%)
244. Item Content Omitted. (True; NS
    56.9%, CG 84.0%)
256. Item Content Omitted. (True; NS
    65.7%, CG 55.7%)
292. Item Content Omitted. (True; NS 26.1%, CG 18.7%)
316. Item Content Omitted. (True; NS 45.1%, CG
    31.3%)
327. Item Content Omitted.
    (True; NS 41.7%, CG 25.0%)
337. Item Content Omitted. (True; NS 50.2%,
    CG 35.8%)

Anger Proneness (ANP, T Score = 73)

119. Item Content Omitted. (True; NS 39.5%, CG 20.2%)
134. Item Content Omitted. (False; NS 32.5%, CG 20.8%)
155. Item Content Omitted. (True; NS 41.6%, CG 30.7%)
293. Item Content Omitted. (False; NS 18.5%, CG 20.5%)
303. Item Content Omitted. (True; NS 28.6%, CG 18.7%)
318. Item Content Omitted. (True; NS 19.9%, CG
    17.5%)

Behavior-Restricting Fears (BRF, T Score = 43)

    No items that are scored on this scale were answered in the keyed direction.

Juvenile Conduct Problems (JCP, T Score = 63)

  21. Item Content Omitted. (True; NS 47.1%, CG 37.0%)
  66. Item Content Omitted. (True; NS 20.3%, CG 29.8%)
223. Item Content Omitted. (True; NS 12.3%, CG 26.2%)

FIGURE 10-1 Case Example 10-1: Ms. G's MMPI-2-RF Profile, continued.

Disconstraint-Revised (DISC-r, T Score = 69)

   21. Item Content Omitted. (True; NS 47.1%, CG 37.0%)
   42. Item Content Omitted. (True; NS 10.3%, CG 10.2%)
   49. Item Content Omitted. (True; NS 29.6%, CG 18.7%)
   61. Item Content Omitted. (False; NS 61.6%, CG 41.3%)
   66. Item Content Omitted. (True; NS 20.3%, CG 29.8%)
   75. Item Content Omitted. (True; NS 50.3%, CG 33.1%)
  115. Item Content Omitted. (True; NS 55.0%, CG 42.5%)
  190. Item Content Omitted. (False; NS 28.6%, CG 62.3%)
  223. Item Content Omitted. (True; NS 12.3%, CG 26.2%)
  237. Item Content Omitted. (False; NS 27.4%, CG 24.4%)
  292. Item Content Omitted. (True; NS 26.1%, CG 18.7%)
  297. Item Content Omitted. (True; NS 14.4%, CG 1.8%)
  300. Item Content Omitted. (True; NS 26.5%, CG 22.6%)

Negative Emotionality/Neuroticism-Revised (NEGE-r, T Score = 66)

   23. Item Content Omitted. (True; NS 39.0%, CG 17.5%)
   37. Item Content Omitted. (False; NS 56.3%, CG 57.2%)
   73. Item Content Omitted. (False; NS 16.6%, CG 26.2%)
   77. Item Content Omitted. (True; NS 24.8%, CG 37.7%)
  123. Item Content Omitted. (True; NS 28.0%, CG 28.6%)
  134. Item Content Omitted. (False; NS 32.5%, CG 20.8%)
  155. Item Content Omitted. (True; NS 41.6%, CG 30.7%)
  209. Item Content Omitted. (True; NS 32.5%, CG 78.0%)
  234. Item Content Omitted. (False; NS 53.9%, CG 67.2%)
  263. Item Content Omitted.
     (True; NS 64.0%, CG 49.7%)
  293. Item Content Omitted. (False; NS 18.5%, CG 20.5%)
  309. Item Content Omitted. (True; NS 34.0%, CG 44.3%)

End of Report

FIGURE 10-1 Case Example 10-1: Ms. G's MMPI-2-RF Profile.

indicating no endorsement of self-doubt, feelings of worthlessness, inefficacy, or problems with decision making. In other words, she is stress-reactive, becomes angry and aggressive to a clinical degree, but she is not generally distressed and unhappy, nor does she feel bad about herself. This information is not surprising in light of the poor insight Ms. G displayed during the evaluation, and her behavior being highly consistent with her historical functioning.

Next, we interpreted RC1 and the somatic/cognitive domain. Ms. G is likely prone to somatic preoccupation, especially with respect to NUC (80T). It is possible that some of her distress is manifested in somatic complaints. Indeed, at very stressful times, she would frequently complain about various medical problems, without medical evidence or diagnosis to support them, including that she likely had a brain tumor. It is also possible that her high NUC score was the result of withdrawal from opiates. Many of the NUC items concern tremors and bodily shaking.

Finally, Ms. G's Interpersonal Scales were interpreted. Although RC3 was not clinically elevated (61T), it was above average for the setting, and she did express some general suspiciousness of other people. FML was elevated, which is not surprising given both her history and current circumstances. Her SAV elevation (65T) indicated a preference for solitude and introversion, whereas her very high DSF score (78T) suggested a lack of emotional connectivity with others, outright dislike of other people, and preference for not being around them. This level of disaffiliativeness could partly explain her lack of desire to fully connect emotionally with her children and her dismissive and neglectful stance toward them.

Case Conclusion

It was the forensic examiner's opinion that Ms. G. exhibited a number of current deficits that rendered her unable to adequately meet her children's needs. Her own emotional, substance abuse, and anger problems, along with her lack of full insight into them, were deemed to be safety issues for her children. Her poor parental judgment was deemed pervasive and warranted significant improvement to ensure adequate welfare for her children. Moreover, she had significantly limited empathy for her children and the effects that her behavior had on them. The family court judge eventually ordered Ms. G to follow an intense intervention protocol to improve her mental health, judgment, and insight, as well as to maintain sobriety and gain adequate parental skills before further consideration for reunification would take place.

CONCLUSIONS

The MMPI-2-RF can certainly have a place in parental fitness evaluations provided the forensic examiner has a good understanding of its role and articulates this to the legal decision maker. In this case, the MMPI-2-RF reflected the mother's approach to the evaluation as well as her significant emotional, behavioral, and interpersonal problems. It also raised some potential concerns about somatization not available in other information sources. The general profile also indicated significantly poor insight, supporting the impressions from the interview.

Chapter 11

Personal Injury and Disability Determination

Differing substantially from the criminal arena, civil litigation is tasked with examining liability between a plaintiff (who brings the lawsuit) and a defendant (the respondent to the lawsuit). Plaintiffs file a civil complaint (tort or lawsuit), claiming that the defendant harmed them in a particular fashion (e.g., injury or damages to property). The court utilizes a series of procedures to establish the veracity of the claim, and, if successful, awards compensatory damages (often in the form of a monetary award). Civil procedure establishes the manner in which the plaintiff files the complaint and how the matter is investigated through the pretrial phase of the case. Psychologists become involved in civil cases when the plaintiff makes a claim that the defendant's actions (or failure to act in a neglect case) resulted in psychological damages (as well as any physical or financial damages). The psychologist may be retained by the plaintiff's counsel early on in the case to investigate whether there is enough evidence to substantiate the psychological basis of the claim (e.g., whether the defendant's actions indeed resulted in psychological damages, such as posttraumatic stress disorder [PTSD]). A psychologist may also be retained by the defendant's counsel, as the adversarial nature of the litigation process affords the defendant an opportunity to have the plaintiff evaluated by his or her retained expert for the purposes of examining the claim. Once retained, the psychologist usually conducts a forensic psychological evaluation and may be asked to prepare a report detailing the findings of the assessment. In some instances, psychologists will introduce and substantiate their position through other means of discovery, most notably a deposition.

Regardless of the retaining side, the psychologist is tasked with providing objective information about the plaintiff's psychological functioning in relation to the damages stemming from the defendant's actions (or inactions depending on the nature of the lawsuit). It is important for the psychologist working in this arena to have some knowledge of the statutes, regulations, standards, and case law pertaining to matters such as the standard defining negligent infliction of emotional distress. These matters vary to some degree by jurisdiction.

SPECIFIC AREAS OF CIVIL LITIGATION

Numerous types of civil litigation disputes have the potential to involve a psychological aspect of the claim. The current chapter will focus on two areas of civil litigation: personal injury litigation and disability/workers' compensation claims. Other areas of civil litigation that may have a psychological component include employment discrimination or harassment and issues related to the Americans with Disabilities Act (see Baker, Vasquez, & Shullman, 2013; Foote & Lareau, 2013; Wygant & Lareau, 2015, for a discussion of these issues).

Personal Injury Litigation

A civil tort begins with a claim filed by a plaintiff that the defendant has caused physical or emotional damage (or both) in one of three ways: negligence, defamation, or intentional behavior. Negligence occurs when a defendant unintentionally causes harm to a plaintiff when that behavior could have foreseeably harmed the individual and the defendant's conduct fell below the standard of care of a reasonable and careful person. If this claim is substantiated in court, the plaintiff is entitled to compensation as a result of the damage, which can include financial awards to compensate economic losses, pain and suffering, and present and future lost earnings. Defamation occurs when a defendant makes a false statement about a plaintiff (either through spoken [slander] or written statements [libel]) that causes damage to that individual's reputation. The plaintiff can seek compensation if the loss of reputation causes economic losses, emotional suffering, or present and future lost earnings. Finally, intentional lawsuits require that the defendant acted in an intentional manner that caused harm to the plaintiff. Examples of behavior that constitute intentional torts include assault, battery, false imprisonment, and intentionally inflicting emotional distress.

Disability and Workers' Compensation

Disability and workers' compensation programs were designed to provide for workers who are injured either physically and/or emotionally through the course of their employment (Wygant & Lareau, 2015). The three types of disability programs in the United States include private disability insurance, employer group disability, and Social Security Disability. Contractual language in the policy often defines what constitutes a disability, which essentially requires that owing to the injury, the individual is not able to work (or work to full capacity). In contrast to personal injury litigation, in most disability cases, the source of the injury is not as relevant as the mere presence of the disability. To be awarded payments, disability claimants have to provide proof of the disability, the validity of which is determined by the insurance company. Social Security Disability determinations are different in that the definition of the disability is much more limited and often requires the individual to have a severe disability. Thus, rather than determining whether the individual can perform his or her usual job duties, the determination is focused on whether he or she can perform any gainful activities such as employment.

Workers' compensation programs differ from disability programs in that they provide compensation for workers who are sick or injured on the job. Workers' compensation programs do not require the employer to be responsible for the injury. Workers are compensated with a percentage of their wages and medical expenses if they can demonstrate that they are genuinely injured and unable to perform their work duties (Piechowski, 2013). Acceptance of workers' compensation payments relinquishes the ability of the worker to file a law suit against the employer for negligence.

CONDUCTING A CIVIL FORENSIC EVALUATION

Regardless of which party retains the psychologist, the goal of a personal injury evaluation is the same: assessing whether (and to what extent) the alleged intentional or negligent behavior of the defendant harmed the plaintiff (Foote & Lareau, 2013). These evaluations require the clinician to comprehensively assess both the present functioning of the plaintiff, as well as his or her functioning before the alleged conduct of the defendant. Wygant and Lareau (2015) noted four basic issues that must be determined in a personal injury assessment:

1. Whether the plaintiff was actually psychologically harmed.
2. Whether the defendant's conduct or another source caused the plaintiff's harm.
3. The extent of impairment to the plaintiff if the conduct of the defendant resulted in the injury.
4. What would be needed to return the plaintiff to his or her prior level of functioning.

Also, a thorough assessment of response bias and symptom feigning is a critical part of the evaluation, since civil litigation presents a substantial motivation for the plaintiff or disability litigant to distort symptoms.

Two particular disorders are prominent in civil forensic cases that involve emotional damages: major depressive disorder and PTSD. PTSD is unique in the forensic arena because it is one of the few diagnoses that explicitly links an incident to the onset of the traumatic response. If the plaintiff is diagnosed with PTSD stemming from the alleged conduct of the defendant, the diagnosis itself implies that the emotional consequences arose out of the tortious conduct (e.g., negligence cases such as automobile accidents).

Wygant and Lareau (2015) discussed several important issues pertaining to PTSD in civil forensic cases. One matter that complicates the assessment of PTSD in forensic cases is that the symptoms are almost entirely established through self-report. Further complicating the matter, these symptoms are well known and easy to research on the Internet. At some level, that makes PTSD easier to feign, particularly if the assessment relies overly on self-report. The assessment must include a thorough consideration of alternative sources of distress that may be present in the plaintiff's life before and since the traumatic event. One should also consider that most individuals exposed to a trauma do not go on to develop PTSD (Breslau et al., 1998), and most that do develop the condition recover from its symptoms, even without the benefit of treatment (American Psychiatric Association, 2010). Wygant and Lareau (2015) cautioned the forensic clinician to be aware of the diagnostic controversies and relevant literature regarding DSM-5 PTSD in civil litigation.

CONSIDERATIONS FOR USING THE MMPI-2-RF IN PERSONAL INJURY AND DISABILITY EVALUATIONS

Personal injury and disability determination cases involve the assessment of the plaintiff's (or claimant's) current psychological functioning. As previously noted, much of the psychopathology involved in civil litigation and disability cases is focused on internalizing disorders, such as depression and PTSD. As such, the MMPI-2-RF, which provides a comprehensive evaluation of internalizing psychopathology (see Sellbom, 2016b; Sellbom, Ben-Porath, & Bagby, 2008) can play an important role in corroborating information gathered during a clinical interview and from other collateral sources. Moreover, if administered before the clinical interview, the MMPI-2-RF results can inform the process by generating inquiries and clinical hypotheses to explore.

The MMPI-2-RF does a good job of capturing the various components of depression. In elaborating on Watson's (2005) model of internalizing disorders, Sellbom, Ben-Porath, and Bagby (2008) found that RCd was differentially associated with distress disorders (which includes depression), whereas RC7 was associated with fear-based disorders (e.g., panic disorder). They also found that RC2, which captures anhedonia, was uniquely associated with depression and social anxiety disorder. Thus, elevations on both RCd and RC2 provide strong evidence of depression. Simms et al. (2005) also found that RCd and RC2 were significantly associated with Structured Clinical Interview for DSM-III-R-diagnosed depression. Several of the Internalizing SP Scales can also be utilized to differentiate depression from other internalizing disorders and can be conceptually aligned with major depressive disorder criteria (see Watson et al., 2011; and Table 11-1).

Wolf and Miller (2014) provided a good review of the MMPI-2-RF assessment of PTSD in forensic assessment. They recommend that the MMPI-2-RF be utilized as part of a multimethod assessment process that incorporates a clinical interview, trauma-specific measures, and collateral sources. Although MMPI-2-RF scales are conceptually aligned with many of the PTSD symptoms (see Table 11-2), Wolf and Miller (2014) noted that its strength in PTSD assessments is its ability to detect invalid responding and psychiatric comorbidities. It should be noted that the MMPI-2-RF, like any self-report personality measure (including trauma-focused measures), cannot establish the presence of a traumatic event (i.e., Criterion A). They can only be used to examine the various posttraumatic symptoms consistent with PTSD.

TABLE 11-1

Conceptual Alignment of Major Depressive Disorder Symptoms
and MMPI-2-RF Scales

Major Depressive Disorder symptom	MMPI-2-RF Scales
Depressed mood indicated by feelings of sadness, emptiness, hopelessness	RCd, HLP
Markedly diminished interest or pleasure	RC2, SAV
Significant weight loss/gain, or decrease/increase in appetite	RC1, GIC
Insomnia/hypersomnia	MLS
Psychomotor agitation/retardation	RC9 (+/−), ACT (+/−)
Fatigue or loss of energy	RC1, MLS
Feelings of worthlessness/excessive or inappropriate guilt	RCd, HLP, SFD
Poor concentration, indecisiveness	COG, NFC
Death/suicidal ideation	SUI

Note. ACT = Activation; COG = Cognitive Complaints; GIC = Gastrointestinal Complaints; HLP = Helplessness/Hopelessness; MLS = Malaise; MMPI-2-RF = Minnesota Multiphasic Personality Inventory-2-Restructured Form; NFC = Inefficacy; RC1 = Somatic Complaints; RC2 = Low Positive Emotions; RC9 = Hypomanic Activation; RCd = Demoralization; SAV = Social Avoidance; SFD = Self-Doubt; SUI = Suicidal/Death Ideation.

Several studies have examined the MMPI-2-RF and PTSD. Sellbom, Lee, et al. (2012) examined the relationship between the MMPI-2-RF and several PTSD measures and found that RCd was the best individual predictor of global PTSD symptoms. They also found that the AXY Scale was the best overall marker of the DSM-IV PTSD symptom clusters (re-experiencing, avoidance, and hyperarousal). Wolf et al. (2008) examined a sample of male and female veterans with the MMPI-2 RC Scales and either the Structured Clinical Interview for DSM-III-R (Spitzer, Williams, Gibbon, & First, 1989) or the Clinician Administered PTSD Scale (CAPS; Blake et al., 1995). They found that the RCd and RC8 Scales were the strongest predictors of PTSD among the male veterans, and RCd and RC1 were the strongest predictors of PTSD among the female veterans. Arbisi, Polusny, Erbes, Thuras, and Reddy (2011) found that the AXY Scale added incrementally to the RC Scales in the prediction of PTSD in a sample of National Guard members who served in Iraq. Lawson, Wright, and Fitzgerald (2013) found that RC7 was associated with PTSD in a sample of female sexual harassment litigants. Additionally, four studies have examined the ability of the MMPI-2-RF Validity Scales to detect feigned symptoms of PTSD (Goodwin et al., 2013; Marion et al., 2011; Mason et al., 2013; Rogers et al., 2011). Collectively, these studies support the use of F-r and Fp-r in detecting feigned PTSD.

TABLE 11-2

Conceptual Alignment of PTSD Symptoms and MMPI-2-RF Scales

PTSD cluster/symptom	MMPI-2-RF Scales
B. Intrusion symptoms	
B1. Recurrent, intrusive recollections	RC7, AXY
B2. Recurrent distressing dreams	AXY
B3. Reliving the experience	AXY
B4. Distress to exposure trauma cues	RC7, AXY
B5. Physiological reactivity to trauma	RC1, AXY
C. Avoidance symptoms	
C1. Avoidance of distressing memories, thoughts, feelings	RC2, RCd
C2. Avoidance of activities/places	SAV, BRF
D. Negative alterations in cognitions and mood	
D1. Inability to recall aspects of trauma	COG
D2. Persistent/exaggerated beliefs about oneself, others, world	RC3, RCd, SFD, HLP
D3. Persistent/distorted cognitions about trauma	RCd
D4. Persistent negative emotional state	RCd, RC7, ANP
D5. Diminished interest or participation	RC2, SAV
D6. Feeling of detachment/estrangement	DSF
D7. Inability to experience positive emotions	RC2
E. Hyperarousal	
E1. Irritability/outbursts of anger	RC7, ANP, AGG
E2. Reckless or self-destructive behavior	RC4, AGG, SUB
E3. Hypervigilance	RC6, RC9, AXY, ACT
E4. Exaggerated startle response	RC1, RC9, AXY
E5. Problems with concentration	COG
E6. Sleep disturbance	MLS

Note. ACT = Activation; AGG = Aggression; ANP = Anger Proneness; AXY = Anxiety; BRF = Behavior Restricting Fears; COG = Cognitive Complaints; DSF = Disaffiliativeness; HLP = Helplessness/Hopelessness; MLS = Malaise; MMPI-2-RF = Minnesota Multiphasic Personality Inventory-2-Restructured Form; RC1 = Somatic Complaints; RC2 = Low Positive Emotions; RC3 = Cynicism; RC4 = Antisocial Behavior; RC6 = Ideas of Persecution; RC7 = Dysfunctional Negative Emotions; RC9 = Hypomanic Activation; RCd = Demoralization; SAV = Social Avoidance; SFD = Self-Doubt; SUB = Substance Abuse.

Given the secondary gain of financial awards of lawsuits and disability, these evaluations require a thorough and systematic assessment of response bias and malingering. The MMPI-2-RF Validity Scales (see Chapter 3 for a thorough review) are useful in evaluating the credibility of the claims of symptoms by the plaintiff or claimant. A number of studies have specifically examined the MMPI-2-RF Validity Scales in civil forensic settings (see Nguyen et al., 2015; Schroeder et al., 2012; Sellbom, Wygant, et al., 2012;

Tarescavage et al., 2013; Wygant et al., 2009, 2011; Youngjohn, Weshba, Stevenson, Sturgeoun, & Thomas, 2011). These studies can guide the assessment of response bias in personal injury and disability assessments.

The MMPI-2-RF includes two relevant comparison groups that can provide some context for the evaluee's test results. These two groups include forensic disability claimant and forensic neuropsychological examination litigant/claimant. The disability claimant comparison group includes non-head injury cases.

Although we have not covered it in this book, we will note that many neuropsychologists employ the MMPI-2-RF in forensic neuropsychological evaluations. Two recent surveys of clinical neuropsychologists found that the MMPI-2-RF is the most widely used measure of symptom validity in neuropsychological evaluations (Martin et al., 2015; Schroeder et al., 2016). Martin et al. (2015) found that RBS and FBS-r were the most widely cited sources in the test for capturing invalid self-report in neuropsychological evaluations.

CASE EXAMPLE 11-1

Case Background

The plaintiff in this case, Ms. H, is a 25-year-old African American female who was involved in an automobile accident in March 2010, during which time she was physically injured (fractured clavicle and significant abrasions) and the driver of her vehicle was fatally injured. The plaintiff was 21 years old at the time and traveling with two friends on a university spring break trip. She was a passenger in the backseat of the vehicle with two of her friends in the front seat. While traveling on the highway, a tractor trailer truck experienced a mechanical malfunction that resulted in a large piece of the truck striking their vehicle, leading to a major accident. The driver of Ms. H's vehicle was fatally injured and both she and her other friend were significantly injured.

Following the accident, Ms. H recovered from her physical injuries and sought mental health treatment for emotional distress. She completed over 10 sessions of individual psychotherapy aimed at alleviating PTSD symptoms and was prescribed antidepressant medication. Her trauma history included a previous, relatively minor automobile accident when she was a teenager. She had previously completed a brief period of counseling in her early teens after her mother died from cancer. She denied any behavioral problems, legal difficulties, or significant use of alcohol and drugs.

The evaluation was requested by the defense (insurance company for the at-fault driver) to address the following questions:

1. Did the plaintiff experience any psychological difficulties as a result of the March 2010 vehicular accident? If so, in what ways and to what extent? Does she continue to experience psychological difficulties?
2. What were the consequences of the psychological difficulties? In what ways has the plaintiff attempted to mitigate the negative effects of the psychological difficulties? Do you have any recommendations for the plaintiff to further mitigate the negative effects of the psychological difficulties?
3. What factors in the plaintiff's history, if any, contributed to these psychological difficulties? If some factors may have contributed, what are those factors, and how may they have contributed? Was the March 2010 vehicular accident the proximal cause of any psychological difficulties the plaintiff experienced?

MMPI-2-RF Results

We utilized the Forensic Disability Claimant comparison group for this case. As noted, this comparison group includes a substantial proportion of individuals who were involved in personal injury lawsuits involving motor vehicle injuries. The other comparison group that might be close to matching the context of the current case would be the Forensic Neuropsychological Examination Litigant/Claimant group. We elected not to use this group because the litigant in this case did not experience head trauma and she did not undergo a neuropsychological evaluation.

PROTOCOL VALIDITY

Ms. H responded to each item (CNS = 0), and she responded consistently to the items throughout the test (VRIN-r = 58, TRIN-r = 57T). Her score on F-r (88T) would be characterized in the *Manual for Administration, Scoring, and Interpretation* as reflecting "possible" overreporting, but this score could also be reflecting significant emotional turmoil. Her scores on the remaining overreporting scales (Fp-r, Fs, FBS-r, RBS) were all well below their respective cut scores. Given her psychiatric history and the results on SIRS-2 (Rogers, Sewell, & Gillard, 2010), which indicated Genuine Responding, Ms. H's score on F-r was not considered to be strong evidence of response bias. There was no evidence of underreporting on L-r or K-r. Overall, her profile was considered valid for interpretation.

CLINICAL INTERPRETATION

The interpretive strategy explained in Chapter 1 begins by examining the domain of the highest score on the H-O Scales. We see that Ms. H had a significant elevation on EID (75T) with low scores on the other two scales. Thus, this interpretation will begin by examining all the scales within the internalizing domain. Consistent with her high score on EID, Ms. H had significant elevations on RCd (73T) and RC2 (73T). The combination of these two scores suggests that she experiences significant emotional turmoil, general dissatisfaction with life, anhedonia, and has limited ability to cope. Diagnostically, these two scales are consistent with major depressive disorder (Sellbom, Ben-Porath, & Bagby, 2008; Sellbom et al., 2012; Simms et al., 2005). Sellbom et al. (2012) noted that RCd was the best individual predictor of global PTSD symptoms, although RCd could also be associated with symptoms of depression. They noted that when the scale is co-elevated with RC2, there is potential for PTSD and depression comorbidity. In the DSM-5, PTSD includes a new symptom cluster (D) labeled Negative Alterations in Cognition and Mood (American Psychiatric Association, 2013). Two of the specific criteria for D include persistent negative emotional state (D4), which is captured by RCd (Wolf & Miller, 2014), and persistent inability to experience positive emotions (D5), which is captured by RC2.

Turning to the Internalizing SP Scales, we see that Ms. H hit the ceiling on AXY (100T), which suggested significant dysfunction in the area of intrusive ideation and hypervigilance and is consistent with Criterion B, Intrusion Symptoms. This scale was the best overall predictor of the DSM-IV PTSD symptom clusters in Sellbom et al. (2012). During the clinical interview (which included the CAPS-5), Ms. H endorsed having experienced significant difficulties owing to intrusive memories, flashbacks, and nightmares, as

Minnesota Multiphasic
Personality Inventory-2
Restructured Form®

Score Report

MMPI-2-RF®

Minnesota Multiphasic Personality Inventory-2-Restructured Form®

Yossef S. Ben-Porath, PhD, & Auke Tellegen, PhD

Name:	Ms. H
ID Number:	11
Age:	25
Gender:	Female
Marital Status:	Never Married
Years of Education:	16
Date Assessed:	10/20/2014

ALWAYS LEARNING   **PEARSON**

FIGURE 11-1 Case Example 11-1: Ms. H's MMPI-2-RF Profile, continued.

239

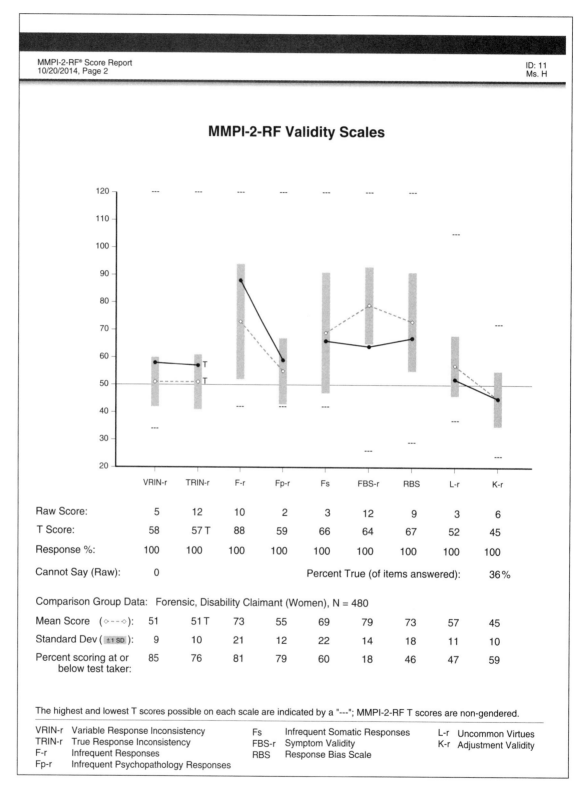

MMPI-2-RF Validity Scales

	VRIN-r	TRIN-r	F-r	Fp-r	Fs	FBS-r	RBS	L-r	K-r
Raw Score:	5	12	10	2	3	12	9	3	6
T Score:	58	57 T	88	59	66	64	67	52	45
Response %:	100	100	100	100	100	100	100	100	100

Cannot Say (Raw):   0   Percent True (of items answered):   36%

Comparison Group Data: Forensic, Disability Claimant (Women), N = 480

Mean Score (◇--◇):	51	51 T	73	55	69	79	73	57	45
Standard Dev (±1 SD):	9	10	21	12	22	14	18	11	10
Percent scoring at or below test taker:	85	76	81	79	60	18	46	47	59

The highest and lowest T scores possible on each scale are indicated by a "---"; MMPI-2-RF T scores are non-gendered.

VRIN-r	Variable Response Inconsistency	Fs	Infrequent Somatic Responses	L-r	Uncommon Virtues
TRIN-r	True Response Inconsistency	FBS-r	Symptom Validity	K-r	Adjustment Validity
F-r	Infrequent Responses	RBS	Response Bias Scale		
Fp-r	Infrequent Psychopathology Responses				

FIGURE 11-1 Case Example 11-1: Ms. H's MMPI-2-RF Profile, continued.

MMPI-2-RF Higher-Order (H-O) and Restructured Clinical (RC) Scales

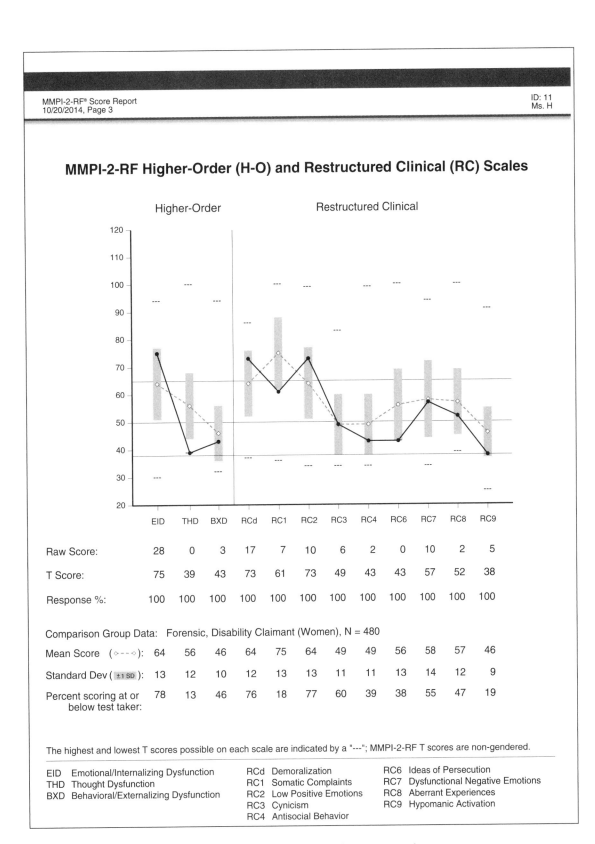

	EID	THD	BXD	RCd	RC1	RC2	RC3	RC4	RC6	RC7	RC8	RC9
Raw Score:	28	0	3	17	7	10	6	2	0	10	2	5
T Score:	75	39	43	73	61	73	49	43	43	57	52	38
Response %:	100	100	100	100	100	100	100	100	100	100	100	100

Comparison Group Data: Forensic, Disability Claimant (Women), N = 480

Mean Score (◇---◇):	64	56	46	64	75	64	49	49	56	58	57	46
Standard Dev (±1 SD):	13	12	10	12	13	13	11	11	13	14	12	9
Percent scoring at or below test taker:	78	13	46	76	18	77	60	39	38	55	47	19

The highest and lowest T scores possible on each scale are indicated by a "---"; MMPI-2-RF T scores are non-gendered.

EID Emotional/Internalizing Dysfunction	RCd Demoralization	RC6 Ideas of Persecution
THD Thought Dysfunction	RC1 Somatic Complaints	RC7 Dysfunctional Negative Emotions
BXD Behavioral/Externalizing Dysfunction	RC2 Low Positive Emotions	RC8 Aberrant Experiences
	RC3 Cynicism	RC9 Hypomanic Activation
	RC4 Antisocial Behavior	

FIGURE 11-1 Case Example 11-1: Ms. H's MMPI-2-RF Profile, continued.

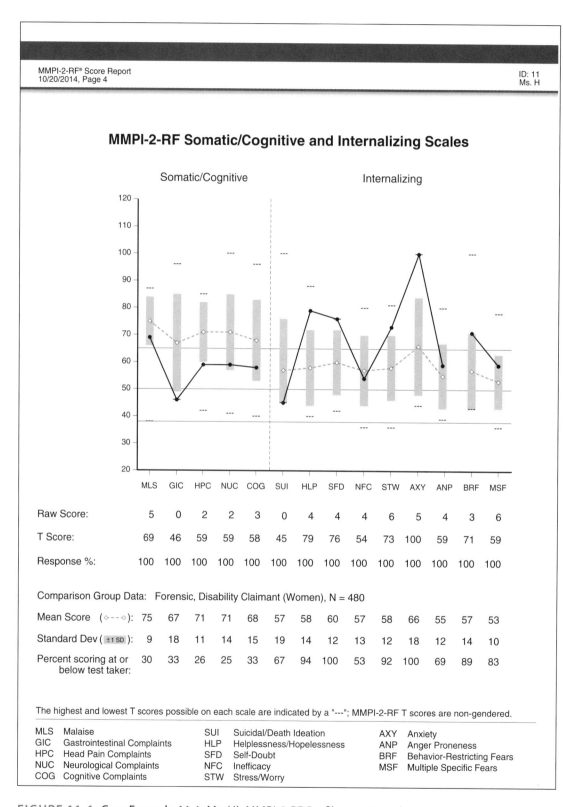

MMPI-2-RF Somatic/Cognitive and Internalizing Scales

Somatic/Cognitive   Internalizing

	MLS	GIC	HPC	NUC	COG	SUI	HLP	SFD	NFC	STW	AXY	ANP	BRF	MSF
Raw Score:	5	0	2	2	3	0	4	4	4	6	5	4	3	6
T Score:	69	46	59	59	58	45	79	76	54	73	100	59	71	59
Response %:	100	100	100	100	100	100	100	100	100	100	100	100	100	100

Comparison Group Data: Forensic, Disability Claimant (Women), N = 480

	MLS	GIC	HPC	NUC	COG	SUI	HLP	SFD	NFC	STW	AXY	ANP	BRF	MSF
Mean Score (◇--◇):	75	67	71	71	68	57	58	60	57	58	66	55	57	53
Standard Dev (±1 SD):	9	18	11	14	15	19	14	12	13	12	18	12	14	10
Percent scoring at or below test taker:	30	33	26	25	33	67	94	100	53	92	100	69	89	83

The highest and lowest T scores possible on each scale are indicated by a "---"; MMPI-2-RF T scores are non-gendered.

MLS	Malaise	SUI	Suicidal/Death Ideation	AXY	Anxiety
GIC	Gastrointestinal Complaints	HLP	Helplessness/Hopelessness	ANP	Anger Proneness
HPC	Head Pain Complaints	SFD	Self-Doubt	BRF	Behavior-Restricting Fears
NUC	Neurological Complaints	NFC	Inefficacy	MSF	Multiple Specific Fears
COG	Cognitive Complaints	STW	Stress/Worry		

FIGURE 11-1 Case Example 11-1: Ms. H's MMPI-2-RF Profile, continued.

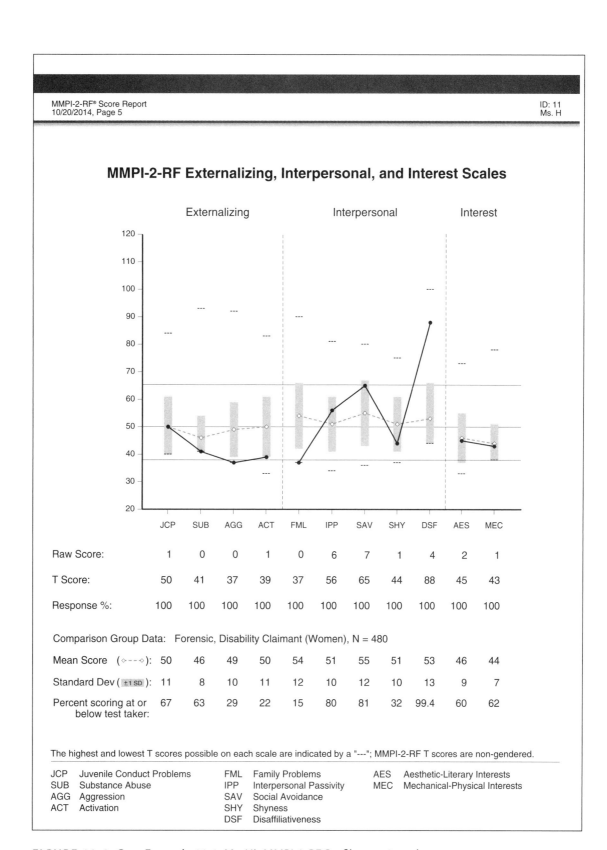

MMPI-2-RF Externalizing, Interpersonal, and Interest Scales

	Externalizing				Interpersonal					Interest	
	JCP	SUB	AGG	ACT	FML	IPP	SAV	SHY	DSF	AES	MEC
Raw Score:	1	0	0	1	0	6	7	1	4	2	1
T Score:	50	41	37	39	37	56	65	44	88	45	43
Response %:	100	100	100	100	100	100	100	100	100	100	100

Comparison Group Data: Forensic, Disability Claimant (Women), N = 480

Mean Score (◇--◇):	50	46	49	50	54	51	55	51	53	46	44
Standard Dev (±1 SD):	11	8	10	11	12	10	12	10	13	9	7
Percent scoring at or below test taker:	67	63	29	22	15	80	81	32	99.4	60	62

The highest and lowest T scores possible on each scale are indicated by a "---"; MMPI-2-RF T scores are non-gendered.

JCP	Juvenile Conduct Problems	FML	Family Problems	AES	Aesthetic-Literary Interests
SUB	Substance Abuse	IPP	Interpersonal Passivity	MEC	Mechanical-Physical Interests
AGG	Aggression	SAV	Social Avoidance		
ACT	Activation	SHY	Shyness		
		DSF	Disaffiliativeness		

FIGURE 11-1 Case Example 11-1: Ms. H's MMPI-2-RF Profile, continued.

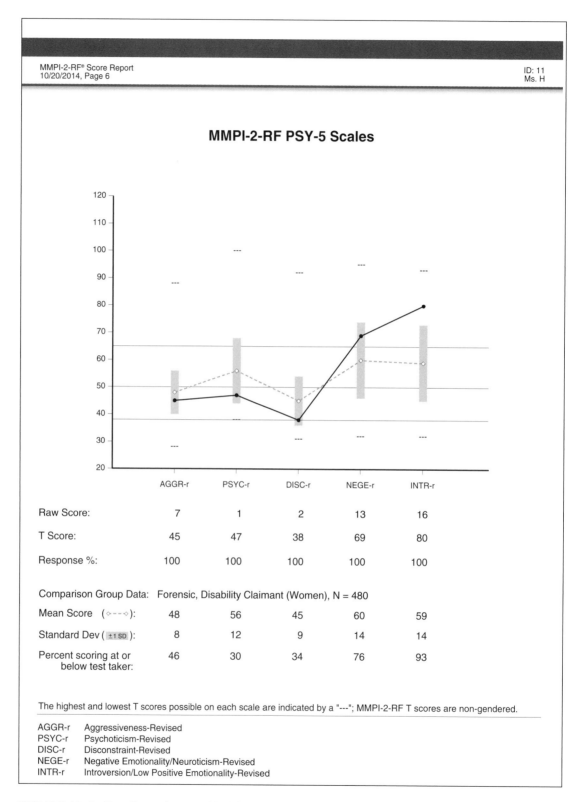

MMPI-2-RF PSY-5 Scales

	AGGR-r	PSYC-r	DISC-r	NEGE-r	INTR-r
Raw Score:	7	1	2	13	16
T Score:	45	47	38	69	80
Response %:	100	100	100	100	100

Comparison Group Data: Forensic, Disability Claimant (Women), N = 480

Mean Score ($\diamond$---$\diamond$):	48	56	45	60	59
Standard Dev (±1 SD):	8	12	9	14	14
Percent scoring at or below test taker:	46	30	34	76	93

The highest and lowest T scores possible on each scale are indicated by a "---"; MMPI-2-RF T scores are non-gendered.

AGGR-r	Aggressiveness-Revised
PSYC-r	Psychoticism-Revised
DISC-r	Disconstraint-Revised
NEGE-r	Negative Emotionality/Neuroticism-Revised
INTR-r	Introversion/Low Positive Emotionality-Revised

FIGURE 11-1 Case Example 11-1: Ms. H's MMPI-2-RF Profile, continued.

MMPI-2-RF T SCORES (BY DOMAIN)

PROTOCOL VALIDITY

Content Non-Responsiveness	0	58	57 T			
	CNS	VRIN-r	TRIN-r			

Over-Reporting	88	59		66	64	67
	F-r	Fp-r		Fs	FBS-r	RBS

Under-Reporting	52	45				
	L-r	K-r				

SUBSTANTIVE SCALES

Somatic/Cognitive Dysfunction		61	69	46	59	59	58	
		RC1	MLS	GIC	HPC	NUC	COG	

Emotional Dysfunction	75	73	45	79	76	54		
	EID	RCd	SUI	HLP	SFD	NFC		
		73	80					
		RC2	INTR-r					
		57	73	100	59	71	59	69
		RC7	STW	AXY	ANP	BRF	MSF	NEGE-r

Thought Dysfunction	39	43	
	THD	RC6	
		52	
		RC8	
		47	
		PSYC-r	

Behavioral Dysfunction	43	43	50	41		
	BXD	RC4	JCP	SUB		
		38	37	39	45	38
		RC9	AGG	ACT	AGGR-r	DISC-r

Interpersonal Functioning		37	49	56	65	44	88
		FML	RC3	IPP	SAV	SHY	DSF

Interests		45	43
		AES	MEC

Note. This information is provided to facilitate interpretation following the recommended structure for MMPI-2-RF interpretation in Chapter 5 of the *MMPI-2-RF Manual for Administration, Scoring, and Interpretation*, which provides details in the text and an outline in Table 5-1.

FIGURE 11-1 Case Example 11-1: Ms. H's MMPI-2-RF Profile, continued.

ITEM-LEVEL INFORMATION

Unscorable Responses

The test taker produced scorable responses to all the MMPI-2-RF items.

Critical Responses

Seven MMPI-2-RF scales--Suicidal/Death Ideation (SUI), Helplessness/Hopelessness (HLP), Anxiety (AXY), Ideas of Persecution (RC6), Aberrant Experiences (RC8), Substance Abuse (SUB), and Aggression (AGG)--have been designated by the test authors as having critical item content that may require immediate attention and follow-up. Items answered by the individual in the keyed direction (True or False) on a critical scale are listed below if her T score on that scale is 65 or higher. The percentage of the MMPI-2-RF normative sample (NS) and of the Forensic, Disability Claimant (Women) comparison group (CG) that answered each item in the keyed direction are provided in parentheses following the item content.

Helplessness/Hopelessness (HLP, T Score = 79)

   135. Item Content Omitted. (True; NS 24.2%, CG 45.0%)
   169. Item Content Omitted. (True; NS 4.3%, CG 27.3%)
   214. Item Content Omitted. (True; NS 10.4%,
      CG 26.3%)
   336. Item Content Omitted. (True; NS 38.0%, CG
      33.8%)

Anxiety (AXY, T Score = 100)

   79. Item Content Omitted. (True; NS 6.2%, CG 36.7%)
  146. Item Content Omitted. (True; NS 1.8%, CG 17.5%)
  228. Item Content Omitted. (True; NS 17.3%, CG 51.3%)
  275. Item Content Omitted. (True; NS 5.0%, CG
     28.3%)
  289. Item Content Omitted. (True; NS 12.7%, CG 44.8%)

User-Designated Item-Level Information

The following item-level information is based on the report user's selection of additional scales, and/or of lower cutoffs for the critical scales from the previous section. Items answered by the test taker in the keyed direction (True or False) on a selected scale are listed below if her T score on that scale is at the user-designated cutoff score or higher. The percentage of the MMPI-2-RF normative sample (NS) and of the Forensic, Disability Claimant (Women) comparison group (CG) that answered each item in the keyed direction are provided in parentheses following the item content.

Ideas of Persecution (RC6, T Score = 43)

    No items that are scored on this scale were answered in the keyed direction.

FIGURE 11-1 Case Example 11-1: Ms. H's MMPI-2-RF Profile, continued.

Hypomanic Activation (RC9, T Score = 38)

39. Item Content Omitted. (True; NS 51.0%, CG 50.2%)
61. Item Content Omitted. (False; NS 61.6%, CG 41.9%)
72. Item Content Omitted. (True; NS 81.5%, CG 78.8%)
244. Item Content Omitted. (True; NS 56.9%, CG 70.4%)
256. Item Content Omitted. (True; NS 65.7%, CG 58.8%)

Behavior-Restricting Fears (BRF, T Score = 71)

20. Item Content Omitted. (True; NS 2.5%, CG 5.2%)
56. Item Content Omitted. (True; NS 5.7%, CG 30.2%)
90. Item Content Omitted. (True; NS 15.7%, CG 30.8%)

Juvenile Conduct Problems (JCP, T Score = 50)

96. Item Content Omitted. (True; NS 18.8%, CG 33.5%)

Negative Emotionality/Neuroticism-Revised (NEGE-r, T Score = 69)

37. Item Content Omitted. (False; NS 56.3%, CG 76.5%)
56. Item Content Omitted. (True; NS 5.7%, CG 30.2%)
73. Item Content Omitted. (False; NS 16.6%, CG 51.0%)
116. Item Content Omitted. (True; NS 40.0%, CG 60.6%)
123. Item Content Omitted. (True; NS 28.0%, CG 50.6%)
134. Item Content Omitted. (False; NS 32.5%, CG 45.2%)
146. Item Content Omitted. (True; NS 1.8%, CG 17.5%)
167. Item Content Omitted. (True; NS 43.7%, CG 39.2%)
206. Item Content Omitted. (True; NS 41.6%, CG 45.8%)
209. Item Content Omitted. (True; NS 32.5%, CG 70.0%)
234. Item Content Omitted. (False; NS 53.9%, CG 86.5%)
263. Item Content Omitted. (True; NS 64.0%, CG 69.4%)
309. Item Content Omitted. (True; NS 34.0%, CG 63.3%)

FIGURE 11-1 Case Example 11-1: Ms. H's MMPI-2-RF Profile, continued.

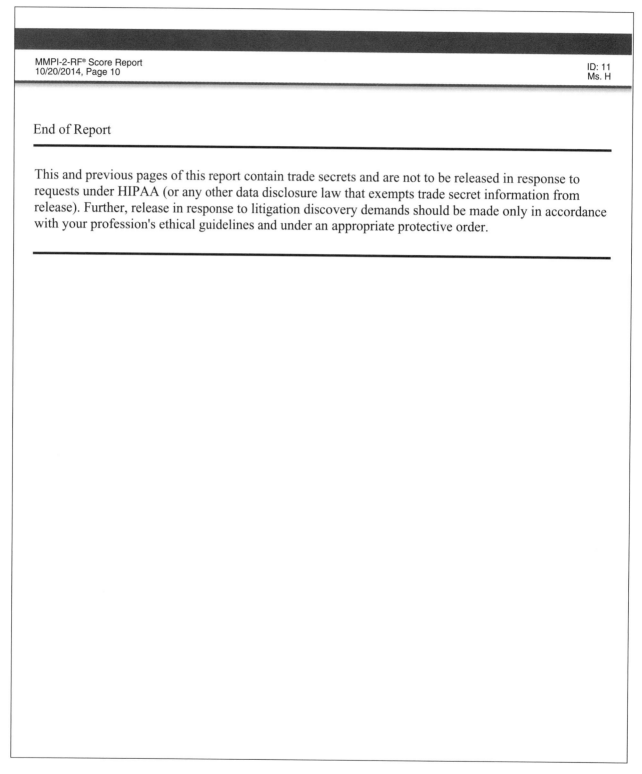

End of Report

FIGURE 11-1 Case Example 11-1: Ms. H's MMPI-2-RF Profile.

well as emotional and physical volatility in response to reminders of the accident. She also reported significant feelings of helplessness and hopelessness (HLP = 79T), self-doubt and insecurity (SFD = 76T), as well as a heightened level of stress and worry (STW = 73T). Moreover, her score on BRF (71T) suggested that she restricts activities because of her level of fearfulness, which is consistent with the avoidance criteria for PTSD (C2) in the DSM-5. From a clinical perspective, it is important to note that she did not endorse any of the suicidal ideation items. Finally, there are significant elevations on the two internalizing PSY-5 Scales, NEGE-r (69T) and INTR-r (80T). These scores are consistent with the internalizing subtype of PTSD found by Miller, Kaloupek, Dillon, and Keane (2004) and suggest that she experiences significant negative emotions and few positive emotions. Her score on INTR-r is also consistent with significant social avoidance, anhedonia, and feelings of detachment.

Since none of the remaining H-O Scales were elevated, we next examine whether any other RC Scales were elevated. Although none were in the elevated range, her score on RC1 (61T) was over one standard deviation above the normative sample, suggesting that a review of the Somatic/Cognitive Specific Problems Scales may reveal some somatically related symptoms. We see that she has an elevated score on MLS (69T), which suggests that she likely experiences a sense of poor health, fatigue, and low energy. This finding is consistent with her complaints of poor sleep regulation and fatigue during the clinical evaluation.

None of her scores reflect externalizing proclivities, which is consistent with her history. Ms. H had no indications of conduct problems as a child or adolescent, as well as no history of significant substance misuse or aggressive behavior. This is particularly important in the case of most diagnostic impressions, which require that the symptom picture is not the result of substance misuse. However, she had significantly low scores on RC9 and DISC-r, which suggests that she may be overcontrolled with respect to her behavior.

The final step in our interpretation is to review the interpersonal domain. The only RC Scale in this domain (RC3) was in the average range. On the Interpersonal SP Scales, we see that Ms. H had a significant elevation on DSF (88T) and SAV (65). Taken together, these scales suggest that she avoids social situations and likely feels cut off and alienated from others; she might outright dislike being around other people. Consistent with PTSD, these two scales could reflect avoidance (Criterion C2) and feelings of detachment and estrangement from others (Criterion D6). Her scores on the two Interest SP Scales did not provide any diagnostic impressions.

Overall, Ms. H's MMPI-2-RF results were valid and suggested that she is experiencing significant emotional turmoil. Diagnostically, her RC Scale results were reflective of possible depression and/or PTSD symptoms. In addition to the MMPI-2-RF, the plaintiff completed two trauma measures: the Trauma Symptom Inventory, Second Edition (Briere, 2010) and the Clinician Administered PTSD Scale for DSM-5 (CAPS-5; Weathers et al., 2013). She produced a valid TSI-2 profile that included elevated scores on scales capturing anxiety and trauma-related symptoms (intrusive ideations, avoidance, and somatic preoccupation), as well as depressed mood. The CAPS-5 yielded a positive diagnosis of PTSD.

Case Outcome

The defense-retained psychological evaluation indicated a diagnosis of PTSD and major depressive disorder. Ms. H impressed as genuine in her presentation during the evaluation, and her psychological test results were valid, with no indications of feigning. The evaluator opined that there was a high likelihood that Ms. H's present psychological difficulties resulted from the vehicular accident in March 2010. Indeed, she continued to experience significant emotional disturbance four years after the accident, despite receiving psychological treatment and antidepressant medication.

The case settled during a mediation hearing shortly after the defense findings were presented to the defense counsel.

CONCLUSIONS

The MMPI-2-RF can serve as a useful component of a personal injury or disability evaluation. The test has well-established Validity Scales that can capture the types of symptoms that are likely to be exaggerated in this setting. Moreover, the test can capture an array of psychopathological symptoms often consistent with trauma. The RC and SP Scales are particularly useful in differentiating specific disorder presentations, including depression and PTSD, which are common mental health problems in this setting.

PART IV

Conclusions about the
Forensic Use of the
MMPI-2-RF

Chapter 12

Closing Remarks about the Forensic Use of the MMPI-2-RF

We hope that this book has illustrated the numerous ways in which the MMPI-2-RF can provide useful and important information in a forensic evaluation. The test can generate a breadth of information using a relatively efficient set of items. MMPI-2-RF results can be used to develop hypotheses about an evaluee's psychological functioning that can be assessed during the clinical interview and through other means (e.g., collateral interviews, record review). Test results can also be used to guide the clinician's approach during the evaluation; for instance, the Validity Scales can be very useful in understanding how the evaluee approached the test (and by extension, the overall evaluation). Finally, MMPI-2-RF results can corroborate other information in forming diagnostic, clinical, and forensic opinions.

The MMPI-2-RF has amassed an impressive number of peer-reviewed publications since its release in 2008. Many of these publications pertain to the RC Scales, originally developed for the MMPI-2, but which are identical in the MMPI-2-RF. As noted in Chapter 2, a number of studies have directly examined the validity of MMPI-2-RF scale scores in various forensic settings. Other studies have focused on topics that are directly relevant to forensic assessment (e.g., response bias, psychopathy). This body of work indicates that the MMPI-2-RF can be used with confidence in the formulation of diagnostic impressions, personality characteristics, and behavioral patterns relevant to various forensic contexts. Although not directly addressing psycho-legal questions (like most psychological measures), the MMPI-2-RF can provide useful information that is relevant to these questions (e.g., presence of psychopathology in a competency or disability evaluation).

It is our hope that the overall forensic use of the instrument (Chapters 2 and 3) and the cases we selected help illustrate these points. In this latter vein, eight chapters focused on specific psycho-legal questions that are common in criminal and civil litigation contexts. Each of these presents unique challenges to the use of the MMPI-2-RF as well as illustrates how test results can be helpful in informing case conclusions. For instance, in Chapter 4, we presented MMPI-2-RF results for two competency evaluations with the same defendant (roughly three years apart). The test results provided clear evidence of psychosis, which had worsened by the second evaluation. As a measure of current psychological functioning, the MMPI-2-RF results were directly relevant to establishing the presence of a mental condition (as required in the competency statute) that impacted the defendant's ability to understand the nature and consequences of the proceedings and assist in his defense. In Chapter 5, the MMPI-2-RF results clearly indicated the high potential for a manic episode in a criminal responsibility evaluation. Although the focus of the psycho-legal question pertained to mental state at the time of the offense, evidence of current mania (which was corroborated by the MMPI-2-RF) was a good indication that the person could have been manic at the time of the offense, as she had not been undergoing treatment for the condition. Chapter 6 illustrated an individual undergoing a violence risk assessment who exhibited traits associated with psychopathy. A number of MMPI-2-RF studies have examined the ability of the test to capture psychopathic traits (e.g., Haneveld et al., 2017; Kastner et al., 2012; Sellbom et al., 2005, 2007; Wygant & Sellbom, 2012). The evaluee's scores on the externalizing scales, which have been found to predict future violence (Tarescavage, Glassmire, et al., 2016), were elevated, and in conjunction with other information, they pointed to a high risk of reoffending if released. Similarly, in Chapter 7, we illustrated how the MMPI-2-RF results were suggestive of depression, low self-esteem, and social ineptitude, which were factors in his sexual offending. In Chapter 8, the MMPI-2-RF results were consistent with the offender's emotional instability, interpersonal sensitivity, and substance abuse, which were useful in providing a mitigating formulation of his mental state at the time of the offenses. The case in Chapter 9 illustrated how the MMPI-2-RF can be useful in formulating diagnostic opinions and relevant clinical impressions about parents involved in a disputed child custody proceeding. Similarly, Chapter 10 presented a good example of how the MMPI-2-RF can inform clinical impressions of a parent who demonstrated a current lack of capacity to provide adequate care and welfare for her children. Finally, Chapter 11 illustrated the utility of the MMPI-2-RF to capture the heterogeneous and multifaceted nature of PTSD in a personal injury evaluation.

FUTURE RESEARCH DIRECTIONS FOR THE MMPI-2-RF IN FORENSIC ASSESSMENT

There continues to be a need for more research in particular forensic settings. We believe several areas are of particular importance. First, it will be important to establish the contribution of MMPI-2-RF information in decision making about psycho-legal issues. More research is needed on how clinicians' opinions are influenced by such information, and the degree to which such opinions are valid predictors of relevant outcomes. Although applied research has considerable challenges in that the design cannot easily be manipulated, future research would nevertheless benefit from establishing reliable external outcome criteria in particular forensic contexts. For example, how well do MMPI-2-RF scale scores associate with independent recent mental health ratings of psychopathology in competency to stand trial evaluations? Furthermore, it would be helpful to determine the degree to which MMPI-2-RF information adds incrementally to other sources of information (clinical interview, third party) in forming opinions and, to the extent possible, the validity of such opinions in relation to an external criterion.

Second, several psycho-legal questions involve retrospective mental health assessments. We argued (see Chapters 5 and 8, in particular) that it is a considerable challenge to use MMPI-2-RF information to make conclusions about mental state at the time of the offense. We believe it would be important to design studies to test the degree to which the MMPI-2-RF can postdict such information. For instance, are MMPI-2-RF scale scores associated with reported psychosis in jail booking records at time of arrest?

A third line of research concerns examining the predictive validity of the MMPI-2-RF in predicting forensically relevant outcomes. One area in particular that needs more research is risk assessment. As discussed in Chapters 6 and 7, the MMPI-2-RF assesses a number of dynamic risk factors that have been empirically identified, such as anger, negative emotionality, and substance abuse (Douglas & Skeem, 2005). Tarescavage, Glassmire, et al. (2016) and Wygant et al. (2015) illustrated how the MMPI-2-RF can be used to inform ratings with the HCR-20 model of violence risk assessment. Tarescavage, Glassmire, et al. (2016) also showed some promise for the externalizing scales in predicting future violence. More research is also needed to examine the degree to which the MMPI-2-RF can improve the accuracy of ratings in SPJ guides. Tarescavage, Cappo, et al. (2016) provided some insight into how the MMPI-2-RF may be useful in addressing limitations of SPJ guides, by incorporating an objective measure of underreporting (which is problematic in risk assessment settings), providing multiple objective sources of information, and objective measures of risk factor severity. More work is needed to examine their ideas empirically.

Finally, we think more comparison groups are needed, particularly for specific psycho-legal questions and special forensic populations. It would be helpful to have a presentence sex offender evaluation group in addition to sexual offenders in treatment, as the contextual demands and circumstances are different in preadjudication versus postadjudication evaluations. It would also be helpful to have specific groups for those evaluated for competency to stand trial, criminal responsibility, and mitigation of penalty. Although psychiatric inpatient and prison samples can likely be useful for postconviction risk assessment evaluations, obtaining such groups explicitly from forensic contexts would also be useful. Furthermore, virtually all of these comparison groups come from the United States. It will be helpful to generate comparison groups for forensic settings in other countries, including those that use U.S. norms, such as Australia and New Zealand.

NOTES

1. INTRODUCTION TO THE MMPI-2-RF

1. For instance, suicidal ideation can be viewed as a conceptual facet of demoralization, but the RCd and SUI scales share no items; thus, the latter is not a subscale of the former.
2. There is also a user's guide for the *Police Candidate Interpretive Report* available, but it will not be discussed here.

2. GENERAL CONSIDERATIONS FOR USING THE MMPI-2-RF IN FORENSIC EVALUATIONS

1. This research includes the RC Scales, which were initially released in the MMPI-2 (Tellegen et al., 2003). The scales are identical in the MMPI-2 and MMPI-2-RF. Tellegen and Ben-Porath (2008/2011) presented data showing that MMPI-2-RF scale scores derived from administration of the 567-item MMPI-2 booklet are interchangeable with results obtained from administration of the 338-item MMPI-2-RF booklet, which included virtually identical mean scale elevations and correlations with external criteria. Thus, any research on the MMPI-2 RC Scales will apply equally well to the MMPI-2-RF.
2. It is also noteworthy that the reliability indices upon which these SEM values are generated (internal consistency and test–retest) are not theoretically indicated for Validity Scales, which are not developed to be homogeneous or temporally stable. As such, these SEM values are likely considerable overestimates of actual error rates. Nonetheless, as Ben-Porath (2012a) pointed out, these higher values are considered in interpretive recommendations for the test.

4. COMPETENCY TO STAND TRIAL

1. MMPI-2-RF item content is not represented owing to copyright restrictions and concerns about test security.

2. In the interest of conserving space, the defendant's second MMPI-2-RF profile will be briefly reviewed, noting differences from his earlier results, rather than providing a complete discussion using the interpretive strategy framework.

5. CRIMINAL RESPONSIBILITY

1. This case, as well as the cases presented in Chapters 6, 8, and 10, are derived from Australia or New Zealand. The English-speaking version of the test was used and standardized scores are generated against the U.S. norms. The publisher does not require local norms if deemed sufficiently similar to the U.S. norms for English-speaking countries. As this is indeed the case for Australia and New Zealand, U.S. norms and comparison groups are used.

6. VIOLENCE RISK ASSESSMENT

1. Sexual offending is typically considered a form of violence as well, but the prediction of sexual violence is associated with its own literature and is often considered a separate psycho-legal question. As such, we will cover sexual violence risk assessment separately in Chapter 7.

10. PARENTAL FITNESS

1. The father of these children was also evaluated, but by another psychologist. The father and mother had separated and were individually seeking reunification.

REFERENCES

Ackerman, M. J., & Ackerman, M. C. (1997). Child custody evaluation practices: A survey of experienced professionals (revisited). *Psychological Psychology: Research and Practice, 28,* 137–145.

Ackerman, M. J., & Pritzl, T. B. (2011). Child custody evaluation practices: A 20-year follow-up. *Family Court Review, 49,* 618–628. doi:10.1111/j.1744-1617.2011.01397.x

Adams v. Astrue, Commissioner of Social Security No. 3:11-CV-00378 RE. (U.S. Dist. Ct. July 3, 2012).

American Educational Research Association, American Psychological Association, & National Council on Measurement in Education (1985/1999/2014). *Standards for educational and psychological testing.* Washington, DC: American Psychological Association.

American Psychiatric Association. (2010). *Practice guideline for the treatment of patients with acute stress disorder and posttraumatic stress disorder.* Washington, DC: Author.

American Psychiatric Association. (2013). *Diagnostic and statistical manual of mental disorders* (5th ed.). Washington, DC: Author.

American Psychological Association. (2010). Guidelines for child custody evaluations in family law proceedings. *American Psychologist, 54,* 586–593.

Anderson, J. L., Sellbom, M., Ayearst, L., Quilty, L. C., Chmielewski, M., & Bagby, R. M. (2015). Associations between DSM-5 Section III personality traits and the Minnesota Multiphasic Personality Inventory 2-Restructured Form (MMPI-2-RF) scales in a psychiatric patient sample. *Psychological Assessment, 27,* 811–815. doi:10.1037/pas0000096

Anderson, J. L., Sellbom, M., Bagby, R. M., Quilty, L. C., Veltri, C. O. C., Markon, K. E., & Krueger, R. F. (2013). On the convergence between PSY-5 domains and PID-5 domains and facets: Implications for assessment of DSM-5 personality traits. *Assessment, 20,* 286–294. doi:10.1177/1073191112471141

Anderson, J. L., Sellbom, M., Pymont, C., Smid, W., De Saeger, H., & Kamphuis, J. H. (2015). Measurement of DSM-5 Section II personality disorder constructs using the MMPI-2-RF in clinical and forensic samples. *Psychological Assessment, 27,* 786–800. doi:10.1037/pas0000103

Andrews, D. A., & Bonta, J. (2000). The level of service inventory: Revised. Toronto, ON: Multi-Health Systems.

Andrews, D. A., & Bonta, J. (2010). *The psychology of criminal conduct.* New York, NY: Routledge.

Arbisi, P. A., & Ben-Porath, Y. S. (1995). An MMPI-2 infrequent response scale for use with psychopathological populations: The infrequency-psychopathology scale, F(p). *Psychological Assessment, 7*, 424–431.

Arbisi, P. A., Polusny, M. A., Erbes, C. R., Thuras, P., & Reddy, M. K. (2011). The Minnesota Multiphasic Personality Inventory-2 Restructured Form in National Guard soldiers screening positive for posttraumatic stress disorder and mild traumatic brain injury. *Psychological Assessment, 23*, 203–214. doi:10.1037/a0021339

Arbisi, P. A., Sellbom, M., & Ben-Porath, Y. S. (2008). Empirical correlates of the MMPI-2 Restructured Clinical (RC) Scales in psychiatric inpatients. *Journal of Personality Assessment, 90*, 122–128. doi:10.1080/00223890701845146

Archer, E. M., Hagan, L. D., Mason, J., Handel, R. W., & Archer, R. P. (2012). MMPI-2-RF characteristics of custody evaluation litigants. *Assessment, 19*, 14–20. doi:10.1177/1073191110397469

Archer, R. P., Buffington-Vollum, J. K., Stredny, R. V., & Handel, R. W. (2006). A survey of psychological test use patterns among forensic psychologists. *Journal of Personality Assessment, 87*(1), 84–94. doi:10.1207/s15327752jpa8701_07

Archer, R. P., Handel, R. W., Ben-Porath, Y. S., & Tellegen, A. (2016). *Minnesota Multiphasic Personality Inventory—Adolescent—Restructured Form (MMPI-A-RF): Administration, Scoring, Interpretation, and Technical Manual.* Minneapolis, MN: University of Minnesota Press.

Archer, R. P., Wheeler, E., & Vauter, R. A. (2016). Empirically supported forensic assessment. *Clinical Psychology: Science and Practice, 23*, 348–364. doi:10.1111/cpsp.12171

Baker, N. L., Vasquez, M. J. T., & Shullman, S. L. (2013). Assessing employment discrimination and harassment. In R. K. Otto & I. B. Weiner (Eds.), *Handbook of psychology* (2nd ed., Vol. 11, pp. 225–245). Hoboken, NJ: John Wiley & Sons.

Barefoot v. Estrelle, 463 U.S. 880 (1983).

Barendregt, M., Muller, E., Nijman, H., & de Beurs, E. (2008). Factors associated with experts' opinions regarding criminal responsibility in the Netherlands. *Behavioral Sciences & the Law, 26*(5), 619–631. doi:10.1002/bsl.837

Ben-Porath, Y. S. (2012a). Addressing challenges to MMPI-2-RF-based testimony: Questions and answers. *Archives of Clinical Neuropsychology, 27*, 691–705. doi:10.1093/arclin/acs083

Ben-Porath, Y. S. (2012b). *Interpreting the MMPI-2-RF.* Minneapolis, MN: University of Minnesota Press.

Ben-Porath, Y. S. (2013a). Forensic applications of the Minnesota Multiphasic Personality Inventory-2 Restructured Form. In R. P. Archer & E. M. A. Wheeler (Eds.), *Forensic use of clinical assessment instruments* (2nd ed., pp. 63–107). New York, NY: Routledge.

Ben-Porath, Y. S. (2013b). The MMPI instruments. In S. Koffler, J. Morgan, I. S. Barron, & M. F. Greiffenstein (Eds.), *Neuropsychology: Science and practice, Vol. I* (pp. 256–284). New York, NY: Oxford University Press.

Ben-Porath, Y. S. (2013c). Self-report inventories: Assessing personality and psychopathology. In I. B. Weiner (Series Ed.) & J. R. Graham & J. A. Naglieri (Vol. Ed.), *Handbook of psychology: Vol. 10. Assessment psychology* (2nd ed., pp. 622–644). Hoboken, NJ: Wiley.

Ben-Porath, Y. S. (2016). An update and corrections to Williams and Lally's (2016) analysis of MMPI-2-RF acceptance. *Professional Psychology Research and Practice.* Advance online publication. doi:10.1037/pro0000115

Ben-Porath, Y. S., & Archer, R. P. (2014). The MMPI instruments. In R. P. Archer and S. R. Smith (Eds.), *Personality assessment* (2nd ed., pp. 89–146). New York, NY: Routledge.

Ben-Porath, Y. S., Corey, D. M., & Tarescavage, A. M. (2017). Using the MMPI-2-RF in preemployment evaluations of police officer candidates. In C. L. Mitchell & E. H. Dorian (Eds.), *Police psychology and its growing impact on modern law enforcement* (pp. 51–78). Hershey, PA: IGI Global. doi:10.4018/978-1-5225-0813-7.ch003

Ben-Porath, Y. S., & Flens, J. R. (2012). Butcher and Williams's (this issue) critique of the MMPI-2-RF is slanted and misleading. *Journal of Child Custody, 9,* 223–232. doi:10.108 0/15379418.2012.748605

Ben-Porath, Y. S., & Forbey, J. D. (2003). *Non-gendered norms for the MMPI-2.* Minneapolis, MN: University of Minnesota Press.

Ben-Porath, Y. S., & Tellegen, A. (2008/2011). *MMPI-2-RF (Minnesota Multiphasic Personality Inventory-2 Restructured Form): Manual for administration, scoring, and interpretation.* Minneapolis, MN: University of Minnesota Press.

Bianchini, K. J., Greve, K. W., & Glynn, G. (2005). Review article: On the diagnosis of malingered pain-related disability: Lessons from cognitive malingering research. *Spine Journal, 5,* 404–417.

Blake, D. D., Weathers, F. W., Nagy, L. M., Kaloupek, D. G., Gusman, F. D., Charney, D. S., & Keane, T. (1995). The development of a clinician administered PTSD scale. *Journal of Traumatic Stress, 8,* 75–90. doi: 10.1002/jts.2490080106

Boer, D. P., Hart, S. D., Kropp, P. R., & Webster, C. D. (1997). *Manual for the Sexual Violence Risk-20: Professional guidelines for assessing risk of sexual violence.* Vancouver, BC, Canada: British Columbia Institute on Family Violence and Mental Health, Law, & Policy Institute, Simon Fraser University.

Bonnie, R. (1992). The competence of criminal defendants: A theoretical reformulation. *Behavioral Sciences and the Law, 10,* 291–316.

Borum, R., Otto, R., & Golding, S. (1993). Improving clinical judgment and decision making in forensic evaluation. *Journal of Psychiatry & Law, 21*(1), 35–76.

Bow, J. N., & Quinnell, F. A. (2001). Psychologists' current practices and procedures and child custody evaluations: Five years after American Psychological Association Guidelines. *Professional Psychology: Research and Practice, 32,* 261–268.

Breslau, N., Kessler, R. C., Chilcoat, H. D., Schultz, L. R., Davis, G. C., & Andreski, P. (1998). Trauma and posttraumatic stress disorder in the community: The 1996 Detroit Area Survey of Trauma. *Archives of General Psychiatry, 55,* 626–632.

Bridges, S. A., & Baum, L. J. (2013). An examination of the MMPI-2-RF L-r Scale in an outpatient protestant sample. *Journal of Psychology and Christianity, 32,* 115–123.

Briere, J. (2010). *Trauma Symptom Inventory* (2nd ed.). (TSI-2) professional manual. Odessa, FL: Psychological Assessment Resources.

Budd, K. S. (2001). Assessing parenting competence in child protection cases: A clinical practice model. *Clinical Child and Family Psychology Review, 4,* 1–18. doi:10.1023/A:1009548509598

Budd, K. S. (2005). Assessing parenting capacity in a child welfare context. *Children and Youth Services Review, 27,* 429–444. doi:10.1016/j.childyouth.2004.11.008

Budd, K. S., Connell, M., & Clark, R. J. (2013). Assessment in a child protection context. In R. K. Otto & I. B. Weiner (Eds.), *Handbook of psychology: Vol. 11. Forensic psychology* (2nd ed., pp. 139–171). Hoboken, NJ: John Wiley & Sons.

Burchett, D., & Bagby, R. M. (2014). Multimethod assessment of distortion: Integrating data from interviews, collateral records, and standardized assessment tools. In C. J. Hopwood & R. F. Bornstein (Eds.), *Multimethod clinical assessment* (pp. 345–378). New York, NY: Guilford Press.

Burchett, D. L., & Ben-Porath, Y. S. (2010). The impact of overreporting on MMPI-2-RF substantive scale score validity. *Assessment, 17*, 497–516. doi:10.1177/1073191110378972

Butcher, J. N., Graham, J. R., Ben-Porath, Y. S., Tellegen, A., Dahlstrom, W. G., & Kaemmer, B. (2001). *MMPI-2 (Minnesota Multiphasic Personality Inventory-2): Manual for administration, scoring, and interpretation (rev ed.).* Minneapolis, MN: University of Minnesota Press.

Butcher, J. N., Hass, G. A., Greene, R. L., & Nelson, L. D. (2015). *Using the MMPI-2 in forensic assessment.* Washington, DC: American Psychological Association.

Capwell, D. F. (1945a). Personality patterns of adolescent girls: I. Girls who show improvement in IQ. *Journal of Applied Psychology, 29*, 212–228.

Capwell, D. F. (1945b). Personality patterns of adolescent girls: II. Delinquents and nondelinquents. *Journal of Applied Psychology, 29*, 289–297.

Chmielewski, M., Zhu, J., Burchett, D., Bury, A. S., & Bagby, R. M. (2017). The comparative capacity of the Minnesota Multiphasic Personality Inventory-2 (MMPI-2) and MMPI-2 Restructured Form (MMPI-2-F) validity scales to detect malingering in a disability claimant sample. *Psychological Assessment, 29*, 199–207. doi:10.1037/pas0000328

Chu, C. M., & Ogloff, J. R. (2012). Assessing alleged child sexual abusers in noncriminal contexts: proposed guidelines for practice. *Psychiatry, Psychology and Law, 19*(4), 464–481. doi:10.1080/13218719.2011.599109

Clegg, C., Fremouw, W., Horacek, T., Cole, A., & Schwartz, R. (2010). Factors associated with treatment acceptance and compliance among incarcerated male sex offenders. *International Journal of Offender Therapy and Comparative Criminology, 6*, 880–897. doi:10.1177/0306624X10376160

Cofer, C. N., Chance, J., & Judson, A. J. (1949). A study of malingering on the MMPI. *Journal of Psychology, 27*, 491–499.

Committee on Psychological Testing (2015). Including Validity Testing, for Social Security Administration Disability Determinations; Board on the Health of Select Populations; Institute of Medicine. Washington, DC: National Academies Press.

Conidi, F. (2015, Jan/Feb). Concussions and the National Football League. *Practical Neurology*, 33–38.

Conroy, M. A., & Murrie, D. C. (2007). Risk assessment with sexual offenders. In M. A. Conroy & D. C. Murrie (Ed.), *Forensic assessment of violence risk: A guide for risk assessment and risk management* (pp. 179–201). New York, NY: Wiley.

Conroy, M. A., & Witt, P. H. (2013). Evaluation and management of sexual offenders. In R. K. Otto & I. B. Weiner (Eds.), *Handbook of psychology: Vol. 11. Forensic psychology* (2nd ed., pp. 332–356). Hoboken, NJ: John Wiley & Sons.

Cooke, G., & Norris, D. M. (2011). Child custody and parental fitness. In E. Y. Drogin, F. M. Dattilio, R. L. Sadoff, & T. G. Guthiel (Eds.), *Handbook of forensic assessment: Psychological and psychiatric perspectives* (pp. 433–458). Hoboken, NJ: John Wiley & Sons.

Crighton, A. H., Marek, R. J., Dragon, W. R., & Ben-Porath, Y. S. (2015). Utility of the MMPI- 2-RF Validity Scales in the detection of simulated underreporting: Implications of incorporating a manipulation check. *Assessment*. Advance online publication. doi:10.1177/1073191115627011

Cunningham, M. D., & Goldstein, A. M. (2013). Sentencing determinations in death penalty cases. In R. K. Otto & I. B. Weiner (Eds.), *Handbook of psychology: Vol. 11. Forensic psychology* (2nd ed., pp. 473–514). Hoboken, NJ: John Wiley & Sons.

Dahlstrom, W. G., Welsh, G. S., & Dahlstrom, L. E. (1975). *An MMPI handbook: Vol. II. Research applications.* Minneapolis, MN: University of Minnesota Press.

Daubert v. Merrell Dow Pharmaceuticals, 727 F. Supp. 570 (S. D. Cal. 1989), aff'd, 951F.2d 1128 (9th Cir. 1990), vacated 1123 S. Ct. 2786 (1993).

Definitions for chapter: Incompetency. Kentucky Revised Statue §504.060 (2005).

Douglas, K. S., Cox, D. N., & Webster, C. D. (1999). Violence risk assessment: Science and practice. *Legal and Criminological Psychology, 4*(2), 149–184. doi:10.1348/135532599167824

Douglas, K. S., Hart, S. D., Groscup, J. L., & Litwack, T. R. (2013). Assessing violence risk. In I. Weiner & R. K. Otto (Eds.), *The handbook of forensic psychology* (4th ed., pp. 385–442). Hoboken, NJ: John Wiley & Sons.

Douglas, K. S., Hart, S. D., Webster, C. D., & Belfrage, H. (2013). *HCR-20 version 3: Assessing risk for violence.* Burnaby, BC, Canada: Mental Health, Law and Policy Institute, Simon Fraser University.

Douglas, K. S., Ogloff, J. R., & Hart, S. D. (2003). Evaluation of a model of violence risk assessment among forensic psychiatric patients. *Psychiatric Services, 54,* 1372–1379. doi:10.1176/appi.ps.54.10.1372

Douglas, K. S., & Skeem, J. L. (2005). Violence risk assessment: Getting specific about being dynamic. *Psychology, Public Policy, and Law, 11,* 347–383.

Dusky v. United States, 362 U.S. 402 (80 S. Ct. 788, 1960).

Emmers-Sommer, T. M., Allen, M., Bourhis, J., Sahlstein, E., Laskowski, K., Falato, W. L., Ackerman, J., et al. (2004). A meta-analysis of the relationship between social skills and sexual offenders. *Communication Reports, 17,* 1–10. doi:10.1080/08934210409389369

Erikson, S. T., Lilienfeld, S. O., & Vitacco, M. J. (2007). A critical examination of the suitability and limitations of psychological tests in family court. *Family Court Review, 45,* 157–174.

Finn, J. A., Arbisi, P. A., Erbes, C. R., Polusny, M. A., & Thuras, P. (2014). The MMPI-2 Restructured form Personality Psychopathology Five Scales: Bridging DSM-5 Section 2 personality disorders and DSM-5 Section 3 personality trait dimensions. *Journal of Personality Assessment, 96,* 173–184. doi:00223891.2013.866569

Foote, W. E., & Lareau, C. R. (2013). Psychological evaluation of emotional damages in tort cases. In R. K. Otto & I. B. Weiner (Eds.), *Handbook of psychology* (2nd ed., Vol. 11, pp. 172–200). Hoboken, NJ: John Wiley & Sons.

Forbey, J. D., & Ben-Porath, Y. S. (2007). A comparison of the MMPI-2 Restructured Clinical (RC) and Clinical Scales in a substance abuse treatment sample. *Psychological Services, 4,* 46–58. doi:10.1037/1541-1559.4.1.46

Forbey, J. D., Ben-Porath, Y. S., & Gartland, D. (2009). Validation of the MMPI-2 Computerized Adaptive version (MMPI-2-CA) in a correctional intake facility. *Psychological Services, 6,* 279–292. doi:10.1037/a0016195

Forbey, J. D., Lee, T. T. C., Ben-Porath, Y. S., Arbisi, P. A., & Gartland, D. (2013). Associations between MMPI-2-RF Validity Scale scores and extra-test measures of personality and psychopathology. *Assessment, 20,* 448–461. doi:10.1177/1073191113478154

Frye v. United States, 293 F.1012 (D.C. Cir. 1923).

Gallo, F. J., & Halgin, R. P. (2011). A guide for establishing a practice in police preemployment postoffer psychological evaluations. *Professional Psychology: Research and Practice, 42*(3), 269–275. doi:10.1037/a0022493

Gervais, R. O., Ben-Porath, Y. S., Wygant, D. B., & Green, P. (2007). Development and validation of a Response Bias Scale (RBS) for the MMPI-2. *Assessment, 14,* 196–208. doi:10.1177/1073191106295861

Gervais, R. O., Ben-Porath, Y. S., Wygant, D. B., & Sellbom, M. (2010). Incremental validity of the MMPI-2-RF over-reporting scales and RBS in assessing the veracity of memory complaints. *Archives of Clinical Neuropsychology, 25,* 274–284. doi:10.1093/arclin/acq018

Gervais, R. O., Wygant, D. B., Sellbom, M., & Ben-Porath, Y. S. (2011). Associations between Symptom Validity Test failure and scores on the MMPI-2-RF Validity and Substantive Scales. *Journal of Personality Assessment, 93,* 508–517. doi:10.1080/00223891.2011.594132

Glassmire, D. M., Jhawar, A., Burchett, D., & Tarescavage, A. M. (2016). Evaluating item endorsement rates for the MMPI-2-RF F-r and Fp-r scales across ethnic, gender, and diagnostic groups with a forensic inpatient unit. *Psychological Assessment.* Advance online publication. doi:10.1037/pas0000366

Goldstein, A. M., Morse, S. J., & Packer, I. K. (2013). Evaluation of criminal responsibility. In R. K. Otto & I. B. Weiner (Eds.), *Handbook of psychology: Vol. 11. Forensic psychology* (2nd ed., pp. 440–472). Hoboken, NJ: John Wiley & Sons.

Goodwin, B. E., Sellbom, M., & Arbisi, P. A. (2013). Post-traumatic stress disorder in veterans: The utility of the MMPI-2-RF Validity Scales in detecting over-reported symptoms. *Psychological Assessment, 25,* 671–678. doi:10.1037/a0032214

Gottfried, E. D., Anestis, J. C., Dillon, K. H., & Carbonell, J. J. (2016). The associations between Minnesota Multiphasic Personality Inventory-2-Restructured Form and self-reported physical and sexual abuse and posttraumatic symptoms in a sample of incarcerated women. *International Journal of Forensic Mental Health.* Advance online publication. doi:10.1080/14999013.2016.1228088

Gough, H. G. (1954). Some common misconceptions about neuroticism. *Journal of Consulting Psychology, 18,* 287–292.

Gould, J. W., & Martindale, D. A. (2013). Child custody evaluations: Current literature and practical applications. In I. Weiner (Series Ed.) & R. K. Otto (Vol. Ed.), *Handbook of psychology: Vol. 11. Forensic psychology* (2nd ed., pp. 101–138). New York, NY: Wiley.

Graham, J. R. (2012). *MMPI-2: Assessing personality and psychopathology* (5th ed.). New York, NY: Oxford University Press.

Green, P. (2003). *The Word Memory Test.* Seattle, WA: Green's Publishing.

Greene, R. L. (2011). *MMPI-2/MMPI-2-RF: An interpretive manual* (3rd ed.). New York, NY: Allyn & Bacon.

Grisso, T. (2014). *Competence to stand trial evaluations: Just the basics.* Sarasota, FL: Professional Resource Press.

Grossi, L. M., Green, D., Belfi, B., McGrath, R. E., Griswald, H., & Schreiber, J. (2015). Identifying aggression in forensic inpatients using the MMPI-2-RF: An examination of MMPI-2-RF scale scores and estimated psychopathy indices. *International Journal of Forensic Mental Health, 14,* 231–244. doi:10.1080/14999013.2015.1108943

Handel, R. W., & Archer, R. P. (2008). An investigation of the psychometric properties of the MMPI-2 Restructured Clinical (RC) Scales with mental health inpatients. *Journal of Personality Assessment, 90,* 239–249. doi:10.1080/00223890701884954

Handel, R. W., Ben-Porath, Y. S., Tellegen, A., & Archer, R. P. (2010). Psychometric functioning of the MMPI-2-RF VRIN-r and TRIN-r Scales with varying degrees of randomness, acquiescence, and counter-acquiescence. *Psychological Assessment, 22,* 87–95. doi:10.1037/a0017061

Haneveld, E. K., Kamphuis, J. H., Smid, W., & Forbey, J. D. (2017). Using MMPI-2-RF correlates to elucidate the PCL-R and its four facets in a sample of male forensic psychiatric patients. *Journal of Personality Assessment, 99,* 398–407. doi:10.1080/00223891.2016.1228655

Hanson, R. K., & Morton-Bourgon, K. E. (2009). The accuracy of recidivism risk assessments for sexual offenders: A meta-analysis of 118 prediction studies. *Psychological Assessment, 21,* 1–21. doi:10.1037/a0014421

Hanson, R. K., & Thornton, D. (1999). *Static–99: Improving actuarial risk assessments for sex offenders* (User Rep. No. 1999–02). Ottawa, ON, Canada: Department of the Solicitor General of Canada.

Hanson, R. K., Thornton, D., Helmus, L. M., & Babchishin, K. M. (2016). What sexual recidivism rates are associated with Static-99R and Static-2002R scores? *Sexual Abuse: A Journal of Research and Treatment, 28,* 218–252. doi:10.1177/1079063215574710

Hare, R. D. (2016). Psychopathy, the PCL-R, and criminal justice: Some new findings and current issues. *Canadian Psychology/Psychologie canadienne, 57*(1), 21–34. doi:10.1037/cap0000041

Harkness, A. R., & McNulty, J. L. (1994). The Personality Psychopathology Five (PSY-5): Issues from the pages of a diagnostic manual instead of a dictionary. In S. Strack & M. Lorr (Eds.), *Differentiating normal & abnormal personality* (pp. 291–315). New York: Springer.

Hart, S. D. (1998). The role of psychopathy in assessing risk for violence: Conceptual and methodological issues. *Legal & Criminological Psychology, 3,* 121–137. doi:10.1111/j.2044-8333.1998.tb00354.x

Hart, S. D., Cox, D. N., & Hare, R. D. (1995). *Manual for the Psychopathy Checklist—Screening Version (PCL–SV).* Toronto, ON, Canada: Multi-Health Systems.

Hart, S., Kropp, P. R., Laws, D. R., Klaver, J., Logan, C., & Watt, K. A. (2003). *The risk for sexual violence protocol (RSVP).* Burnaby, BC, Canada: Mental Health, Law, and Policy Institute, Simon Fraser University.

Hathaway, S. R., & McKinley, J. C. (1943). *The Minnesota Multiphasic Personality Inventory manual.* New York, NY: Psychological Corporation.

Hathaway, S. R., & Monachesi, E. D. (1953). *Analyzing and predicting juvenile delinquency with the MMPI.* Minneapolis: University of Minnesota Press.

Hathaway, S. R., & Monachesi, E. D. (1957). The personalities of predelinquent boys. *Journal of Criminal Law, Criminology, and Political Science, 48,* 149–163.

Heilbrun, K., Grisso, T., & Goldstein, A. (2008). *Foundations of forensic mental health assessment*. New York, NY: Oxford University Press.

Heilbrun, K., & Heilbrun, A. B. (1995). Risk assessment with the MMPI-2 in forensic evaluations. In Y. S. Ben-Porath, J. R. Graham, G. C. N. Hall, R. D. Hirshman, & M. S. Zaragoza (Eds.), *Forensic applications of the MMPI-2* (pp. 160–178). Thousand Oaks, CA: Sage.

Helmus, L., Thornton, D., Hanson, R. K., & Babchishin, K. M. (2012). Improving the predictive accuracy of Static-99 and Static-2002 with older sex offenders: Revised age weights. *Sexual Abuse: A Journal of Research and Treatment, 24,* 64–101. doi:10.1177/1079063211409951

Hoelzle, J. B., Nelson, N. W., & Arbisi, P. A. (2012). MMPI-2 and MMPI-2-Restructured Form Validity Scales: Complementary approaches to evaluate response validity. *Psychological Injury and Law, 5,* 174–191. doi:10.1007/s12207-012-9139-2

Huss, M. T. (2013). *Forensic psychology: Research, clinical practice, and applications* (2nd ed.). Hoboken, NJ: John Wiley & Sons.

Ingram, P. B., & Ternes, M. S. (2016). The detection of content-based invalid responding: A meta-analysis of the MMPI-2-Restructured Form's (MMPI-2-RF) over-reporting validity scales. *Clinical Neuropsychologist, 30,* 473–496 doi:10.1080/13854046.2016.1187769

Jones, A., & Ingram, M. V. (2011). A comparison of selected MMPI-2 and MMPI-2-RF Validity Scales in assessing effort on cognitive tests in a military sample. *Clinical Neuropsychologist, 25,* 1207–1227. doi:10.1080/13854046.2011.600726

Jones, A., Ingram, M. V., & Ben-Porath, Y. S. (2012). Scores on the MMPI-2-RF Scales as a function of increasing levels of failure on cognitive symptom validity tests in a military sample. *Clinical Neuropsychologist, 26,* 790–815. doi:10.1080/13854046.2012.693202

Kastner, R. M., & Sellbom, M. (2012). Hypersexuality in college students: The role of psychopathy. *Personality and Individual Differences, 53,* 644–649. doi:10.1016/j.paid.2012.05.005

Kastner, R. M., Sellbom, M., & Lilienfeld, S. O. (2012). A comparison of the psychometric properties of the Psychopathic Personality Inventory Full-Length and Short-Form Versions. *Psychological Assessment, 24,* 261–267. doi:10.1037/a0025832

Kauffman, C. M., Stolberg, R., & Madero, J. (2015). An examination of the MMPI-2-RF (Restructured Form) with the MMPI-2 and MCMI-III in child custody litigants. *Journal of Child Custody, 12,* 129–151. doi:10.1080/15379418.2015.1057354

Kotov, R., Krueger, R. F., Watson, D., Achenbach, T. M., Althoff, R. R., Bagby, M., Brown, T. A., et al. (2017). The Hierarchical Taxonomy of Psychopathology (HiTOP): A dimensional alternative to traditional nosologies. *Journal of Abnormal Psychology, 126,* 454–477. doi: 10.1037/abn0000258

Kovacs, M., & Garrison, B. (1985). Hopelessness and eventual suicide: a 10-year prospective study of patients hospitalized with suicidal ideation. *American Journal of Psychiatry, 1*(42), 559–563. doi:10.1176/ajp.142.5.559

Kutchen, T. J., Wygant, D. B., Tylicki, J. L., Dieter, A. M., Veltri, C. O., & Sellbom, M. (2017). Construct validity of the MMPI-2-RF Triarchic Psychopathy Scales in correctional and collegiate samples. *Journal of Personality Assessment, 99,* 408–415. doi:10.1080/00223891.2016.1238829

Lally, S. J. (2003). What tests are acceptable for use in forensic evaluations? A survey of experts. *Professional Psychology: Research and Practice, 34,* 491–498.

Lawson, A. K., Wright, C. V., & Fitzgerald, L. F. (2013). The evaluation of sexual harassment litigants: Discrepancies in the diagnosis of post-traumatic stress disorder. *Law and Human Behavior, 37,* 337–347. doi:10.1037/lhb0000024

Lees-Haley, P. R., English, L. T., & Glenn, W. J. (1991). A Fake Bad Scale on the MMPI-2 for personal injury claimants. *Psychological Reports, 68,* 203–210.

Leichsenring, F., & Leibing, E. (2003). The effectiveness of psychodynamic therapy and cognitive behavior therapy in the treatment of personality disorders: A meta-analysis. *American Journal of Psychiatry, 160,* 1223–1232. doi:10.1176/appi.ajp.160.7.1223

Lykken, D. T. (1995). *The antisocial personalities.* Hillsdale, NJ: Lawrence Erlbaum Associates.

Loevinger, J. (1972). Some limitations of objective personality tests. In J. N. Butcher (Ed.), *Objective personality assessment: Changing perspectives* (pp. 45–58). New York: Academic Press.

Makita v. Sprowles. (New South Wales Ct. App., Australia, 2001).

Mann, R. E., Hanson, R. K., & Thornton, D. (2010). Assessing risk for sexual recidivism: Some proposals on the nature of psychologically meaningful risk factors. *Sexual Abuse: A Journal of Research and Treatment, 22,* 191–217.

Marion, B. E., Sellbom, M., & Bagby, R. M. (2011). The detection of feigned psychiatric disorders using the MMPI-2-RF overreporting Validity Scales: An analog investigation. *Psychological Injury and Law, 4,* 1–12. doi:10.1007/s12207-011-9097-0

Marion, B. E., Sellbom, M., Salekin, R. T., Toomey, J. A., Kucharski, T., & Duncan, S. (2013). An examination of the association between psychopathy and dissimulation using the MMPI-2-RF Validity Scales. *Law and Human Behavior, 37,* 219–230. doi:10.1037/lhb0000008

Martin, P. K., Schroeder, R. W., & Odland, A. P. (2015). Neuropsychologists' validity testing beliefs and practices: A survey of North American professionals. *Clinical Neuropsychologist, 29,* 741–776. doi:10.1080/13854046.2015.1087597

Martindale, D. A., & Gould, J. W. (2004). The forensic model: Ethics and scientific methodology applied to custody evaluations. *Journal of Child Custody: Research, Issues, and Practices, 1,* 1–22.

Martindale, D. A., & Gould, J. W. (2007). Custody evaluation reports: The case for empirically-derived information. *Journal of Forensic Psychology Practice, 7,* 87–99.

Mason, L. H., Shandera-Ochsner, A. L., Williamson, K. D., Harp, J. P., Edmundson, M., Berry, D. T. R, & High, W. M. (2013). Accuracy of MMPI-2-RF Validity Scales for identifying feigned PTSD symptoms, random responding, and genuine PTSD. *Journal of Personality Assessment, 95,* 585–593. doi:10.1080/00223891.2013.819512

Mattson, C. A., Powers, B. K., Halfaker, D., Akenson, S. T., & Ben-Porath, Y. S. (2012). Predicting drug court completion with the MMPI-2-RF. *Psychological Assessment, 24,* 937–943. doi:10.1037/a0028267

McAnulty, R. D., McAnulty, D. P., Sipp, J. E., Demakis, G. J., & Heggestad, E. D. (2014). Predictive validity of the MMPI-2 in a residential treatment program. *Journal of Personality Assessment, 96,* 604–609. doi:10.1080/00223891.2014.880061

McBride, W. F., Crighton, A. H., Wygant, D. B., & Granacher, R. P. (2013). It's not all in your head (or at least your brain): Association of traumatic brain lesion presence and location with performance on measures of response bias in forensic evaluation. *Behavioral Sciences and the Law, 31,* 779–788. doi:10.1002/bsl.2083

Megargee, E. I., & Mendelsohn, A. (1962). A cross-validation of twelve MMPI indices of hostility and control. *Journal of Abnormal & Social Psychology, 65,* 431–438.

Melton, G. B., Petrila, J., Poythress, N. G., & Slobogin, C. (2007). *Psychological evaluations for the courts: A handbook for mental health professionals and lawyers.* New York, NY: Guilford Press.

Michigan v. Espinoza, No. 297574 (Mich. Ct. App. Sept. 27, 2011).

Miller, H. A. (2001). *M-FAST: Miller Forensic Assessment of Symptoms Test professional manual.* Odessa, FL: Psychological Assessment Resources.

Miller, M. W., Kaloupek, D. G., Dillon, A. L., & Keane, T. M. (2004). Externalizing and internalizing subtypes of combat-related PTSD: A replication and extension using the PSY-5 Scales. *Journal of Abnormal Psychology, 113,* 636–645.

Milner, J. S. (1986). *The Child Abuse Potential Inventory: Manual* (2nd ed.). DeKalb, IL: Psytec.

Milner, J. S. (1994). Assessing physical child abuse risk: The Child Abuse Potential Inventory. *Clinical Psychology Review, 14,* 547–583. doi:10.1016/0272-7358(94)90017-5

Monahan, J. (2013). Violence risk assessment. In R. K. Otto & I. B. Weiner (Eds.), *Handbook of psychology: Vol. 11. Forensic psychology* (2nd ed., pp. 541–555). Hoboken, NJ: John Wiley & Sons.

Moran, R. (1981). *Knowing right from wrong: The insanity defense of Daniel McNaughten.* New York, NY: Free Press.

Mulvey, E. P., & Lidz, C. W. (1985). Back to basics: A critical analysis of dangerousness research in a new legal environment. *Law and Human Behavior, 9*(2), 209–219. doi:10.1007/BF01067052

Neal, T. M., & Grisso, T. (2014). Assessment practices and expert judgment methods in forensic psychology and psychiatry: An international snapshot. *Criminal Justice and Behavior, 41,* 1406–1421. doi:0093854814548449

Nguyen, C. T., Green, D., & Barr, W. B. (2015). Evaluation of the MMPI-2-RF for detection of over-reported symptoms in civil forensic and disability setting. *Clinical Neuropsychologist, 29,* 255–271. doi:1080/13854046.2015.1033020

Nicholson, R. A., & Kugler, K. E. (1991). Competent and incompetent criminal defendants: A quantitative review of comparative research. *Psychological Bulletin, 109,* 355–370.

Norman, W. (1972). Psychometric considerations for a revision of the MMPI. In J. N. Butcher (Ed.), *Objective personality assessment: Changing perspectives* (pp. 59–83). New York, NY: Academic Press.

Otto, R. K., Buffington-Vollum, J. K., & Edens, J. F. (2003). Child custody evaluation. In A. M. Goldstein & I. B. Weiner (Eds.), *Handbook of psychology* (Vol. 11, pp. 179–208). Hoboken, NJ: John Wiley & Sons.

Phillips, T. R., Sellbom, M., Ben-Porath, Y. S., & Patrick, C. J. (2014). Further development and construct validation of MMPI-2-RF indices of global psychopathy, fearless-dominance, and impulsive-antisociality in a sample of incarcerated women. *Law and Human Behavior, 38,* 34–46. doi:10.1037/lhb0000040

Piechowski, L. D. (2013). Disability and workers compensation. In R. K. Otto & I. B. Weiner (Eds.), *Handbook of psychology* (2nd ed., Vol. 11, pp. 201–224). Hoboken, NJ: John Wiley & Sons.

Pinsoneault, T. B., & Ezzo, F. R. (2012). A comparison of MMPI-2-RF profiles between child maltreatment and non-maltreatment custody cases. *Journal of Forensic Psychology Practice, 12,* 227–237. doi:10.1080/15228932.2012.674469

Pirelli, G., Gottdiener, W. H., & Zapf, P. A. (2011). A meta-analytic review of competency to stand trial research. *Psychology, Public Policy and Law, 17,* 1–53.

Quinsey, V. L., Harris, G. T., Rice, M. E., & Cormier, C. A. (1998). *Violent offenders: Appraising and managing risk.* Washington, DC: American Psychological Association.

Quinsey, V. L., Jones, G. B., Book, A. S., & Barr, K. N. (2006). The dynamic prediction of antisocial behavior among forensic psychiatric patients: A prospective field study. *Journal of Interpersonal Violence, 21*(12), 1539–1565. doi:10.1177/0886260506294238

R v. Verdins, 16 VR 269 (Victoria Ct. App., Australia, 2007).

Resendes, J., & Lecci, L. (2012). Comparing the MMPI-2 scale scores of parents involved in parental competency and child custody assessments. *Psychological Assessment, 24,* 1054–1059. doi:10.1037/a0028585

Rice, A. K., Boccaccini, M. T., Harris, P. B., & Hawes, S. W. (2014). Does field reliability for Static-99 scores decrease as scores increase? *Psychological Assessment, 26,* 1085–1095. doi:10.1037/pas0000009

Rock, R. C., Sellbom, M., Ben-Porath, Y. S., & Salekin, R. T. (2013). Concurrent and predictive validity of psychopathy in a batterers intervention sample. *Law and Human Behavior, 37,* 145–154. doi:10.1037/lhb0000006

Rogers, R. (2018). Detection strategies for malingering and defensiveness. In R. Rogers (Ed.), *Clinical Assessment of Malingering and Deception* (4th ed.). New York, NY: Guilford Press.

Rogers, R., Bagby, R. M., & Dickens, S. E. (1992). *Structured Interview of Reported Symptoms: Professional manual.* Odessa, FL: Psychological Assessment Resources.

Rogers, R., & Bender, S. D. (2013). Evaluation of malingering and related response styles. In R. K. Otto & I. B. Weiner (Eds.), *Handbook of psychology* (2nd ed., Vol. 11, pp. 517–540). Hoboken, NJ: John Wiley & Sons.

Rogers, R., Gillard, N. D., Berry, D. T., & Granacher, R. P. (2011). Effectiveness of the MMPI-2-RF validity scales for feigned mental disorders and cognitive impairment: A known-groups study. *Journal of Psychopathology and Behavioral Assessment, 33,* 355–367. doi:10.1007/s10862-011-9222-0

Rogers, R., & Granacher, R. P. (2011). Conceptualization and assessment of malingering. In E. Y. Drogin, F. M. Dattilio, R. L. Sadoff, & T. G. Guthiel (Eds.), *Handbook of forensic assessment: Psychological and psychiatric perspectives* (pp. 659–678). Hoboken, NJ: John Wiley & Sons.

Rogers, R., & McKee, G. R. (1995). Use of the MMPI-2 in the assessment of criminal responsibility. In Y. S. Ben-Porath, J. R. Graham, G. C. N. Hall, R. D. Hirshman, & M. S. Zaragoza (Eds.), *Forensic applications of the MMPI-2* (pp. 103–126). Thousand Oaks, CA: Sage.

Rogers, R., Sewell, K. W., & Gillard, N. D. (2010). *SIRS-2: Structured Interview of Reported Symptoms: Professional manual.* Odessa, FL: Psychological Assessment Resources.

Rogers, R., Tillbrook, C. E., & Sewell, K. W. (2004). *Evaluation of Competency to Stand Trial–Revised professional manual.* Lutz, FL: Psychological Assessment Resources.

Romero, I. E., Toorabally, N., Burchett, D., Tarescavage, A. M., & Glassmire, D. M. (2017). Mapping the MMPI-2-RF substantive scales onto internalizing, externalizing, and thought dysfunction dimensions in a forensic inpatient setting. *Journal of Personality Assessment, 99*, 351–362. doi:10.1080/00223891.2016.122368

Salekin, R. T. (2002). Psychopathy and therapeutic pessimism: Clinical lore or clinical reality? *Clinical Psychology Review, 22*(1), 79–112. doi:10.1016/S0272-7358(01)00083-6

Salekin, R. T., Worley, C., & Grimes, R. D. (2010). Treatment of psychopathy: A review and brief introduction to the mental model approach for psychopathy. *Behavioral Sciences & the Law, 28*(2), 235–266. doi:10.1002/bsl.928

Schall v. Martin, 467 U.S. 253 (1984).

Schroeder, R. W., Baade, L. E., Peck, C. P., VonDran, E., Brockman, C. J., Webster, B. K., & Heinrichs, R. J. (2012). Validation of the MMPI-2-RF Validity Scales in criterion group neuropsychological samples. *Clinical Neuropsychologist, 26*, 129–146. doi:10.1080/138 54046.2011.639314

Schroeder, R. W., Martin, P. K., & Odland, A. P. (2016). Expert beliefs and practices regarding neuropsychological validity testing. *Clinical Neuropsychologist, 30*(4), 515–535. doi: 10.1080/13854046.2016.1177118

Sellbom, M. (2011). Elaborating on the construct validity of the Levenson Self-Report Psychopathy Scale in incarcerated and non-incarcerated samples. *Law and Human Behavior, 35*, 440–451. doi:10.1007/s10979-010-9249-x

Sellbom, M. (2012). The MMPI-2-RF is ready for the Daubert challenge: Evidence, implications, and recommendations for use in court testimony. *Journal of Psychological Practice, 17*, 151–179.

Sellbom, M. (2014). A factor mixture model approach to elaborating on offender mental health classification with the MMPI-2-RF. *Journal of Personality Assessment, 96*, 293–305. doi:10.1080/00223891.2013.843538

Sellbom, M. (2016a). Elucidating the validity of the externalizing spectrum of psychopathology in correctional, forensic, and community samples. *Journal of Abnormal Psychology, 125*, 1027–1038. doi:10.1037/abn0000171

Sellbom, M. (2016b). Mapping the MMPI-2-RF Specific Problems scales onto Extant Psychopathology Structures. *Journal of Personality Assessment.* doi:10.1080/00223891. 2016.1206909

Sellbom, M. (In press). Using the MMPI-2-RF to characterize defendants evaluated for competency to stand trial and criminal responsibility. *International Journal of Forensic Mental Health.*

Sellbom, M., & Anderson, J. L. (2013). The Minnesota Multiphasic Personality Inventory-2. In R. P. Archer & E. M. A. Wheeler (Eds.), *Forensic uses of clinical assessment instruments* (2nd ed., pp. 21–62). New York, NY: Routledge.

Sellbom, M., Anderson, J. L., & Bagby, R. M. (2013). Assessing DSM-5 Section III personality traits and disorders with the MMPI-2-RF. *Assessment, 20*, 709–722. doi:10.1177/1073191113508808

Sellbom. M., & Bagby, R. M. (2008). Validity of the MMPI-2-RF (Restructured Form) L-r and K-r Scales in detecting underreporting in clinical and nonclinical samples. *Psychological Assessment, 20*, 370–376. doi:10.1037/a0012952

Sellbom, M., & Bagby, R. M. (2010). The detection of over-reported psychopathology with the MMPI-2-RF (Restructured Form) Validity Scales. *Psychological Assessment, 22*, 757–767. doi:10.1037/a0020825

Sellbom, M., Bagby, R. M., Kushner, S., Quilty, L. C., & Ayearst, L. E. (2012). Diagnostic construct validity of MMPI-2 Restructured Form (MMPI-2-RF) scale scores. *Assessment, 19*(2), 176–186. doi:10.1177/1073191111428763

Sellbom, M., & Ben-Porath, Y. S. (2005). Mapping the MMPI-2 Restructured Clinical (RC) Scales onto normal personality traits: Evidence of construct validity. *Journal of Personality Assessment, 85,* 179–187. doi:10.1207/s15327752jpa8502_10

Sellbom, M., Ben-Porath, Y. S., & Bagby, R. M. (2008). On the hierarchical structure of mood and anxiety disorders: Confirmatory evidence and elaboration of a model of temperament markers. *Journal of Abnormal Psychology, 117,* 576–590. doi:10.1037/a0012536

Sellbom, M., Ben-Porath, Y. S., Baum, L. J., Erez, E., & Gregory, C. (2008). Predictive validity of the MMPI-2 Restructured Clinical (RC) Scales in a batterers' intervention program. *Journal of Personality Assessment, 90,* 129–135. doi:10.1080/0022 3890701845153

Sellbom, M., Ben-Porath, Y. S., & Graham, J. R. (2006). Correlates of the MMPI-2 Restructured Clinical (RC) Scales in a college counseling setting. *Journal of Personality Assessment, 86,* 89–99. doi:10.1207/s15327752jpa8601_10

Sellbom, M., Ben-Porath, Y. S., Graham, J. R., Arbisi, P. A., & Bagby, R. M. (2005). Susceptibility of the MMPI-2 Clinical, Restructured Clinical (RC), and Content Scales to overreporting and underreporting. *Assessment, 12,* 79–85. doi:10.1177/1073191104273515

Sellbom, M., Ben-Porath, Y. S., Lilienfeld, S. O., Patrick, C. J., & Graham, J. R. (2005). Assessing psychopathic personality traits with the MMPI-2. *Journal of Personality Assessment, 85,* 334–343. doi:10.1207/s15327752jpa8503_10

Sellbom, M., Ben-Porath, Y. S., McNulty, J. L., Arbisi, P. A., & Graham, J. R. (2006). Elevation differences between MMPI-2 Clinical and Restructured Clinical (RC) Scales: Frequency, origins, and interpretative implications. *Assessment, 13,* 430–441. doi:10.1177/1073191106293349

Sellbom, M., Ben-Porath, Y. S., Patrick, C. J., Wygant, D. B., Gartland, D. M., & Stafford, K. P. (2012). Development and construct validation of MMPI-2-RF measures assessing global psychopathy, fearless-dominance, and impulsive-antisociality. *Personality Disorders: Theory, Research, and Treatment, 3,* 17–38. doi:10.1037/a0023888

Sellbom, M., Ben-Porath, Y. S., & Stafford, K. P. (2007). A comparison of measures of psychopathic deviance in a forensic setting. *Psychological Assessment, 19,* 430–436. doi:10.1037/1040-3590.19.4.430

Sellbom, M., Drislane, L. E., Johnson, A. K., Goodwin, B. E., Phillips, T. R., & Patrick, C. J. (2016). Development and validation of MMPI-2-RF scales for indexing triarchic psychopathy constructs. *Assessment, 23,* 527–543. doi:10.1177/1073191115590853

Sellbom, M., Graham, J. R., & Schenk, P. (2006). Incremental validity of the MMPI-2 Restructured Clinical (RC) Scales in a private practice sample. *Journal of Personality Assessment, 86,* 196–205. doi:10.1207/s15327752jpa8602_09

Sellbom, M., & Hopwood, C. J. (2016). Evidence-based assessment in the 21st century: Comments on the special series papers. *Clinical Psychology: Science and Practice, 23*(4), 403–409. doi:10.1111/cpsp.12183

Sellbom, M., & Lee, T. T. C. (2013). Assessment of anxiety symptoms using the MMPI-2, MMPI-2-RF, and MMPI-A. In D. McKay & E. A. Storch (Eds.), *Handbook of assessing variants and complications in anxiety disorders* (pp. 139–162). New York, NY: Springer.

Sellbom, M., Lee, T. T. C., Ben-Porath, Y. S., Arbisi, P. A., & Gervais, R. O. (2012). Differentiating PTSD symptomatology with the MMPI-2-RF (Restructured Form) in a forensic disability sample. *Psychiatry Research, 197,* 172–179. doi:10.1016/j.psychres.2012.02.003

Sellbom, M., Smid, W., De Saeger, H., Smit, N., & Kamphuis, J. H. (2014). Mapping the Personality Psychopathology Five domains onto DSM-IV personality disorders in Dutch clinical and forensic samples: Implications for the DSM-5. *Journal of Personality Assessment, 96,* 185–192. doi.org/10.1080/00223891.2013.825625

Sellbom, M., & Smith, A. (2017). Assessment of DSM-5 Section II personality disorders with the MMPI-2-RF in a nonclinical sample. *Journal of Personality Assessment, 99,* 384-397. doi:10.1080/00223891.2016.1242074

Sellbom, M., Toomey, A., Wygant, D., Kucharski, L. T., & Duncan, S. (2010). Utility of the MMPI-2-RF (Restructured Form) Validity Scales in detecting malingering in a criminal forensic setting: A known-groups design. *Psychological Assessment, 22,* 22–31. doi:10.1037/a0018222

Sellbom, M., Wygant, D. B., & Bagby, R. M. (2012). Utility of the MMPI-2-RF in detecting non-credible somatic complaints. *Psychiatry Research, 197,* 295–301. doi:10.1016/j.psychres.2011.12.043

Sharf, A. J., Rogers, R., Williams, M. M., & Henry, S. A. (2017). The effectiveness of the MMPI-2-RF in detecting feigned mental disorders and cognitive deficits: A meta-analysis. *Journal of Psychopathology and Behavioral Assessment, 39,* 441–455.

Simms, L. J., Casillas, A., Clark, L. A., Watson, D., & Doebbeling, B. I. (2005). Psychometric evaluation of the Restructured Clinical Scales of the MMPI-2. *Psychological Assessment, 17,* 345–358. doi:10.1037/1040-3590.17.3.345

Skeem, J., & Golding, S. (1998). Community examiners' evaluations of competence to stand trial: Common problems and suggestions for improvement. *Professional Psychology: Research and Practice, 29,* 357–367.

Sleep, C. C., Petty, J. A., & Wygant, D. B. (2015). Framing the results: Assessment of response bias through select self-report measures in psychological injury evaluations. *Psychological Injury and Law, 8,* 27–39. doi:10.1007/s12207-015-9219-1

Slick, D. J., Sherman, E. M. S., & Iverson, G. L. (1999). Forum: Diagnostic criteria for malingered neurocognitive dysfunction: Proposed standards for clinical practice and research. *Clinical Neuropsychologist, 13,* 545–561.

Solomon, D., Morgan, B., Asberg, K., & McCord, D. M. (2014). Treatment implications based on measures of child abuse potential and parental mental health: Are we missing an intervention opportunity. *Children and Youth Services Review, 43,* 153–159. doi:10.1016/j.childyouth.2014.05.016

Spitzer, R. L., Williams, J. B. W., Gibbon, M., & First, M. D. (1989). *Structured Clinical Interview for DSM-III-R—Patient version (SCID-P).* New York, NY: New York State Psychiatric Institute.

Stafford, K. P., & Sellbom, M. (2013). Competency to stand trial. In R. Otto (Ed.), *Handbook of psychology: Vol. 11. Forensic psychology* (pp. 412–439). New York, NY: Wiley.

Stredny, R. V., Archer, R. P., & Mason, J. A. (2006). MMPI-2 and MCMI-III characteristics of parental competency examinees. *Journal of Personality Assessment, 87,* 113–115. doi:10.1207/s15327752jpa8701_10

Sutherland, A. A., Johnstone, L., Davidson, K. M., Hart, S., Cooke, D. J., Kropp, P. R., & Stocks, R. (2012). Sexual violence risk assessment: An investigation of the interrater reliability of professional judgements made using the risk for sexual violence protocol. *International Journal of Forensic Mental Health, 11,* 119–133. doi:10.1080/14999013.2012.690020

Sutker, P. B., & Allain, N. (1973). Incarcerated and street heroin addicts: A personality comparison. *Psychological Reports, 32,* 243–246.

Tarescavage, A. M., Cappo, B., & Ben-Porath, Y. S. (2016). Assessment of sex offenders with the Minnesota Multiphasic Personality Inventory-2-Restructured Form (MMPI-2-RF). *Sexual Abuse: A Journal of Research and Treatment.* Advance online publication. doi:10.1177/1079063216667921

Tarescavage, A. M., Glassmire, D. M., & Burchett, D. (2016). Introduction of a conceptual model for integrating the MMPI-2-RF into HCR-20-V3 violence risk assessments and associations between the MMPI-2-RF and institutional violence. *Law and Human Behavior, 40,* 626–637. doi:10.1037/lhb0000207

Tarescavage, A. M., Luna-Jones, L., & Ben-Porath, Y. S. (2014). Minnesota Multiphasic Personality Inventory-2-Restructured Form (MMPI-2-RF) predictors of violating probation after felonious crimes. *Psychological Assessment, 26,* 1375–1380. doi:10.1037/pas0000022

Tarescavage, A., Wygant, D. B., Gervais, R. O., & Ben-Porath, Y. S. (2013). Association between the MMPI-2 Restructured Form (MMPI-2-RF) and malingered neurocognitive dysfunction among non-head injury disability claimants. *Clinical Neuropsychologist, 27,* 313–335. doi:10.1080/13854046.2012.744099

Tellegen, A., & Ben-Porath, Y. S. (2008/2011). *MMPI-2-RF (Minnesota Multiphasic Personality Inventory-2 Restructured Form): Technical manual.* Minneapolis, MN: University of Minnesota Press.

Tellegen, A., Ben-Porath, Y. S., McNulty, J. L., Arbisi, P. A., Graham, J. R., & Kaemmer, B. (2003). *MMPI-2 Restructured Clinical (RC) Scales: Development, validation, and interpretation.* Minneapolis, MN: University of Minnesota Press.

Tellegen, A., Ben-Porath, Y. S., & Sellbom, M. (2009). Construct validity of the MMPI-2 Restructured Clinical (RC) Scales: Reply to Rouse, Greene, Butcher, Nichols, & Williams. *Journal of Personality Assessment, 91,* 211–221. doi:10.1080/00223890902794192

Tombaugh, T. N. (1996). *Test of Memory Malingering (TOMM).* New York, NY: Multi-Health Systems.

Wall, T. D., Wygant, D. B., & Gallagher, R. W. (2015). Identifying overreporting in a correctional setting: Utility of the MMPI-2 Restructured Form Validity Scales. *Criminal Justice and Behavior, 42,* 610–622. doi:10.1177/0093854814556881

Watson, C., Quilty, L. C., & Bagby, R. M. (2011). Differentiating bipolar disorder from major depressive disorder using the MMPI-2-RF: A receiver operating characteristics (ROC) analysis. *Journal of Psychopathology and Behavioral Assessment, 33,* 368–374. doi:10.1007/s10862-010-9212-7

Watson, D. (2005). Rethinking the mood and anxiety disorders: A quantitative hierarchical model for DSM–V. *Journal of Abnormal Psychology, 114,* 522–536.

Weathers, F. W., Blake, D. D., Schnurr, P. P., Kaloupek, D. G., Marx, B. P., & Keane, T. M. (2013). *The Clinician-Administered PTSD Scale for DSM-5 (CAPS-5)* [Interview]. National Center for PTSD. Retrieved from the www.ptsd.va.gov

Webster, C. D., Douglas, K. S., Eaves, D., & Hart, S. D. (1997). *HCR–20: Assessing risk for violence* (Version 2). Vancouver, BC, Canada: Mental Health, Law, and Policy Institute, Simon Fraser University.

Webster, C. D., & Hucker, S. J. (2007). *Violence risk: Assessment and management.* Hoboken, NJ: John Wiley & Sons.

Wiggins, C. W., Wygant, D. B., Hoelzle, J. B., & Gervais, R. O. (2012). The more you say the less it means: Over-reporting and attenuated criterion validity in a forensic disability sample. *Psychological Injury and Law, 5,* 162–173. doi:10.1007/s12207-012-9137-4

Wiggins, J. S. (1959). Interrelationships among MMPI measures of dissimulation under standard and social desirability instructions. *Journal of Consulting Psychology, 23,* 419–427.

Witt, P. H., Dattilio, F. M., & Bradford, J. M. (2011). Sex offender evaluations. In E. Drogin, F. M. Dattilio, R. L. Sadoff, & T. G. Gutheil (Eds.), *Handbook of forensic assessment: Psychological and psychiatric perspectives* (pp. 97–120). Hoboken, NJ: John Wiley & Sons.

Wolf, E. J., & Miller, M. W. (2014). The Minnesota Multiphasic Personality Inventory-2 Restructured Form and posttraumatic stress disorder: Forensic applications and considerations. *Psychological Injury and Law, 7,* 143–152. doi:10.1007/s12207-014-9193-z

Wolf, E. J., Miller, M. W., Orazem, R. J., Weierich, M. R., Castillo, D. T., Milford, J., Kaloupek, D. G., et al. (2008). The MMPI-2 Restructured Clinical Scales in the assessment of posttraumatic stress disorder and comorbid disorders. *Psychological Assessment, 20,* 327–340. doi:10.1037/a0012948

Wood v. Haler, Director, Texas Department of Criminal Justice, Correctional Institutions Division. Civil No. SA-01-CA-423-OG (U.S. Dist. W. D. Texas, San Antonio Div. May 10, 2011).

Wygant, D. B., Anderson, J. L., Sellbom, M., Rapier, J. L., Allgeier, L. M., & Granacher, R. P. (2011). Association of MMPI-2 Restructured Form (MMPI-2-RF) Validity Scales with structured malingering criteria. *Psychological Injury and Law, 4,* 13–23. doi:10.1007/s12207-011-9098-z

Wygant, D. B., Applegate, K. C., & Wall, T. D. (2015). Assessing facets of personality and psychopathology in violent offenders. In C. A. Pietz & C. A. Mattson (Eds.), *Violent offenders: Understanding and assessment* (pp. 384–408). New York, NY: Oxford University Press.

Wygant, D. B., Arbisi, P. A., Bianchini, B. J., & Umlauf, R. L. (2017). Waddell nonorganic signs: New evidence suggests somatic amplification among outpatient chronic pain patients. *Spine Journal, 17,* 505–510. doi:10.1016/j.spinee.2016.10.018

Wygant, D. B., Ben-Porath, Y. S., & Arbisi, P. A. (2004, May). *Development and initial validation of a scale to detect infrequent somatic complaints.* Poster presented at the 39th Annual Symposium on Recent Developments of the MMPI-2/MMPI-A, Minneapolis, MN.

Wygant, D. B., Ben-Porath, Y. S., Arbisi, P. A., Berry, D. T. R., Freeman, D. B., & Heilbronner, R. L. (2009). Examination of the MMPI-2 Restructured Form (MMPI-2-RF) Validity Scales in civil forensic settings: Findings from simulation and known group samples. *Archives of Clinical Neuropsychology, 27,* 671–680. doi:10.1093/arclin/acp073

Wygant, D. B., & Granacher, R. P. (2015). Assessment of validity and response bias in neuropsychiatric evaluations. *NeuroRehabilitation, 36,* 427–438.

Wygant, D. B., & Lareau, C. R. (2015). Civil and criminal forensic psychological assessment: Similarities and unique challenges. *Psychological Injury and Law, 8,* 11–26. doi:10.1007/s12207-015-9220-8

Wygant, D. B., & Sellbom, M. (2012). Viewing psychopathy from the perspective of the Personality Psychopathology Five model: Implications for DSM-5. *Journal of Personality Disorders, 26,* 717–726. doi:10.1521/pedi.2012.26.5.717

Wygant, D. B., Sellbom, M., Ben-Porath, Y. S., Stafford, K. P., Freeman, D. B., & Heilbronner, R. L. (2007). The relation between symptom validity testing and MMPI-2 scores as a function of forensic evaluation context. *Archives of Clinical Neuropsychology, 22*(4), 489–499. doi:10.1016/j.acn.2007.01.027

Wygant, D. B., Sellbom, M., Gervais, R. O., Ben-Porath, Y. S., Stafford, K. P., Freeman, D. B., & Heilbronner, R. L. (2010). Further validation of the MMPI-2 and MMPI-2-RF Response Bias Scale: Findings from disability and criminal forensic settings. *Psychological Assessment, 22,* 745–756. doi:10.1037/a0020042

Wygant, D. B., Walls, B. D., Brothers, S. L., & Berry, D. T. R. (2018). Assessment of malingering and defensiveness on the MMPI-2 and MMPI-2-RF. In R. Rogers (Ed.), *Clinical assessment of malingering and deception* (4th ed., pp. 267–279). New York, NY: Guilford Press.

Youngjohn, J. R., Weshba, R., Stevenson, M., Sturgeon, J., & Thomas, M. L. (2011). Independent validation of the MMPI-2-RF Somatic/Cognitive and Validity Scales in TBI litigants tested for effort. *Clinical Neuropsychologist, 25,* 463–476. doi:10.1080/13854046.2011.554444

Zapf, P. A., Golding, S. L., Roesch, R., & Pirelli, G. (2013). Assessing criminal responsibility. In I. B. Weiner & R. K. Otto (Eds.), *The handbook of forensic psychology* (4th ed., pp. 315–384). Hoboken, NJ: John Wiley & Sons.

Zapf, P. A., & Roesch, R. (2009). *Evaluation of competence to stand trial.* New York, NY: Oxford University Press.

INDEX

MARTIN SELLBOM, PhD, is an associate professor of clinical psychology in the Department of Psychology at the University of Otago, Dunedin, New Zealand. His research focuses on psychopathy and other personality disorders, the broader integration of personality and psychopathology, and personality assessment with the MMPI-2-RF. As a registered psychologist in Australia and New Zealand, he has extensive clinical experience in forensic psychological assessment and teaches professional workshops and webinars on the use of the MMPI-2-RF in forensic settings. His work has been featured in more than 150 book chapters and peer-reviewed journal articles, and he has authored or coauthored over 200 professional presentations.

DUSTIN B. WYGANT, PhD, is a professor of psychology in the Department of Psychology at Eastern Kentucky University in Richmond, Kentucky, and serves as Director of Clinical Training for the doctoral program in clinical psychology. His primary research interests include the conceptualization of the psychopathic personality and the DSM-5 alternative model of personality disorders. His research has been featured in more than 55 book chapters and peer-reviewed journal articles, and he has authored or coauthored over 200 professional presentations and workshops. As a licensed psychologist in Kentucky and Ohio, he maintains an active forensic consultation practice and routinely completes forensic psychological evaluations in criminal and civil cases. He regularly teaches professional workshops in the area of MMPI assessment, forensic assessment, and substance abuse.

YOSSEF S. BEN-PORATH, PhD, is professor of psychological sciences at Kent State University. He received his doctoral training at the University of Minnesota and has been involved extensively in MMPI research for more than 30 years. He is a codeveloper of the MMPI-2-RF and coauthor of test manuals, books, book chapters, and articles on the MMPI instruments. He is editor-in-chief of the journal *Psychological Assessment*. His clinical practice involves supervision of assessments at Kent State's Psychological Clinic, consultation to agencies that screen candidates for public safety positions, and provision of consultation and expert witness services in forensic cases.

Drs. Sellbom, Wygant, and Ben-Porath are paid consultants for the University of Minnesota Press, publisher of the MMPI-2-RF.